WITHDRAWN

Telling Time

Carol Jacobs

Telling Time

• • • • • • • • • • • • • •

Lévi-Strauss,
Ford,
Lessing,
Benjamin,
de Man,
Wordsworth,
Rilke

The Johns Hopkins University Press

Baltimore and London

© 1993 The Johns Hopkins University Press
All rights reserved
Printed in the United States of America
on acid-free paper

The Johns Hopkins University Press
2715 North Charles Street
Baltimore, Maryland 21218–4319
The Johns Hopkins Press Ltd., London

Library of Congress Cataloging-in-Publication Data
Jacobs, Carol.
    Telling time : Lévi-Strauss, Ford, Lessing, Benjamin, de Man, Words-
worth, Rilke / Carol Jacobs.
        p.   cm.
    ISBN 0-8018-4477-0 (hc)
    1. Criticism.   I. Title.
PN81.J282   1992
801'.95—dc20   92-21456

A catalog record of this book is available from the British Library

*For my mother—the first feminist in my
life—who made all the difference*

Contents

· · · · · · · · · · · · · · ·

Acknowledgments

· · · · · · · · · · · · ·

I would like to thank the American Council of Learned Societies for the grant that made possible, many years ago, the writing of the Rilke chapter.

I am enormously grateful to the John Simon Guggenheim Foundation for the fellowship that enabled me to complete a substantial part of this book in more recent years.

Once again my thanks to the Camargo Foundation in Cassis, France, where I resided and worked on the manuscript for a semester in great peace. And in memory of Jean-François Gagneux, who was so much a part of that aura.

Imre Szeman did the fine work on the index.

Several of the chapters that follow were published previously. Chapter 2 first appeared in *Agenda* 27, no. 4, and 28, no. 1 (1989/90): 67–76; chapter 3 in *Glyph* 3 (Spring 1978): 32–51; chapter 4 in *Modern Language Notes* 102 (Spring 1987): 483–521; chapter 5 in *Modern Language Notes* 90 (December 1975): 755–66; and chapter 6 in *Reading de Man Reading,* ed. Lindsay Waters and Wlad Godzich (Minneapolis: University of Minnesota Press, 1989), 105–20.

Telling Time

Prologue:
Telling, Time

I know that of all problems, none disquieted
him more, and none concerned him more than
the profound one of time. Now then, this is the
only problem that does not figure in the pages of
The Garden. He does not even use the word which
means *time*. . . . *The Garden of Forking Paths* is an
enormous guessing game, or parable, in which
the subject is time. The rules of the game forbid
the use of the word itself. To eliminate a word
completely, to refer to it by means of inept
phrases and obvious paraphrases, is perhaps the
best way of drawing attention to it.

—Borges, "The Garden of Forking Paths"

This is not a book *about* time. At least time
is not the explicit subject matter about which—as though it were
some-thing—I could venture here to tell. Nor do the texts read
here necessarily present time as their fundamental thematic preoccupation. If the thematic unity seemingly promised by the title is
lacking, what holds together such generically, culturally, and historically disparate texts: poetry, anthropology, the aesthetic treatise,
fiction, and critical theory ranging over four national cultures and
some two-and-a-half centuries?

In a sense the disparity among these texts is the point of this volume, for it makes all the more remarkable that they have this in
common: time may not rigorously unite them as their ostensible
referent, but time is still telling. Time is what their narrations are
about—not necessarily as subject matter but as the condition of the
possibility of telling and as the crisis that it endures. It figures as

3

the critical matrix that makes such writings thinkable, even when that matrix is not made explicitly accessible to the reader. *Telling, Time:* no doubt, this is what I could have, more properly, entitled the book. The comma would have insisted on an awkward rupture in a phrase that is otherwise rather reassuring: "telling time" is, after all, a common, everyday expression that speaks of skills mastered by every schoolchild, confirming our powers both of telling and of situating ourselves unproblematically in time. But, since titles are meant to take the reader in, I left the turn of speech intact.

Still, each of the authors read here does touch on certain temporal and narrative conventions, if only as a tangent touches a circle. They perform, however, not only a traditional relation between telling and time but also a rupture within this telling. A call is made to a structure of temporality—often as history, as memoir, as narrative of recollection or imitation—a temporality that has a before and after, in which sequence and progression are taken for granted, and in which a belated text seems to assimilate its past or at least make off with an appropriate recompense.

Thus Ford Madox Ford writes literary memoirs. Or, in what seems the radical gesture of impressionist fiction, where he ostentatiously denigrates the sequential story, his narration still preserves the impressions of the narrator and thus repeats the sequence in another form. Lévi-Strauss's *Tristes Tropiques,* also a memoir, preoccupies itself with the question of retelling, of repeating a past, and finding its origins. Lessing creates fictional histories as the frame for his narration, tales of the original followed by imitation, copies, plagiarisms, and, at the very heart of his treatise, a prescription for imitation in the arts that presupposes two different modes of temporal ordering. Wordsworth sets forth "Tintern Abbey" and *The Prelude* as autobiographies and opens the Immortality Ode with nostalgia for an era lost. Benjamin, briefly at least, speaks of conventional translation that might follow the original in order to communicate its content to the reader. De Man speaks of and performs illusions of progress through sequences in which a certain enlightenment seems the reward for critical reading. Rilke, too, poses, if only to deflect it, the conventional mirror with its lure of reflecting what was outside and previous.

Somewhere in each of these texts, then, not always at the outset but always as a recurrent possibility, is a temporality of sequence accompanied by a linguistic medium of recuperation. Yet, always, too, the urgent and compelling question—never quite satisfactorily answered and persistently at odds with that recuperation—of what each text is *about*. What is Ford's impressionism, Lévi-Strauss's anthropology? What is imitation in the arts for Lessing or autobiography and recollection for Wordsworth, translation for Benjamin or criticism for de Man? How are we to understand the mirror that Rilke makes metaphorical for poetry? Each text ponders the nature of its own enterprise in terms of a temporality ironically posited which it casts aside for preoccupations with theoretical issues of another order or, perhaps we should say, with theoretical questionings that are bound to undo that first order.

More often than not these writers situate themselves with respect to history, designating both their positions in it and the implications of pretensions to write it. Thus, Lévi-Strauss contemplates not only his own personal history but also the relation of ethnography to human history and the history of the planet earth. He closes his volume from the perspective of an apocalypse that renders all of these irrelevant. Ford poses in much of his critical work as a conventional literary historian, but his theoretical performance of Impressionism is calculated to blast us out of historical complacency. This is particularly evident in *The Good Soldier*, where a return to the historical context of the novel's pivotal scene takes us to the Marburg Colloquy. There, the crucial subject matter for discussion unsettles the linguistic presuppositions of all historical documentation: for Luther, his friends, and his enemies simply refuse to agree on the representational force of language and leave that indecision to haunt theology for many years to come. De Man's "Rhetoric of Temporality" frames its initial argument in a literary history that will later be all too pointedly ironized. Lessing, too, upsets the principles of naive historical discourse: he fictionalizes the history of the writing of his own treatise, belabors discussions of originality in the history of the arts, and finally turns to reading Homer's exemplary progressions. In each case the authority to reproduce the past is disempowered, giving way to the complexities of figural language, of writing, and of interpretation. It is not that Lévi-Strauss, Ford, de Man, and Lessing jettison history: rather, their irony with respect to its conventional conceptualization redefines its possibilities in rethinking the relation of telling to truth.

None of these authors confronts such issues more decisively than Walter Benjamin, although of all the texts written on in the chapters to follow, "The Task of the Translator" may approach the question the least directly. Nevertheless, we might turn to another piece where Benjamin, in no uncertain terms, casts aside what he calls "historicism." In the work that is often regarded as his clearest political statement, the "Theses on the Philosophy of History,"[1] the last text we have from Benjamin's hand, he repeatedly marks the complicity of "historicism" with fascism through the former's temporality of sequence, illusion of progress, and its claims to recuperate the past "as it actually was" (VI).

Thus writing in the critical historical moment of 1940, Benjamin rails against the politicians' "stubborn faith in progress" (X) against those who "let the sequence of events run through [their] fingers like a rosary" (XVIII), against belief in an apparent "causal connection of different moments of history" (XVIII). For Benjamin, neither truth nor the past can be held fast, and Gottfried Keller's "The truth will not run away from us" is marked as the point where Benjamin's "historical materialism" beats its way through conventional historicism (V). Where historicism promises an " 'eternal' image" of the past, Benjamin speaks rather of an "experience" with the past that "blasts open [the] continuum of history" (XVI). Only thus is "a revolutionary chance [offered] in the struggle for the oppressed past" (XVII).

In a passage whose difficulty makes it as elusive as the image to which it refers, Benjamin writes: "The true image of the past *rushes hurriedly* by. Only as an image that flashes up precisely never to be seen again in the moment of its cognizability is the past to be grasped [*festzuhalten*]" (V). This, and not the conservative grasp of "historicism," sets the stage for Benjamin's writings. Benjamin returned again and again, although differently, to this strange figure of the moment in which memory of the past is seized in the present, in which recognition takes place always coincident with irretrievable disappearance. Often he writes of this encounter between past and present in terms of a "constellation." The "historical materialist" "seizes the constellation into which his own epoch has stepped with an earlier epoch that is totally determined" (XVIII). This is an encounter in which shock, redemption, and a revolution of sorts have their place (XVII)—and, if we are willing to think of the *Theses* in relation to his earlier work, also reading.

In the 1933 "Doctrine of the Similar,"[2] in an argument too complex to set forth here, Benjamin shifts from a temporality of sequence (never explicitly underscored as such) to that of the constellation. The opening pages of that essay insist on linear temporal sequences ("course of time," "uniform direction")—on a "history" of man's production of similarities, for example, or on "natural correspondences" that precede and stimulate a response, on an already present similarity which is in turn imitated, and, above all and repeatedly, on an originary state that is followed by interpretation (II.1.205–6). But as Benjamin offers the example of the constellation, of the actual reading of the stars, the scenario of historian or reader appearing belatedly to unproblematically interpret what was already present is abruptly abandoned. Moreover, perception is no longer a question of possession—a possession that until now in "The Doctrine of the Similar" had only been spoken of in a narrative fiction. The perception of similarity is suddenly bound to an instantaneous flash. "The perception [of similarity] is in every case bound to a flashing up. It rushes hurriedly by. . . . It offers itself to the eye just as fleetingly, transitorially as a star constellation. The perception of similarities therefore appears bound to a moment of time [*Zeitmoment*]. It is like the supervention [*Dazukommen*] of the third, of the astrologer to the conjunction of two stars that wishes to be grasped in a moment [*Augenblick;* literally, blink of the eye]" (II.1.206–7). Thus the astrologer does not perceive the constellation or name it from outside. Nor is any reward made present to hand (II.1.207). Rather, the moment of interpretation, what Benjamin calls the perception of similarities, is one in which the reader-astrologer completes and is assimilated into the constellation in a flash.

One might ponder why "The Theses on the Philosophy of History" presents the "historical materialist's" revolutionary redemption of the past through its relation to the present in an image so surprisingly similar to—indeed almost identical to—this scene of reading. To put it another way: why is the political for Benjamin an act of reading, and why is a certain mode of reading always political? (And perhaps not only for Benjamin. What follows poses less as an answer to these questions than as a prolegomenon to the possibility of an answer). Perceiving similarities, in any case, inscribes the reader, just as the historical materialist's thinking is crystallized in the encounter between present and past. This suggests, at the very least, that what is at stake in such performances (certainly in the chapters to follow) can only be approached, not by appropriating a text or the past in the name of truth and as one's own, but through a practice of disparate readings.

The same story and yet never the same. "Historicism" is inevitably, as Benjamin puts it, "blasted," but the constellation that takes place in the confrontation of past and present, text and reader, is always a shock, revolutionary, and never predictable. It always puts into question, but forever differently, all that conservative "historicism" stands for. Benjamin, then, cannot speak for the other authors read here. The conventional temporality they glance off of says everything and nothing of what they are actually about. We have to mark the constellations ever anew, not in the mode of imitation but as encounter.

Nowhere is the pretense to a certain historicism more seductive than in Ford Madox Ford, in whose work the delineation of temporal scope is so precise and limited. Even the titles of Ford Madox Ford's critical works create a sense of unproblematical confrontation with a particular past—titles such as *Portraits from Life, Memories and Impressions, Joseph Conrad: A Personal Remembrance, Thus to Revisit, The March of Literature from Confucius to Modern Times, The English Novel, From the Earliest Days to the Death of Joseph Conrad.* Here is a writer with a fix on history, with a self-appointed mission to remember and reflect on it. Promises abound to record for us both the spirit of former times and of his own age. Let us leave aside that this prolific author of memoirs was repeatedly (and with good reason) attacked for his inaccuracies.

Ford accounts for these—and goes far beyond merely accounting for them with his theory of Impressionism. It is the theory of Impressionism on which I insist—not just restating it, like so many before me—but actually reading it in at least some of its resonances. And it is in light of that theory that one must consider Ford's most famous novel, *The Good Soldier.* Ford elaborates a number of "techniques," but none is as crucial as the "time-shift." Time and time again he disdains an adherence to fact and does so in the name of a storytelling that moves backwards and forward, simulating the order and way in which the past returns to our minds. For, despite his superficial pretensions to traditional historical sequencing, Ford favors what appears a more truthful reproduction of the narrating consciousness. This is how Ford's readers have come to understand him, with no sacrifice of the basic tenets of either the linear flow of time or the mimetic intentions of narrative. They simply substitute—as Ford often seems to—reproducing *impressions*, the way in which life is remembered by the observer, for what Ford calls reproducing *life* in words.

And yet, despite his claims to an accuracy of impressions that surpasses historical convention, to a force of sincerity that surpasses objective truthfulness, Ford is far more concerned with the impression of truth than with the truth of impression. Moreover, in

Ford's critical works (which he quite openly declares fictions), with complex parodic and ironic sleights of hand, he calls on us to rethink his texts in terms both of uncanny self-deflections and especially in terms of the semiotic and rhetorical operations of language.

The Good Soldier is the quintessential "Impressionist" novel. It performs Ford's techniques with such precision that his critics never tire of finding there what he has told them they would find. They rearrange the tale chronologically; they point out and fill in the narrator's gaps in memory; they explain away John Dowell's errors. But the temporal dilemmas John Dowell confronts exceed such recuperative critical gestures, and his predicament openly and from the beginning carries over to his readers. On the one hand, Dowell calls on us to puzzle things out, to fit the pieces together, claiming to have provided all the necessary facts. Dowell's memories are fragments, and he often forgets to remember and therefore forgets to arrange his memories in their proper place. On the other, and far more crucial, is the declared originary ignorance of all he never saw and never knew to begin with. None of this is fundamentally problematic, for if we cannot get straight the story of what happened to the Dowells and Ashburnhams, we are at least guaranteed, it would seem, an accurate rendering of the way and the order in which Dowell fails to remember.

Except that what *The Good Soldier* relentlessly insists on—interspersed with these questions of memory and narrative sequence—is a concern that throws even this possibility on its head. That concern is the way in which language functions. Talk functions less as that which expresses or releases an already present dangerous passion than as that which generates it in all its incarnations. This takes place not only in the context of the tale but also in its telling. Over and over and in many different ways we are told of a language in which no semiological or epistemological certainty can be vouchsafed. This comes to its richest theoretical implications in a scene that asks us to turn to history and all that the historical text might promise. It is a reference to a period on which Ford was something of an expert, having researched for many years a volume on Henry VIII. In a complex chain of ironical events, Ford has one of his characters mimic an autobiographical moment in which historical facts are mis-cited. When we turn to the actual historical event it turns out to be the 1529 conference at Marburg, where heated and endless discussion left unanswered how to determine the difference between literal and figurative language, an understanding without which neither history, nor biography, nor Impressionism can function. It is not as though, then, if Dowell could only have gotten it right and gotten it straight, if his memory had only served him correctly enough to overcome the temporal resistance that the past offers to every narrative, we might have fully understood. The point is that what seems a temporal barrier to regaining past time is always and repeatedly overtaken by forces far more formidable.

It is due to such forces that *Tristes Tropiques* is something of a hall of mirrors (the author himself will use the phrase), what we tend to call a "fun house," however inappropriate that may be for a book entitled *Sad Tropics*. Lévi-Strauss starts out backwards, inevitably confusing his ends and beginnings as, perhaps, any author writing of the past must do. Still, this is not exclusively attributable to the narrative structure of recapitulation. Those confusions of beginnings and ends, departures and destinations, are also Europe and South America, anthropologist and native, science and its object. And Lévi-Strauss is above all contemplating the nature of anthropology, asking what significance it might hold as he looks to his past.

Anthropology here is, of course, not only a matter of looking to that past two decades prior to the writing of *Tristes Tropiques* when Lévi-Strauss found himself in South America; it is also the question of looking to what we think of somehow as a return to an earlier era of humankind, to our own point of origin. The primitives, then, are as much self as other, and Lévi-Strauss is quick to identify himself with them. He defines his own anthropological endeavor as the failed quest of the young Indian engaged in the puberty rites of exposing himself to a dangerous wilderness, a quest in which the desire for power is left unsatisfied.

Unsatisfied, because there is inevitably an insurmountable disjunction between present and unrecuperable past. There is no way to reconstitute either the exotic or former times from a debris that inevitably slips through one's fingers. Is this because of the historical gap between twentieth-century explorer and an exoticism pure only hundreds of years prior? What looks like the wedge of intervening time becomes the inexorability of an epistemological double-bind: the fundamental unknowability of the anthropologist's scientific object either as past or as other.

And yet Lévi-Strauss will insist—for he can never free himself from this question—on two elaborate metaphors for anthropology, one of which seems to escape this skepticism. The passages are doubles of one another, both set on a geological stage that marks the distance between two rock formations. The fact that they dramatically present almost inverse conceptions of anthropological knowledge is symptomatic of what is to come, where one can trace the oscillation between remembering and forgetting, a scientific self-certainty and a melancholic despair, between meaning and what the anthropologist will finally call "entropology."

Just prior to entering the New World proper, Lévi-Strauss proposes the description of a sunset as a test of his future skills: to fix the real world in writing, to communicate it to others, to counteract the passage of time. As one might expect, the anthropologist both succeeds and fails. For if he seems to capture the most fleeting of structures, the subtlest of detail with elaborate reflection, what he in turn describes bespeaks cataclysmic scenes in which the object and its reflection are indistinguishable, in which structures dissolve and writing is obliterated. As with the geological metaphors, it is when anthropology seeks an adequate figure of itself that things go amiss.

When Lévi-Strauss finally arrives in South America and confronts his object, the reader is no doubt relieved to be free of the uncertainties of theoretical speculations. For hundreds of pages protracted descriptions of various tribes follow with little sense of hesitation, as though the opening chapters were themselves a rite of passage. We seem launched into a realm of retelling in which neither the other nor the past is problematic to the writer. Nevertheless, it is the Caduveo whom Lévi-Strauss encounters, the first tribe he reflects on in detail, those whose designed faces have significantly enough found their place on the cover of so many editions. And with the Caduveo what was formerly presented as a fundamentally temporal problem becomes rethought in terms of space.

First, prefatory to describing the Indians, is the extraordinary claim to powers that can reconstitute an ideal repertoire of the customs of all human societies set forth in a periodic table—with all its implicit assumptions about iterability, representation, and scientific reduction. Then follows Lévi-Strauss's fascination with the way in which the Caduveo women paint themselves, surely not in scientific tables, but with an art that splits and deforms the human face as well as many of the anthropologist's claims for systematicity. The designs neither reproduce the human visage nor one another, as one might have expected, and their fundamental asymmetry belies all attempts to reestablish the static harmony of a golden age implicit in the structuralist dream.

If Lévi-Strauss's attempts to capture the Caduveo in writing repeat the temporal involutions of the opening chapters in spatial terms, the remarkable closing pages of the volume pitch us to a cosmological theater of precipitous temporal slippage toward a future that reduces what came before to utter insignificance.

Not altogether different forces are at play in Lessing's *Laocoön*, although it takes getting away from the clichés attached to the text to see that. As any student of German literature can tell you, *Laocoön* is about the relation of time and space to the arts. The famous sixteenth chapter distinguishes the literary work from the visual arts in that literature, composed as it is of signs that follow one after another, must take actions rather than bodies as its proper objects. Despite traditional critical lore from Goethe to the present, this is hardly Lessing's first or last word on the relation between time and language. Or one might say that there is indeed one object that changes continually in the course of time and that is Lessing's text itself, which repeatedly represents itself in temporal frames of before and after to then redefine the performance of its language. *Laocoön* is framed in the guise of other temporal questions. It opens, for example, with a polemical attack. Polemics take no direct relation to an outside referent as their point of departure; they speak by way of undoing a previous work. The previous work in question is, significantly enough, a history. In attacking this work Lessing dazzles us with a fictive history of his own writing, pretending in the opening and the closing sections to have all but completed his treatise before the publication of Winckelmann's *History of the Art of Antiquity,* a text that explicitly presents *Laocoön*'s main thesis. Lessing tells us that polemics are no path to truth, but rather, a mode of struggle in which contradiction emerges. In fabricating the relation between Winckelmann's essay and his own, Lessing ironizes conventional history as representation, the essence of a text envisaged as its content, and the value of originality—of saying something first, of being the source rather than the imitation.

All this is elaborated further in another histrionic struggle, with historical questions of originality once again as its ostensible base. Lessing asks if the sculptors of Laocoön copied Virgil or whether it was the other way around. Although Winckelmann's earlier volume, *Thoughts on the Imitation of the Greek Works,* has nothing to say as to the historical priority of either the poet or the sculptors of the famous statue of Laocoön and his sons, Lessing invents a position for Winckelmann and takes the other side of the argument. As Lessing speaks for Virgil's historical priority, as he insists that it must be the sculptors who imitated the poet, he metaphorically speaks of his own priority with respect to Winckelmann. The lengthy argument gets entangled in questions of how to interpret Pliny and of how to read altogether, of how to understand the meaning of *similiter* ("similarly") in particular and the power of analogy in general. It is these issues of reading and figuration which, while upsetting once again (and as in Ford) the concept of linear, content-determined history, unhinge as well the concepts of controlled rhetorical language and authorship.

The frame of *Laocoön* is repeated at its interior, where the temporality of the written word is bound once again to questions of mimesis. In the closing sections of the body of the treatise Lessing ponders the place of the ugly and the disgusting in literature. The wisdom by which the temporal structure of language brings about dispersal of what it reproduces makes these otherwise questionable topics acceptable in literature, theoretically at least. Yet as Lessing belabors the semiotics of the disgusting, as he provides his reader with first-hand examples, as he more specifically probes the ways in which hunger can be represented, the logic of the essay's mimetic rules disintegrates.

As we circle around the pivotal section in which the definitive word on time and language is ostensibly uttered, implicitly at issue is always the very crux of the treatise and how its premises go awry. But even in section 16, where the relation between temporal and literary concepts is clearly established, in the very examples taken from Lessing's exemplary Homeric text, cited to prove his point, another story is told. At this moment, when he sets out to insist that Homer's narration through progressive temporal stages is better than giving us the thing itself, Lessing offers an allegorical reading in which power and interpretation are at stake. Here, as elsewhere, there is a multifaceted dissipation of authority—political, authorial, and readerly power alike. All this is bound to the force of allegory understood as a displacement in time and language.

For Paul de Man representation, allegory, and interpretation are also key concerns—although in a very different scenario. I have written here of that enigmatic essay "The Rhetoric of Temporality," which from its first publication in 1969 had such an impact on theoretical studies. I have placed it in the perspective of the Rousseau essays in *Allegories of Reading*, where matters appear to be more straightforward. In both, the issue of how one writes and how one reads cannot be separated, and each is critically determined by temporal questions.

One is struck in the opening essays on Rousseau by a sense of progression—the sense of a step-by-step increase in knowledge both within each essay and also in moving from one to the next. De Man seems to pose and solve questions one after another, each depending on what came before. He seems to learn from each of his mis(readings) and to move on to a state of higher enlightenment. Moreover, the subject matter starts with the fundamental questions of naming and advances to confront the self and then the act of interpretation. A multiple progression, then, is always at stake, at once in that to which the essays refer and to their act of referring, at once to their gesture of referring and ours of understanding.

The experience is one of being pitched ahead almost, or perhaps indeed, before we know it, to a higher level of critical understanding which is inevitably a more advanced level of error—an experience we will learn again to mistrust both from Wordsworth and from Rilke. For the movements sketched above are readable both as progress and as repetition—an ironical fall back into repeating a former mistake, albeit at a higher level of reflection.

Time—or at least the metaphor of temporality—is the driving force, as de Man will put it. Sequence or linear temporal order is the illusion which makes naming, reading, and understanding possible. It is that which gives apparent structure to much of *Allegories of Reading* and, no doubt, to all reading in general. It marks the repeated and uncontrolled discrepancy between the constative assertions and the performative thrust they generate. (De Man himself will speak of such interference between the two in reading Rousseau's *Social Contract* and also the fourth *Promenade*.) One can arrive at these conclusions by summary and paraphrase of the essays at hand. But it is only in working through de Man's particular enactments that one has a sense of the ungovernable relationship between self and self-definition, between author and rhetoric.

The earlier essay, "The Rhetoric of Temporality," certainly tests the powers of critical authority to define both its object and its own act of reading, for this is what the essay is about both in content and as performance. One has to reflect on not only the key terms— *allegory, symbol,* and *irony*—in all their implications for defining the literary text, but also the way in which this essay is put together. What seems a gesture of clarification—the division of the essay into

two parts—operates as a call to read the relationship between the
two. They ostensibly concern different literary modes, but they are
written in such a manner that their own allegorical, symbolic, and
ironic gestures must be understood to get beyond the flat, definitional, and assertive tonality that sometimes seems to control the
essay. De Man relates allegory and irony in that they have time as
their constitutive category—caught in the predicament of noncoincidence with their source. But this temporal dimension is precisely
what unhinges the relationship of the two sections of the essay,
which otherwise might be left to create an aura of satisfying conclusions untouched by an irony that invades the coherent historical
stories de Man pretends to tell.

   If the category of history is less explicit in the particular works of
Benjamin, Wordsworth, and Rilke read here, the conditions of its
narrative are no less at stake. Benjamin's essay on translation may
make a call—not to the historical—but to the "suprahistorical," but
like allegory and irony in de Man's terms, translation too marks a
telling noncoincidence with its source. When Walter Benjamin
writes of translation, he inevitably begins, given his topic, with the
temporal dilemma of anteriority that opens "The Rhetoric of Temporality" and that haunts so many of the other texts read here.
"The Task of the Translator" meditates the traditional temporal sequencing we cannot avoid attributing to translation. For translation
presupposes an original that guarantees its purpose. From the beginning, however, Benjamin ironizes the teleology of original and
translation both in relation to meaning and in relation to one another. Through metaphors of organic plant life, he elaborates an
expectation of linear development which he then systematically
disappoints. He speaks of winning back pure language only to insist that it is at once suprahistorical and also emancipated from all
sense of communication. As in de Man and Lessing, then, as in
Ford and Lévi-Strauss, the temporal structure of this mode of language has much to say about critical understanding.
   In an image borrowed from the Kabbalah that echoes the messianic hopes of restoring the broken fragments of original Being
and original history, Benjamin tells us that translation can never
bring about that which transcends the broken fragment. Translation—and for Benjamin all language is a translation of sorts—can
never make a lost beginning whole again, can neither restore the
past nor promise a conventionally conceived future redemption.
The past too is language. As Benjamin cites it, "In the beginning

was the word." Its destiny is a translation that ironically offers revelation, not as meaning, but as meaning lunging from abyss to abyss.

What seems the narrow and particular problem of translation,
what seems the description of a technical linguistic activity, is made
in Benjamin's essay explicitly metaphorical for criticism. It is exemplary no less for the way in which all writing takes place, and in
this regard a poet like Wordsworth may be seen to perform something akin to "translation," however much his lines appear to cling
to the originary.

Perhaps nowhere is this more evident than in "Tintern Abbey,"
where the sense of immediate experience of a particular natural
scene and its resonance in later memory seems the inescapable
point. Yet this poem, to which every reader of Wordsworth feels
compelled to return, is an elaborate questioning of such immediacy
and an insistence, rather, on the inevitable distancing implicit in
recollection, repetition, and reflection. If that is the case, Wordsworth nevertheless claims to achieve an increased level of conscious
understanding, that which he will call "thought," as recompense for
parting with his pantheistic beginnings. Something similar takes
place in the Immortality Ode, where recollection is rethought in
relation to mortality. There, the poet celebrates a mode of language
he calls "questionings," quite the contrary of the conventional celebration of childhood—a questioning that replaces the melancholic
sense of originary loss that opens the ode. In "Tintern Abbey" too,
Wordsworth accepts perplexity in place of the immediacy of nature
and a false sublime.

"Tintern Abbey" goes on to meditate another form of dubious
memory, one that is rooted in the love Wordsworth proclaims for
his sister Dorothy, tinged as his tone is with an egotistical and mor-
alistic superiority. The attempt to find himself by having Dorothy
relive the stages of his own progression culminates in a thrust to
the future in which the poet's death will leave his sister the task of
remembering him. And here remembrance is quite different from
its former emanation in the poem. Much might be said of its relation to Wordsworth's famous passage on Imagination in the sixth
book of The Prelude. As in The Prelude, so in the closing lines of "Tintern Abbey" the light of the senses and of sense goes out. Remembrance is no longer a matter of internal perception, nor is it a path
to the sublime. Like the "questionings" of the Immortality Ode, it
causes vanishings, as a recollection that displaces the past and pres-

ent in the name of a future that marks those displacements and not much more.

There is an uncanny repetition of this rupture into the future in a brief poem of Rainer Maria Rilke written a century and a quarter later. It is one of the *Sonnets to Orpheus*, and it sets out to define what mirrors are—mimesis perhaps, poetry certainly. How literature operates is bound to a peculiar concept of time, a link announced in the opening stanza, where mirrors are called "interstices of time," so that the poetic and the temporal are mutually defining or, perhaps, mutually liberating. The text inevitably works through what mirrors or literature is not. Much energy throughout Rilke's work, not only the poetry but also the fiction and the letters as well, goes towards exorcising mystified notions of language, and these fourteen lines are no exception. They think through, however tersely, definition, representation, and reflection; and the one, whether intentionally or not, inevitably becomes the other. The sonnet closes with an extraordinary encounter between the figure of Narcissus and another, emblematic of beauty. The temporal dimensions of the rapid narrative are barely comprehensible and are traced through only in an ungraspable enactment of literary self-deflection as a gap in time.

Less enigmatically, this is the enterprise of each of the texts we will read. Time and telling are inextricably bound but there are no theoretical morals to be drawn here. Critical and literary language as well as their readings are enmeshed in and defined by a passage of time that has already taken place and the lurch to a future that repeats the dilemma once again. It is these interstices of time that make such reflection both possible and unthinkable and totally inadequate to its pretensions. Each of these writers speaks of this both literally and figuratively, but above all in spectacularly different performances whose crucial implications are yet to be grasped.

1

● ● ● ● ● ● ● ●

Architectures
of Oblivion:
Lévi-Strauss's
Tristes Tropiques

● ● ● ● ● ● ● ● ● ● ● ● ● ●

Eugenio Donato, *in memoriam*

The Art of Anthropology

In reading a volume it makes sense to first cast an eye at the table of contents—a summary offered at the end of a book in French and an overture to what is to come in English, a "sort of small-scale image" (68F, 63E),[1] as Lévi-Strauss puts it in another context. In the case of *Tristes Tropiques*, while one hopes to grasp the clear structure of the whole, one is caught in a certain dilemma by this enterprise, for the space of those opening pages is marked erratically now by ends, now by beginnings. The first part is entitled "The End of Voyages," but the first chapter is called "Departure." Here we are carried along on the memory of so many departures that, like Lévi-Strauss, we can ultimately draw no lines of demarcation, floating along among dates that span the decades between 1934 and its writing: "I arrived in Marseilles ready to embark for Santos. Afterwards I knew other departures and all of them have blended together in my memory, where only a few images are preserved" (66F, 61E). If "The End of Voyages" paradoxically speaks of embarkations, the next section, which happens to reflect on Lévi-Strauss's various beginnings as an anthropologist, moves towards an image of closure, the setting of the sun as a privileged metaphor.

All of this leaves the point of his storytelling somewhat in suspense. One despairs of knowing where Lévi-Strauss is coming from or what he is trying to get at. How is one to understand his seeming inability to locate a beginning, uncertain as he is that there is such a point—that of civilization, as we shall see, of his career, of *Tristes Tropiques?* He starts out fifteen years after leaving Brazil, and once again by describing the departure for his major trip, and again in speaking of several later voyages, and over again by telling of his first interests in anthropology.

Somehow in this muddle of an overture (it takes Lévi-Strauss four sections and 150 pages to finally arrive at a detailed ethnographic description of the inhabitants of the New World) is a remarkable meditation on the question "What is anthropology?"—a question that has everything to do with the space between departure and destination, origin and end. For it is not simply a preoccupation with literal voyages that is intriguing here. Woven throughout these false starts and this forth and back between commencement and conclusion is a continual preoccupation with the relation between Europe and America, between the ethnographer and his subject.

Perhaps it goes without saying that not only these chapters but the entire book is played out between the Old World and the New, that it is less the so-called primitives of South America that are the subject matter of the book than their encounters with the European ethnographer. Both of these lay a claim in the logic of Lévi-Strauss's tale to an originary position of sorts. The primitive peoples he studies lie closer to a state (albeit now corrupted) of "earthly paradise" (80F, 74E) in a landscape apparently "emerging at the beginning of creation" (101F, 91E), primeval innocence and virginity of landscape.[2] And yet it is, of course, Europe that is the point of departure, physically, autobiographically, and scientifically. It is, after all, the voice of Lévi-Strauss that narrates.

But who is this European who, with unveiled contempt, claims for himself, already in the opening paragraphs, a more authentic understanding of his object of study than those who come after, those who make it impossible "for the reader to assess the value of the evidence" (14F, 17E), who do not devote themselves to "discovering hitherto unknown facts after years of study" (14F, 17E)? On the one hand, there is the repeated disdain[3] from the vantage point of the rigorous scientist. On the other, when Lévi-Strauss speaks of himself as anthropologist, he does so on occasion from a twilight in which he figures himself as an Indian.

Today I sometimes wonder if anthropology did not attract me, without my realizing this, by reason of the structural affinity between the civilizations it studies and my own thought. I have no aptitude for keeping a field prudently cultivated from which, year after year, I gather in the harvest. I have a neolithic intelligence. Like native bush fires, it sets, sometimes, unexplored areas ablaze; it may fertilize them in order to snatch a few crops from them, and then leave behind a devastated terrain. (57F, 53E)

Surely there is something facetious in insisting on a "neolithic kind of intelligence"[4] when the preceding lines rehearse in detail the anthropologist's virtuosity in the rigors of the French *agrégation* and other similar academic triumphs. And yet the image of leaving the earth devastated in one's wake, of destroying the ground of the harvest, will have a certain resonance.

That resonance can be located in the comparison that Lévi-Strauss elaborates over several pages between the rites of puberty among North American tribes and similar gestures in the context of European society.

Among a great many North American tribes, the social prestige of each individual is determined by the circumstances surrounding the ordeals to which adolescents must submit themselves at the age of puberty. Some set themselves adrift [*s'abandonnent*] without food on a solitary raft; others go to seek solitude in the mountains, exposed to face wild beasts, to the cold, and to the rain. For days, *weeks, or months* on end, as the case may be, they deprive themselves of food, consuming only coarse food, or *fasting* for long periods. . . . Everything is a pretext for calling forth the beyond. . . . Even when they do not resort to such extremes, they at least *exhaust* themselves with *pointless tasks* [*travaux gratuits*]: plucking out body hairs, one by one, or pine branches until they are stripped of all their needles, or hollowing out blocks of stone. (40F, 39–40E; emphasis mine)

This practice of the Indians of North America is, on the one hand, proposed as a counterpart to the "quest for power" so much in "vogue in contemporary French society, in the unsophisticated form of the relationship between the public and 'its' explorers" (41F, 40E). Such travelogue authors, who return with their "scraps of hackneyed information" (14F, 18E), appear as the ironized doubles of those who

in the dazed, weakened, or delirious state into which these ordeals plunge them . . . hope to enter into communication with the supernatural world. Touched by the intensity of their sufferings and their prayers, a magic animal will be forced to appear to them; a vision will reveal to them which one will henceforth be their guardian spirit at the same time as the name by which they will be known and the particular power held by their protector which will give them their privileges and rank within their social group. (40–41F, 40E)

And yet, of course, as is evident from the first page of *Tristes Tropiques*, it is Lévi-Strauss who long before has with far greater fidelity repeated the ritual, the fasting, the hardship, the exhaustion with pointless tasks (40F, 39–40E; see also 434-5F, 376E).

> Adventure has no place in the profession of ethnography; it is merely one of its limitations [servitude]: it weighs on his effective work with the loss of *weeks* or *months* on the way; idle hours when the informant slips away; *hunger, exhaustion*, sickness perhaps; and always the thousand and one *dreary tasks* [*corvées*] which eat away the days *to no purpose* (13F, 17E; italicized phrases echo those of the citation from 40F, 39–40E)·

Let me digress here to underscore that the European anthropologist turns to the New World to define himself. If the ethnographer describes the Indian myth, it is equally true that the Indian myth describes the ethnographer. Anthropology has something to do with this inversion, a reorientation or perhaps disorientation of the terms of its discourse.[5]

> And so, it was in Puerto Rico that I first made contact with the United States. . . . It was there, too . . . that I first perceived those features typical of the American town. . . .
> The accidents of journeys often produce ambiguities such as these. Having spent my first weeks on United States soil in Puerto Rico will make me from then on find America in Spain. Just as, several years later, having visited my first English University on a campus with the Neo-Gothic buildings of Dacca in Eastern Bengal now prompts me to look upon Oxford as a kind of India that has succeeded in controlling the mud, the mildew and the ever-encroaching vegetation. (35–36F, 35E)

In this Spain has been colonized by the Americans and England by the Indians. It makes perfect sense, then, that the "village" that Lévi-Strauss presents before all others is that of an overcrowded group of European refugees. We hear of the layout of the boat according to gender, of their sanitary arrangements, of their rituals of showering, toileting, and flirtations (23–24F, 25–26E).

This inverted vision of the Old and New Worlds that opens *Tristes Tropiques* finds exoticism first associated, not with the tribes of South America, but with the scientific figure at the origin of Lévi-Strauss's career.

> I had been a pupil of Georges Dumas at the time of his *Traité de psychologie*. Once a week . . . he gathered the philosophy students together in a room of Sainte Anne Hospital in which the wall opposite the windows was completely covered with joyous paintings by lunatics. One already had the sensation of being exposed to a peculiar kind of exoticism; there was a platform on which Dumas ensconced his robust body, roughly hewn, surmounted by a knobbly head resembling a large root that has been bleached and stripped through a stay on the sea bed. This curious piece of vegetable flotsam, still bristling with little roots, suddenly became humanized (16F, 19E)

At the European point of departure (and we will soon see how Dumas epitomizes at least a certain strain of the French cultural tradition) lies the exotic, an "exotic" that, despite the etymology, does not enter from the outside. At the center, then, of that which produces the anthropologist, there where the European par excellence should stand, raised on a platform, is the exotic Georges Dumas, who, under the scrutiny of Lévi-Strauss, becomes a vegetal anthropological object. (Much later in *Tristes Tropiques* he speaks of wandering along the shore gathering "roots . . . that figured chimeras in order to make [himself] a museum of all this debris" [390F, 338E].) Within the walls of Sainte Anne Hospital, there to contain the alienated of mind, where the ringmaster himself has already been shown as deflected to the fringe, Dumas follows up his lectures on psychology with a manner of circus. The so-called lunatics are now trotted out in performances in which they know quite well—all expectations to the contrary—both how and when to produce their symptoms. They obey—or is it that they thereby control?—their trainer (*dompteur*), the apparent master scientist, as the inversions of marginal and center proliferate:

> The second hour, and occasionally the third, were devoted to the presentation of patients; one was then witness to some extraordinary performances involving the crafty practitioner and his subjects who, after years of confinement, were trained in exercises of this kind, knowing quite well what was expected of them, producing symptoms on command or putting up just enough resistance to give their tamer the opportunity for a display of skill. (16F, 20E)

While Lévi-Strauss enjoys the irony of the situation, we must keep in mind that this also prefigures certain otherwise ironic scenes between the ethnographer and the savage. The exotic and the European, the insane and the scientific, do not hold their own here. Indeed, this is a lesson that Lévi-Strauss has learned outright if not from the *Traité de psychologie* of Georges Dumas then from psychological theories of another order:

> During the period from 1920 to 1930 psychoanalytical theories were diffused in France. They taught me that the static oppositions around which we were advised to construct our philosophical essays and later our teaching—the rational and the irrational, the intellectual and the emotional, the logical and the pre-logical—amounted to no more than a gratuitous game. (59F, 55E)

All the more so the static oppositions of Old World and New, the ethnographer and the primitive, as we have seen.

As Lévi-Strauss portrays himself reenacting Indian puberty rites, then, what distinguishes him from his European successors is an insistence on a certain failure.

> I, white-haired predecessor of those scourers of the bush, am I the only one to have held on to nothing but a handful of ashes? Is mine the only voice to bear witness to the failure of escapism? Like the Indian in the myth, I went as far as the earth allows one to go, and when I arrived at the world's end, I questioned the people, the creatures and things to find once again its deception: "He stood there, in tears praying and moaning. And yet he heard no mysterious sound, nor was he put to sleep in order to be transported, as he slept, to the temple of the magic animals. For him there could no longer be the slightest doubt: no power, from anyone, had fallen to him." (42–43F, 41–42E)

This failure defines Lévi-Strauss's position as anthropologist. It defines his success as well, for it is at this moment that the ethnographer most closely approaches the object of his study, where he can define himself in terms of the Indian in the myth, where the Indian myth speaks of and for Lévi-Strauss.[6] What the myth or this version of it tells is that the quest for power inevitably founders; no communication with the beyond is possible. One can bring back nothing but a handful of ashes, for such dreams inevitably slip through one's fingers.

It is here that Lévi-Strauss begins to describe this failure in terms of an insurmountable temporal disjunction. He shifts from the Indians of the New World to a city of ancient India to see where the dreams might have left "a few shining particles [*parcelles*]" in the hand. Starting at the outskirts of legendary Lahore, a "prisoner of . . . meaningless vastness," Lévi-Strauss moves toward a point he knows must escape him, "this old, this true Lahore" (43F). As an "archaeologist of space" he is compelled to displace himself horizontally rather than searching the depths.

> Prisoner of this meaningless vastness, what I am looking for is already beyond my reach. Where is this old, this true Lahore? In order to get to it, on the far side of these badly laid out and already decrepit suburbs, I still have to go through a kilometer of bazaar. . . . Am I going to finally get hold of it in these dark little streets? . . . In front of this crumbling woodwork, eaten away by the years? I would be able to sense [*deviner*] its lace and fretwork if the approach were not prohibited by the metallic spider web flung out from wall to wall all through the old town by the ramshackle electrical supply system. From time to time, certainly, for several seconds and over the space of a few meters, an image or an echo surges up from the depths of the past. . . . I climb out if only to fall back again immediately into a vast network of avenues brutally cutting through the ruins . . . of 500-year-old houses. . . . Thus I recognized myself, traveller, archaeologist of space, seeking in vain to reconstitute the exoticism with the aid of particles and debris. (43–44F, 42–43E)

Like the metallic spiderwebs of the electric wires, the entire endeavor is cast over with a web of illusion. One cannot rediscover a lost and originary exoticism. What Lévi-Strauss finds is "parcelles et debris." *Parcelles* is the term earlier used for what might yet remain once the dream had slipped through his fingers, once the search for communication with the supernatural had failed: "The dream, 'god of the savages,' as the old missionaries used to say, has always slipped through my fingers like elusive quicksilver. Where did it leave me a few shiny particles [*parcelles brillantes*]? . . . I choose at random a name still steeped in magic according to legend: Lahore" (43F, 42E). The archaeologist of space finds his particles, but they do not enable him to "reconstitute [*reconstituer*]" a past. Exoticism, it would seem, is more present to hand in the context of Sainte Anne's. The particles that remain are bound up, rather, with "debris," a term that, strangely enough for a founder of "structuralism," we will see to be fundamental to Lévi-Strauss's enterprise.[7] Why is it that the exotic cannot be "reconstituted"? Why can one not re-form the authentic whole in gathering up the diverse elements of the past? Why is it that Lévi-Strauss is able to recognize himself precisely insofar as his quest for such a reconstitution is recognized as vain ("Thus I recognized myself, traveller, archaeologist of space, seeking in vain to reconstitute the exoticism with the aid of particles and debris" [44F, 42–43E])? Can this be explained by the narrator's historical position? Is the fragmentation of the exotic attributable to the historical gap between the true Lahore and the twentieth-century traveller, or say, between the true Brazil and its European visitor?

> Then, insidiously, illusion begins to weave its snare. I would like to have lived at the time of *true* [*vrais*] journeys, when a spectacle that was not yet spoiled, contaminated, and cursed would have offered itself in all its splendor; I would like not to have crossed over this boundary myself [*n'avoir pas franchi cette enceinte moi-même*], but as Bernier, Tavernier or Manucci. . . . Once broached, this guessing game has no end. When would one have had to see India? At what period would the study of the Brazilian savages have afforded the purest satisfaction, made them knowable [*les faire connaître*] in their least adulterated state? Would it have been better to arrive in Rio in the eighteenth century with Bougainville, or in the sixteenth with Léry and Thevet? (44F, 43E)

Lévi-Strauss mocks the youthful traveller who has completed his notes in forty-eight hours, hiding the fact that the object of his study has been in touch with missionaries for decades, glossing over the cans in which the apparently virgin natives do their cooking, neglecting to mention the motorboat that brought him to the so-called primitives.

> I open one of these explorer's accounts: such and such a tribe is described as savage and as preserving to this day the customs of some caricature or other of primitive humanity in several superficial chapters; yet I spent weeks of my life as a student in taking notes on works that fifty years ago, sometimes even recently, men of science had devoted to their study, before contact with the whites and the subsequent epidemics had reduced them to a handful of pathetic rootless individuals. (39F, 39E)

But was there a time when European consciousness could have confronted the exotic and have experienced it as not fragmented, as not yet broken up and contaminated by Western thought?[8] (The correlative question is whether the Western eye could ever have been pure in its scientific perspective, as yet untainted by the decay of its object.) Or is there, perhaps, implicit in the very concept of the exotic, despite its aura of wholeness, a fundamental fragmentation? The earlier the voyage, the greater the possibility of "saving a custom," "gaining a holiday," "sharing in an additional belief." And yet, the earlier historical positioning of the predecessors holds no epistemological advantage:

> But I am too familiar with the texts not to know that, in stripping away a century, I am at the same time renouncing information and things of interest that would enrich my reflections [*propres à enrichir ma réflexion*]. And there in front of me is the uncrossable circle [*le cercle infranchissable*]: the less human societies were able to communicate with each other and therefore to corrupt each other through contact, the less their respective emissaries were able to perceive the riches and significance of this diversity. In short, I am prisoner of an alternative: either like some traveller of the olden days, faced with a stupendous spectacle, all, or almost all, of which eluded him . . . ; or modern traveller, chasing after the vestiges of a vanished reality. (44–45F, 43E)

Once one knows the texts (and let us not forget that *connaître* and *savoir* are linked to texts), one is caught in a circle from which there is no escape. (One might reflect here on the symmetry of the phrases, lost in the English, that mark the entrance into this realm—"franchir cette enceinte" and, inherent in the confrontation, the later inability to escape from its epistemological dilemma, "le cercle infranchissable".) The more one moves back in time, the more one loses the information necessary for proper reflection. The less communication and therefore corruption, the less one perceives and understands the significance of what one encounters.[9] One could have seen all and understood nothing, or, as modern travellers, one can chase after the vestiges of a reality that has disappeared (see also 375F, 326E). In any case, as the closing passage of *Tristes Tropiques* will put it, "all effort to understand destroys the object to which we had attached ourselves" (475F, 411E). The anthropologist does, it would seem, leave a devastated territory in his wake.

> I lose on both counts [*sur ces deux tableaux*], and more than may at first appear, for, while I moan when faced with these shadows, am I not impervious to the true spectacle which takes shape at this very moment, for the observation of which my level [*degré*] of humanity is still lacking the required sense? A few hundred years hence, in this

same place, another traveller, as despairing as myself, will mourn the disappearance of what I might have seen, but which escaped me. Victim of a double infirmity: all that I perceive offends me, and I constantly reproach myself for not seeing more. (45F, 43E)

From the perspective of the future, the modern traveller repeats the blindness of his or her predecessors. The "true spectacle" of the moment is never available to a present sensibility that will constitutively always be lacking. It is only centuries from now that what we (fail to) see today may be sensed; and then only as that which has already disappeared.

And so we have perhaps come full circle in our paradox, even if we have found no means of passing beyond it. Lévi-Strauss defines the ethnographer in terms of the Indian in the myth: having arrived at the end of the world, no power from the beyond is granted him. This position is cast in temporal and epistemological terms. The definition of the ethnographer, which, metaphorically, may well be his greatest triumph of proximity to the savage, tells of his inability to communicate with that beyond and that past which is the Indian.[10] One could regard this as a failure in understanding or as the understanding of a necessary failure. Knowledge, in any case, as Lévi-Strauss suggests above, is the force that brings about the effacement of its object, an object separated by a temporal and cultural gap. Intelligibility is coincident with a contact that corrupts. And yet it is that corruption or loss that makes further knowledge possible, makes it possible to enrich one's reflection. What one knows is perpetually in the process of slipping through one's fingers, and it would seem to be the knowing that brings about that inevitable disintegration. At best, one can learn to understand the structure of such epistemological crumbling.

What takes place, of course, in this process of contamination/ knowledge is not only that the Indians become more available to the understanding in taking on a more "adulterated state" (44F, 44E) but also that they become more like the European. The passage that follows in *Tristes Tropiques* is the logical, if puzzling, extension of that fact in an elaborate metaphor. The temporal chasm is no longer that between the twentieth-century explorer and the savages of several centuries earlier in their pure and originary state. It is a question, rather, of coming to terms with a personal temporal gap, that between the events of which Lévi-Strauss writes and the era of their recording two decades later.

Here there is a shift from the general dilemma of the ethnographer to the construct of Lévi-Strauss's individual scene, and we are somehow to understand the latter as the solution to the former. The preceding pages spoke of the ethnographer doomed to find his object already fragmented, reduced to a kind of debris out of which any reconstitution of a lost primitive exoticism would be an illusion. Yet here one is tempted to say that with the passage of time, things take shape by simply falling into place.[11] And yet that is not quite what happens.

> For a long time paralyzed by this dilemma, it seems to me, however, that the cloudy liquid is beginning to settle. Evanescent forms are becoming clearer, the confusion is dissipating slowly. What has happened if not the passage of years? In rolling my memories in the flux, forgetting has done more than wear them away and bury them. The profound edifice that it has constructed of these fragments offers a more stable balance to my steps, a clearer design to my sight. One order has been substituted for another. Between these two cliffs that maintain my gaze and its object at a distance from one another, the years that break them down have begun to pile up the debris. The ridges dwindle, entire faces collapse; times and places collide with each other, become juxtaposed or inverted, like strata dislocated by the tremblings of an aged [planetary] crust. That miniscule detail rises up like a peak, while entire layers of my past cave in without leaving a trace. Events that are without apparent relationship coming from disparate periods and regions slide against one another and suddenly become fixed in the semblance of a small castle the plans of which were thought out by an architect wiser than my own history. . . . From then on the passage is possible. In an unexpected way, between life and myself, time has stretched forth its isthmus; twenty years of forgetting were necessary to bring me into a tête-à-tête with a former experience of which a chase as distant as the other end of the world had once refused me the meaning and robbed me of the immediacy. (45F, 43–44E)

Whereas disintegration and the piling of debris were the point of lamentation in the description both of Lahore and of the ethnographer's constitutive belatedness, here they are the means to bring about order and form. What does it mean to construct an edifice of stability and clear design out of a vocabulary conventionally destined to mark a collapse of structure: *fragments, ruinent* (break down), *debris, s'amenuisent* (dwindle), *s'effondrent* (collapse), *se heurtent* (collide), *tremblements* (quakes), *s'affaisent* (cave in)? Lévi-Strauss is no longer set on recapturing another's historical experience of a virgin past but, rather, on coming to terms with his own past. His is a perspective across the decades that separate him from his early experiences of South America, and what he contemplates at that temporal distance is the relation between his former ethnographic eye and the primitive it beheld. For the scene he delineates is that of two cliffs held at a distance from one another, the one "my gaze," the other, "its object." If he thereby closes the first part of *Tristes Tropiques* with the quasi-triumphant announcement of a finally achieved "tête-à-tête" with his former experience, this is not to say that it brings about the once denied meaning and immediacy of that experience: entire layers of his past cave in without leaving a trace. Nor is this a gesture of recapturing his own past, an act of bringing to consciousness afterward. Whatever takes form here, whatever takes place, is due to a watery tide of oblivion ("le trouble liquide," "[l'oubli] roulant mes souvenirs dans un flux"). It is the flight of time, the two decades of forgetting, that results in an architecture planned by a wisdom and consciousness other than his own ("an architect wiser than my history").[12] Forgetting rolls his memories in its liquid flux, disintegrating both gazer and his object. Gone are the cliffs of the seeing eye and the scientific object, and with them memory.[13] Out of the debris arises form, design, structure.

This is at once the same and quite different from what preceded it. The debris that in Lahore marked the vanishing of the "real" form is now necessary for the appearance of form. The gap that previously was a temporal difference of centuries, separating the eye of the ethnographer from the originary savage, is reprojected on the one hand as a spatial chasm between gaze and object (where, just as before, the confrontation between Indian and European means mutual disintegration), and on the other as the difference of two decades that separates the current narrative perspective from its past.[14] Time, once the obstacle to ethnography, has become that which enables it through an architecture of forgetting.

Given this, how can we possibly situate the long geological description less than twenty pages later, also presented as an image for the kind of knowledge Lévi-Strauss sees himself producing, another metaphor, then, of ethnography? The passages must be placed side by side because it is once again a question of a certain cleft between two pieces of land. To be sure, despite the recurrent landscape of rocky debris and crumbling stone ("debris rocheux" [60F], "éboulements" [61F]), the natural scene of the first passage functions quite differently from the quasi-scientific pretensions in the second.[15] It was not, after all, in that imaginary setting, a question of actual cliffs, an actual waterway, an actual isthmus, but of these as figures for the gazer and his past, the flux of forgetting, the passage of time. The whole sense of that natural allegory was a collapsing of distinctions, a breakdown of the distance between the ethnographer-gazer and his more originary object of study, as well as between the narrator's present and his past. It was disintegration and fragmentation that paradoxically produced structure.

Nothing, it would seem, could be farther from what Lévi-Strauss is about in a chapter entitled "How One Becomes an Ethnographer."

> This intellectual evolution, which I underwent along with other members of my generation, was given a particular nuance because of the intense curiosity which had pushed me in the direction of geology ever since childhood. I still rank among my most precious memories . . . the tracking of the line of contact between two geological strata along the flank of a limestone plateau in Languedoc. . . . This quest, incoherent to an uninformed observer, offers to my eyes the very image of knowledge. (60F, 56E)

Let us note that in the larger context of this passage Lévi-Strauss produces an intellectual autobiography, one in which one cannot imagine entire layers of his past collapsing as before. Effortlessly, rather, he reconstructs for his reader those forces that account for his intellectual evolution and recalls one of his "most precious memories." At the flank of a limestone plateau his careful gaze searches for the line of contact between two geological strata; the eye of the observer is in no more risk of crumbling than the stony object of his scientific eye. This quest for a line of demarcation might well be regarded by a lesser observer as incoherent—not only the line but the quest itself. For the geologist is not only he who completes the particular task called for by his discipline, but also he who understands its vaster epistemological significance as "the very image of knowledge."

> Every countryside presents itself at first as an immense disorder which leaves one free to choose the sense one prefers to give it. But beyond agricultural speculations, geographic accidents, the varied experiences of history and prehistory, isn't the most majestic meaning [sens auguste] of all that which precedes, rules, and in a larger measure explains [explique] all the others. This pale and confused line, this often imperceptible difference in the form and consistency of the rocky debris testify to the fact that there where I today see arid soil two oceans once succeeded one another. Following the

tracks of the evidence of their millenaire stagnation and overcoming [*franchissant*] all obstacles—abrupt cliff walls, stone-falls, scrub bushes, cultivation—indifferent to the paths as well as the barriers, one seems to be acting in a meaningless fashion. Yet the sole aim of this insubordination is to recover a master sense, obscure, no doubt, but of which each of the others is a partial or deformed transposition.

When the miracle occurs, as sometimes happens, when from one side and the other of the secret crevice there rises up side by side two green plants of different species of which each has chosen the most propitious soil, and when at the same moment two ammonites with involutions of unequal complexity are discernable in the rock attesting in their own manner to a distance [*écart*] of several dozen millennia, suddenly space and time merge [*l'espace et le temps se confondent*]. The living diversity of the instant juxtaposes and perpetuates the ages. (60–61F, 56E)

One order has been substituted for another. The architecture of forgetting has been superseded, or is at least counterbalanced, by an architecture of memory. No longer caught in the vicissitudes of liquid flux, the element of water disappears in favor of terra firma. Lévi-Strauss marks with precision and certainty the ground on which he stands, a stability and clarity quite different from that suggested by the "profound edifice" formed of settling debris two chapters earlier. There, "times and places collide[d] with each other," ("les temps et les lieux se heurtent" [45F, 44E]) became juxtaposed or inverted, were like the dislocated strata of monumental earthquakes. Here, "space and time merge" in a scene that celebrates the transition from "disorder" to the recovery of a master sense.[16] However immense the confusion may seem, it is pale and all but imperceptible ("this pale and confused line, this often imperceptible difference," a "secret crevice") and destined to be resolved by a majestic meaning that precedes, determines, and explains everything. Entering the bounds of primitive South America ("avoir franchi cette enceinte" [44F]) meant being caught in an inescapable (epistemological) circle ("le cercle infranchissable" [44F]), but here in southern France there is no longer a problem in overcoming either physical or intellectual obstacles ("franchissant tous les obstacles" [60F]).

Just before Lévi-Strauss conjures up his past geological memory, metaphorical for his epistemological position and ethnographic achievements, he prefaces it with "I convinced myself that beings and things are able to conserve their own values without losing the clarity of the contours that delimit them with respect to one another and that give to each an intelligible structure" (60F, 55–56E). This insistence on the clarity of contours that delimit beings and things—which is to say the human mind and its object—has everything to do with the lines that follow. For what is it that Lévi-Strauss sees when he sees two plants of different species, two ammonites of unequal complexity, split side by side across the obscure cleft? He calls it the difference between two eras (here a separation between several dozen millennia), the living diversity of the present that is able to juxtapose the diversity of two (pre)historical moments before the scientific eye of the narrator.

It should be obvious that the two geological scenes are as remarkably similar in outline as they are different in apparent content: in each a narrative perspective that describes in geological metaphor the relation between two implicit eras—the cliffs as the (primitive) Indian and (twentieth-century) European on the one hand, and the sides of the secret crevice on the other as two eras separated by thousands of years. And what is anthropology, after all (as Lévi-Strauss also puts it), if it is not being able "to reascend the flow of millennia" (435F, 376E)?[17]

At a later moment he implicitly links the two passages by comparing the difference of two settlements side by side (of two human civilizations, therefore) to that found by paleontologists in geological strata:

> In displacing themselves from one point to another without necessarily increasing in number, the inhabitants changed in social type, and the observation side by side of fossilized towns and embryonic cities made possible on the human level and within extremely short temporal limits the study of transformations as striking [*saisissantes*] as those of the paleontologist comparing geological strata in order to follow the phases, extending over millions of centuries, of the evolution of organized beings. (125F, 112E)

Thus, all along we have been shifting through similar scenarios with similar insistence on temporal differentiations: first between primitive Indian and European in general, then between the "real" or ancient Lahore and the contemporary wanderer, then between the South American tribes in their originary state and the twentieth-century ethnographer, who are separated by hundreds of years and available to each other's understanding only at the price of mutual contamination or a losing "of the clarity of the contours that delimit them"—then, finally, Lévi-Strauss's image for his current narrative perspective as he contemplates the cliff of the European eye crumbling together with the cliff of its ethnographic object while the narrative subject renounces recuperation of memory in the name of collapse and forgetfulness. But here the eye of the geologist escapes contamination, crumbling, the oblivion of forgetting. It remembers the past and sees itself seeing, clearly and distinctly, the line of contact between geological strata, the (almost imperceptible) difference or gap between eras. This prowess is in turn guarantor of a master sense which rules and explains all other meaning and functions as "the very image of knowledge"—quite the inverse of the image of knowledge implicit in the relationship between ethnographer and Indian or in the crumbling cliffs of gazer and object caught in the flux of forgetting.[18]

What, then, is Lévi-Strauss's structuralism? How are we to make intelligible, how can we reconcile, such different moments, such different places in *Tristes Tropiques?* For with the second geological metaphor he feels himself "bathed by a more dense intelligibility at the heart of which the centuries and places correspond with one another" (61F, 56–57E). In the earlier passage times and places collided with one another to the point of mutual collapse. Still, in this last geological description, where Lévi-Strauss celebrates his acumen in delineating between two epoques and thereby echoes the earlier, less definitive distinctions between European and primitive, one can find an almost imperceptible line of connection to what came before. In this passage, under the aegis of the chapter title "How One Becomes an Ethnographer," so concerned with place and past, we find a place and past to which we must return. The plateau of which the narrator speaks, the plateau with the hidden (fault) line, is located in the Languedoc.

Once before as Lévi-Strauss also spoke of how he became an ethnographer, the region of Languedoc had a certain resonance.

[Dumas's] courses did not teach a great deal; he never prepared one, conscious as he was of the physical charm exerted by the expressive play of his lips deformed by an inconstant grin and especially his voice, hoarse and melodious—a true siren's voice of which the strange inflections re-echoed not only his natal Languedoc but even more the very archaic modes of the music of spoken French. (16F, 19–20E)

How shall we read the figure of Languedoc? In the later passage it is the ground on which the line of difference between two eras can be absolutely determined as a master sense. In the earlier passage it is the native land of Dumas—Dumas, once again at the origin of Lévi-Strauss's career, whose unscientific lectures were of little intellectual significance, resonating at once with the language of Languedoc and also with an archaic mode of French musicality, above all that figure in whom we have seen the two eras suggested by the European and the exotic to be inextricable. In the plateau of Languedoc, that figure in which Lévi-Strauss establishes his epistemological certainty precisely insofar as he can read a line of differentiation between two time periods, there is another, even more imperceptible rift, then—between the possibility of rigorous scientific narrative and the descriptive seductions of a siren's voice, in which such demarcations are inevitably blurred.

Perhaps this is why Lévi-Strauss now abandons the ground on which he ostensibly founds his science and turns a few pages later to the heavens. This, the seventh chapter of *Tristes Tropiques*, entitled "Sunset," is strikingly bizarre, peculiarly irrelevant, it might seem, to the scientific anthropological project[19]—a long and novelistic passage[20] in which human society is, in all but a few phrases, forgotten. Nevertheless the passage occupies a unique and pivotal position.[21] It is the last of the truly introductory chapters, marking the line of demarcation between what precedes and the third part, entitled "The New World." In many ways it is an overture appearing at the end of those meditations instead of at the beginning, summarizing and raising again the complications with which we have only begun to come to terms. For if what we have encountered so far was a series of reflections on the enterprise of anthropology, Lévi-Strauss presents the eight pages of notes on the setting of the sun as (once again) "the very image of [his] knowledge" (60F, 56E):

> If I found a language to fix these appearances [that were] at the same time unstable and rebellious to all effort of description, if it were given to me to communicate to others the phases and the articulations of a nevertheless unique event and one which would never reproduce itself in the same terms, then, it seemed to me I would have in one single stroke penetrated to the deepest mysteries of my profession: there would be no experience to which the ethnographic inquiry might expose me, however bizarre or peculiar, which I would not one day be able to make graspable in all its significance and consequence [*portée*]. (67F, 62E)

The setting sun is not only the very image of his knowledge but also and above all a test of its possibility, and one in which the parameters of that knowledge have shifted. It is no longer a question of bridging a vast cultural or temporal gap, the temporal gap that might return one to the natives of several centuries before or to one's past experience of them two decades ago. Nor is a shrewd discerning of the relation between millennia at issue. The eye, first of all, has been replaced by the pen, and the temporality is now one of the instant if not of simultaneity.

The language of the anthropologist is the counteractant to the instability of the moment. Its deepest secret lies in finding the right words and thus being able to fix the rebellious articulations of unique events, to reproduce in writing what nature will never reproduce in fact. "Experience," which earlier was to be recaptured only insofar as it crumbled into debris, is here to be preserved in the never-never land of a text which grasps all meaning and in turn makes that significance available to others.

Once again the anthropologist is confronted with rites of passage, but a very different version from that of the Indian at puberty with whom he so passionately identified himself. The risks seem fatuous in relation to those of the earlier scenario, for all takes place here pen in hand, and the results—which we know in advance to be all but guaranteed—are the assurance of a total plenitude of understanding and a hedge against the passage of time that speaks inexorably of our mortality. If the challenge is that of repeating the sunset, Lévi-Strauss notes this even before giving us the particular description, the sunset in turn, is itself a repetition, therefore an image of the possibility of repetition and perhaps of the possibility of describing what one has seen.

> The sunrise is a prelude, its setting an overture that would take place at the end rather than at the beginning as in old operas. The face of the sun announces the moments that are going to follow. . . . But dawn does not judge in advance the continuation of the day. It sets the meteorological action going and says: it is going to rain, it is going to be nice. As for the sunset, it is something else; it is a question of a complete representation with a beginning, a middle, and an end. And this spectacle offers a sort of small scale image of the battles, the triumphs, and the defeats which have succeeded one another for twelve hours in a palpable manner, but also one that is slower. The dawn is nothing but the beginning of the day; dusk is the repetition of it. (68F, 62–63E)

The sunset is an overture that takes place at the end instead of at the beginning. It repeats the events of the day. To be sure, the scale is changed from the original, as well as the speed of events—but it is nevertheless a repetition. And yet these events are given a decidedly agonistic cast, categorized as they are as combats, victories, and defeats. "The play of consciousness" (68F, 63E) is also to be read there, and the two are not without relation to one another.

> To remember [*se souvenir*] is a great sensual pleasure for man but not in so far as memory [*mémoire*] shows itself to be literal, for few would accept to live again the weariness and sufferings that they nevertheless like to recall. Memory [*le souvenir*] is life itself, but of another quality. Thus it is that when the sun goes down toward the polished surface of a calm water, like the farthing of a celestial miser, or when its disk cuts out the crest of mountains like a hard and serrated leaf, man finds preeminently, in a short fantasmagoria, the revelation of the opaque forces, the mists and flashings of which in the depths of himself and throughout the day he has vaguely perceived [*perçu*] the obscure conflicts.
>
> It must have been, then, that very sinister struggles took place in the soul. Because the insignificance of the exterior events did not justify any atmospheric debauchery. Nothing had marked out that day. (69F, 63E)

But Lévi-Strauss is there to mark down the sunset and thus to repeat, as a measure of his future anthropological skills, the repetition of the day. And yet, not quite a duplication of the day—changing the scale, slowing its speed, finding nothing but struggles, as we have noted. Moreover, the way we are to understand the sunset here is determined, it would seem, by the way in which man draws pleasure from memory, only in its nonliterality—refusing to relive the sufferings of the everyday. If the sunset, then, as the play of human consciousness is life of another order, we might expect a suppression of the negative, a counterfeit coin, as it were, that renders bright, hard, and shiny the worn object of its imitation. Yet if man takes great pleasure in remembering, it is not because he remembers pleasure in place of conflict: "very sinister struggles" are, after all, what the sunset reveals to him—cataclysms far greater than anything suggested by the day's non-events. The great pleasure of remembrance requires substitution of recalling for reliving. For what one "remembers" is not at all what we tend to call life—those totally insignificant exterior events—but rather that which one had sensed only in the most obscure manner and which takes place within our own souls. Not that the revelation which the setting sun is makes all of that clear: what man finds at the end of the day in which nothing was to be noted, having come up under himself, as "se sou-venir" might suggest, is the struggle of forces within, which nevertheless remains as opaque as flashes and mist.

This appears as "a short fantasmagoria," not as a conscious act of will, but rather as a revelation that appears to come from outside and seems granted by another. Thus it is as the "farthing of a celestial miser" that the sun moves down toward the water, offering no great illumination, shedding no great light. And who is this celestial miser if not a figure of God, a god who bestows no grandiose gift to mankind, but a coin, which though of a certain value, is not of a very great worth after all? He drops the sun-coin that gives just enough light to remind us that what comes to us of ourselves is in the guise of opacity and all too rapid flashes—to remind us that in the normal course of the day we see nothing of what is really going on, however much we may be bent on recording what we see.

"If it were given" him, Lévi-Strauss writes to preface this passage, to communicate to others what he has seen—but what is given him by that questionable deity is a setting sun at odds with all he sought to achieve, at odds with the iterability of a lived event, at odds with the significance or even pleasure of such iterability,[22] insistent, rather than on the promised reconciliation, on cataclysms not available to the conventional eye. In this natural description, emblematic (or so we are told) of an assured scientific take on ethnography, there are hidden inner struggles, then, precisely in relation to the passage's pretext.

Such conflicts (perhaps the deepest secrets of Lévi-Strauss's profession) intensify as we begin to read this remembrance of the sunset and of the sunset as remembrance:

> At 5:40 P.M. the sky, on the west side, seemed encumbered by a complex edifice, perfectly horizontal below, in the likeness [à l'image de] of the sea from which one would have thought it had been separated [decollé] by an incomprehensible stilting above the horizon or perhaps by the interposition between them of a thick and invisible sheet of crystal. At its top were hanging and were suspended towards the zenith under the effect of an inverted force of gravity, unstable scaffoldings, swollen pyramids, immobilized [figés] frothy bubblings [solidified] in a style of molding that would claim to represent clouds, which clouds themselves would resemble in so far as they evoke the shine and roundness of sculpted and gilded wood. (70F, 64–65E)

Here the very first lines to record the actual sunset are couched in precision of time and place (later it will be "5:45 P.M. *precisely*"

[71F, 66E; emphasis mine]. And yet who cannot fail to sense this apparently exterior event as a fantasmagoria that reveals—had we not done it before—or repeats the obscure conflicts of those earlier meditations on the nature of anthropology? If the crumbling cliffs of the ethnographer's gaze and its object produced a "profound edifice" (45F, 43E) constructed of debris in the waters of forgetfulness, here we find a "complex edifice" that is the very image of the sea. This figure is indeed complex: it not only doubles the one construction, but sets forth as well the lines of demarcation that organized the second geological metaphor. What takes place here and never ceases to disconcert is the play across such lines, hardly as distinct as that which Lévi-Strauss differentiated between the two geological strata. In this skyscape the anthropologist finds a structure with a lower horizontal in the likeness of the ocean but incomprehensibly lifted above the horizon line as though an invisible sheet of glass divided them. "Incomprehensible," "invisible"— these are the key terms,[23] for the narrative delineates a sea and sky whose borders are indeterminable.[24] A cloud formation in the likeness of the sea, but also like a thing of the earth, it mirrors and inverts the sense of terrestrial structure, with "unstable scaffoldings" hanging as though pulled towards the zenith. The moldings are made so to resemble, not clouds, but their imitation, that clouds might resemble them only if they were to imitate human, earthly woodworking. It is the unfinished project of a mad architect who fashions his edifice of clouds and intangible mirrors.

As the night enters, in an act that Lévi-Strauss calls a piece of trickery ("supercherie" [74F, 67E]), cast in metaphors of painting, sculpture, theater, and photography, the illusory realms and lines of distinction proliferate.

> The nocturnal [photographic] plate slowly revealed a marine landscape above the sea, immense screen of clouds fraying out in front of an oceanic sky in parallel peninsulas, like a flat and sandy coast seen from a banking plane flying at a low elevation. . . . The illusion was found to be increased by the last glimmers of the day, which, hitting these cloudy points very obliquely, gave them the appearance of [standing out in] a relief such that they conjured up solid rocks— they too, but at other times sculpted of shadow and light—as though the star would not make use of its glittering graving tools on porphyry and granite but only on feeble and vaporous substances while at the same time conserving the same style in its decline.
>
> Against this backdrop, which resembled a coastal landscape, as the sky progressively cleaned itself one saw beaches, lagoons, myri-

ads of islets and sandbanks appear, invaded by the inert ocean of the sky, which riddled the sheet in the process of decomposition with fjords and inland lakes. And because the sky bordering these cloudy shafts simulated an ocean, and because the sea usually reflects the color of the sky, this celestial tableau was a *reconstitution* of a faraway landscape on which the sun would set again. (73F, 63E; emphasis mine)

The narrator travels across the ocean from one continent to another, at ease in inhabiting both land and sea, which, he assures himself, man has mastered, perhaps overmastered. Yet the whole point of this exercise is to note down what takes place in that third realm of the sky which promises to repeat the substance of the human day and the human realm. And is this not what is unbearable, that the sky—which is at once for us the theological locus (place of the heavenly miser) and a realm we enter only with a certain daring questioning of gravity (as in a banking plane)—mimics and confuses the relation of land and sea and air? For the clouds in the sky look now like land, now like ocean or inland bodies of water, and even now like clouds ("at other times sculpted of shadow and light . . . on feeble and vaporous substances"). In a rapid flicker they become alternately one or the other, dislocating our gaze and even the locus of the setting sun, which threatens to set again in a faraway landscape that is itself created by the sunset's illusion. "Reconstituer," which in the passage about Lahore was the subject for nostalgic complaint, reappears here as a pitch to a future that will mirror but dislocate our present.

In this chapter that culminates a series of theoretical reflections, in this test of imitative accuracy and correct notation, we find a whimsical realm of mimetic chaos and borderlines run wild. And yet, it would seem, there is still space for precise distinctions—although, perhaps, with a certain double-edged irony.

> There are two very distinct phases in a sunset. At the beginning the star is an architect. Afterwards only (when its rays come to be reflected and no longer direct) it transforms itself into a painter. Once it becomes obliterated behind the horizon, the light weakens and makes planes appear which are more complex at each instant. Full light is the enemy of perspective, but between day and night there is a place for an architecture as fantastic as it is temporary. With darkness, everything flattens out again like a marvelously colored Japanese toy. . . .
> Little by little the profound constructions of the evening folded

up. The mass which had occupied the western sky all day appeared
laminated like a metallic leaf which was illuminated from behind by
a fire at first golden, then vermillion, then cherry-red. This was already making the contorted clouds dissolve, scouring and removing
them in a swirl of fragments [*parcelles*] which progressively vanished.
(71–72F, 65–66E)

One would like to think of these phases as distinct, a clear architectural structure only later followed by a darkening obscurity that
flattens and crumbles its structure. The parallel to the certainty of
distinct geological determination on the one hand (the second geological metaphor) and then to the collapse into imaginary geological debris (like the first) is tempting. But the architectural phase of
the sunset with its "complex edifice" and "profound constructions"
echoes, rather, the "profound edifice" between the two cliffs; and
the collapse of distinction which we have reserved for a reading of
that first scenario is here already implicit in the architecture of endless mirrorings.

The conflict between those two geological representations of anthropology is somehow erased in this the model for ethnographic
description. It is simply in the inevitable way of things that structure and fragmentation, delineation and effacement, are inextricably bound, even and especially when one is passionately trying to
mark down that very scene. "It becomes difficult, after that, to follow a spectacle which seem(s) to repeat itself at [such frequent] in-
tervals" (72F, 66E). And as Lévi-Strauss compares this heavenly
theater to the erasure of a text, one cannot help thinking of his
own:

> The apparition developed rapidly, became enriched with details
> and nuances, then everything began to become obliterated laterally,
> from right to left, as though enduring the effects of a dust-cloth
> passed with a sure and slow movement. At the end of several sec-
> onds nothing remained any longer but the scrubbed slate of the sky.
> (73F, 66–67E)

That slate of the sky is copied furiously by the narrator on his
own writing slate, where he strives, as proof of the possibility of his
intelligible transcription, for a sunset that will be identical to what
he observes. Perhaps it was of this passage that Eugenio Donato was
thinking when he wrote: "It would seem that Lévi-Strauss must
originate his words in an authorial voice and then, through an elab-

orate methodological ritual, erase it—leaving in its place only the metaphorical poetical statement of its absence."[25]

In what sense, then, are we to understand the recurrent images of illusion, indecipherability, and inversion, structures that dissolve and demarcations that disorient, the endless plays across the dividing lines of sea, land, and sky, and finally the image of a slate wiped clean? How, moreover, to read the implication that with each duplication that the sunset is, the sun might set again, anew (73F, 68E)?

Perhaps it becomes clearer why dusk tells the future ethnographer of conflicts within his own soul that had previously remained obscure. For the backdrop against which the entire chapter is placed in its opening lines is, "These are rather long and useless cogitations in order to lead up to that morning of February 1934 when I arrived at Marseille ready to embark for the destination of Santos" (66F, 61E). This is the boat that carries Lévi-Strauss on his first trip from the Old World to the New as he retraces, once again, the trajectory from European science to the primitive object, a trajectory which has all along been the preoccupation of his text. Image of the setting sun, body moving from East to West, Lévi-Strauss indeed duplicates the sunset—itself a theater that plays across the dividing line of sky and sea, a passage from above to below the horizon line ("once it becomes obliterated behind the horizon" [71F, 65E]). This is a (rite of) passage that is never definitive, a struggle between the forces of obscurity and clarity, darkness and light, one that takes place while reconstituting a faraway landscape on which the sun will, no doubt, set again.

Designing Natives

Here, appropriately, we enter Part III of *Tristes Tropiques,* a section entitled "The New World." We encounter finally those *Sad Tropics,* the area on two sides of the imaginary demarcation line of the equator and the perpetual turning around such lines suggested by the etymology—*trope.* We encounter as well the Caduveo, the first primitive community to which the anthropologist devotes a protracted description. And unlike the Indian in the myth, Lévi-Strauss seems to have reached the ends of the earth, to have questioned the people, and to have met with a satisfactory measure of success, at least if we are to judge from the voice with which he speaks. Perhaps no mysterious sound has reached his ears, nor has he been "transported . . . to the temple of the magic animals" (43F,

42E). But the opaque forces and sinister struggles (69F, 63E) of "Sunset," the incertitude, anguish, and illusion (73F, 67–68E) associated with that testing of his ability to find a language to immobilize appearances are all but gone. This is no breathless notation of a present that might otherwise pass from his sight, slip through his fingers—nor the desperate chase after the vestiges of a reality that vanished centuries earlier, despite an occasional comentary to the contrary.[26] Nor does one sense a narrative eye that gains its vision only with respect to the crumbling of the anthropologist's past.

And yet, in these chapters so at ease in matter-of-fact reportage, the sole concern is representation. It is less an open preoccupation with depicting the primitive Indian as before than a fascination with the ways in which the natives themselves delineate. This delineation is doubled, not only among the Caduveo, but also in a similar fashion among the Indians of the northwest coast. For in *Structural Anthropology* Lévi-Strauss devotes a crucial chapter entitled "Split [literally, The Doubling of] Representation in the Arts of Asia and America" to comparing their modes of art. Twice doubled, for not only is it a question of what the English renders as "split representation," but this mode of art must in turn be understood in relation to its counterpart in both cultures.

> In both cases sculpture and drawing furnish the two fundamental means of expression; in both cases, sculpture presents a realistic character while drawing is more symbolic and decorative. . . . In both cases masculine art, centered on sculpture, affirms its will to represent, while feminine art . . . is a non-representational art. (*SA* 281F, 255–56E)
>
> As I *noted* then, the art of the Caduveo is *marked* by a dualism: that of men and women, the one sculptors, the other painters; the first attached to a representational and naturalist style, despite the stylization; while the second devote themselves to a non-representational art. Limiting myself to the consideration of this feminine art, I would like to *underline* that the dualism extends to several levels. (217F, 190E; emphases mine)

The art of Lévi-Strauss has pretensions only to the representational, and yet his noting, marking, underlining appear also as arabesques which might inevitably give us pause. It is as though the proliferation of doubling—Northwest Coast / Caduveo, men / women, representational / nonrepresentational—might be destined to corrupt the single-mindedness of the account—as though the will to representation might give way to other designs. Something of this can be traced in Lévi-Strauss's gentle self-irony as he attempts to relate the celebration of the puberty of a Caduveo girl—once again a question of puberty rites, then, but this time of a female.

> During our stay a feast took place to celebrate the puberty of a girl. . . . They began by dressing her in the ancient fashion: her dress of cotton was replaced by a piece of square cloth wrapped round the body under the armpits. They painted her shoulders, her arms, and her face with rich designs, and all the available necklaces were placed around her neck. All of that, moreover, was perhaps less a sacrifice to custom than an attempt to dazzle us [*nous en mettre "plein la vue"*]. (200F, 176E)

It is these designs, a consideration of this feminine art, that interests Lévi-Strauss above all. The vision of the anthropologist is therefore at stake, but not seriously. It soon becomes, however, a question of photographs, not only that of the "adolescent Caduveo girl made ready for her puberty rites" (plate 10F) with which we as readers are presented and implicitly asked to take as authentic, but others as well.

> One teaches young ethnographers that the natives fear letting their image be captured by a photograph and that it is proper to assuage their fear and to compensate them for what they consider a risk by making them a present in the form of an object or money. The Caduveo had perfected the system: not only did they insist on being paid in exchange for letting themselves be photographed, they also compelled me [*m'obligeaient*] to photograph them so that I would [have to] pay them. Hardly a day passed without some woman presenting herself to me in an extraordinary get-up and obliging me, whether I wanted to or not, to render her the homage of a click followed by several milreis. Sparing with my rolls of film, I often limited myself to a simulacre and paid. (200F, 176E)

By taking no pictures, Lévi-Strauss escapes the ignominy he reserves for the untrained collector of photographs, "where the concern for impressions dominates too much to make it possible for the reader to assess the value of the evidence" (14F, 17E).[27] And yet one cannot help thinking back to that scene at Sainte Anne Hospital where, in a complex circus, the roles of ringmaster and trained animals, psychologist and "lunatics," began to overstep their bounds. In this passage that starts out with the controlled hierarchical relationships between teacher and student and between ethnographer and native, to say that the Caduveo had perfected the system is not quite the point. For it is not merely that they insist on payment each time Lévi-Strauss chooses to photograph them. The Indians assume the initiative of deciding when the photographic sessions will take place. The vocabulary of mastery is striking: "exigeaient," "m'obligeaient," "m'imposât" (200F). Moreover, they appear (and it cannot be insignificant that it is always the women, the nonrepresentational artists) in outfits so extraordinary that there can be no question of authenticity, or of an ethnographic image that might record the true Indian. Capitulating to a certain extent, Lévi-Strauss nevertheless imagines himself to regain control of the parodic scene by pretending to take a picture, merely pretending to pay homage. But here the ethnographer is swept up in their theatricality, becoming a caricature of himself, the simulacrum of an image maker. And it is, after all, the Indians who walk away with the milreis, and he who walks away with nothing in the hand.

Put off by an irony he at best half-senses, the narrator immediately reestablishes himself in the traditional position of the scientific observer and relocates the institutions and traits of his scientific object. Thus anthropologist and nature are able to conserve their own values without losing the clarity of the contours that delimit them with respect to one another and that give to each an intelligible structure (60F, 55–56E). The two, it would seem, had threatened to crumble into one, but Lévi-Strauss is quick to redelineate the proper line of demarcation.

> However, it would indeed have been poor ethnography to resist this strategem or even to consider it as a proof of decadence or mercantilism. Because in a transposed form, specific traits of the indigenous society were thus reappearing: independence and authority of women of high birth; ostentation in front of a stranger and the demand of homage from the commoner [du commun]. The attire might be fantastic and improvised: the conduct that inspired it conserved all of its signification. My part was to reestablish it in the context of the traditional institutions. (200F, 176–77E).

This sets the stage for the style of chapter 20, which Lévi-Strauss devotes largely to the art of the Caduveo. The Caduveo attempt to dislocate the logic of ethnographic representation; the ethnographer responds by reestablishing scientific balance and conserving signification. This is the repeated drift of the pages that follow—all in the name of art and other forms of reproduction—although not necessarily in that order. For as though to preempt what he

knows must follow, Lévi-Strauss opens the chapter with the following lines.

> The customs of a people taken as a whole are always marked by a
> style; they form systems. I am persuaded that these systems do not
> exist in an unlimited number and that human societies like the indi-
> viduals—in their games, their dreams, or their deliriums—never
> create in an absolute fashion, but limit themselves to choosing cer-
> tain combinations in an ideal repertoire that it would be possible to
> reconstitute. In making the inventory of all observed customs, of all
> those imagined myths, also those evoked in the games of children
> and adults, the dreams of healthy or sick individuals and the psycho-
> pathological conduct, one would succeed in setting up a sort of peri-
> odic table like that of the chemical elements, where all real or even
> possible customs would appear grouped in families and where we
> would only have to recognize those that the societies had actually
> adopted. (203F, 178E)

That this statement should preface a chapter on the Caduveo is
remarkable, although Lévi-Strauss will go on to insist that it is "particularly appropriate." One might well imagine it as an overture to
the detailed description of the Bororo. There, the obsessive symmetries of the natives might make understandable Lévi-Strauss's
desire to see all ethnographic material reduced to a table, as delirious as that whim might seem.[28] With the Bororo, the layout of their
huts along an east-west axis marks the division of the population
into groups or moieties whose daily roles are strictly and minutely
determined by this division; the second diameter on a north-south
axis then cuts the population into four sections so complex that no
observer has been able to understand its function; there is also a
further division into clans with subgroups of "red" and "black"
(these clans in turn divided into three grades) (251–54F, 220–24E).
"The distribution of the population into clans," he writes "constitutes, no doubt, the most important of these 'deals of the cards'"
(253F, 224E).[29]

But in the case of the Caduveo, the dealing out of the cards is
quite different:

> These reflections are particularly appropriate in the case of the
> Mbaya-Guaicuru of whom . . . the Caduveo of Brazil are today
> [among] the last representatives. Their civilization irresistibly evokes
> that which our society amused itself to dream in one of its tradi-
> tional games and of which the fantasy of Lewis Carroll has so well
> succeeded in drawing out [*dégager*] the model: these Indian knights

resembled [figures of] court cards [*figures de cartes*]. This trait already stood out in their costume: tunics and leather cloaks broadening the shoulders and falling in stiff pleats decorated in black and red with designs . . . where motifs in the form of spades, hearts, diamonds, and clubs recurred.

They had kings and queens, and, like Alice's queen, the latter liked nothing better than to play with the severed heads that their warriors brought back. (203–4F, 178E)

Lévi-Strauss assimilates the Caduveo to our dreams and games for which the periodic table of social customs was also said to account, but their dreams and games are perhaps less traditional and less systematic than those which Lévi-Strauss imagines, less able, as we shall see, to be "inventoried" (203F).

To be sure, the Caduveo seem divided, like the Bororo, in four sections (here suits) and also into red and black. A paragraph later Lévi-Strauss will mark out their division into castes, orders, and branches (204F, 180E). And yet, as he himself tells it, to be among the Caduveo is like entering an *Alice in Wonderland* world. No comparison could seem more inappropriate to follow global assertions about the systematic nature of human culture. In the dream of Alice in Wonderland all that happens seems totally arbitrary, the clear opposition between sense and non-sense repeatedly menaced. This is a realm in which wordplay, and especially the notion of play itself, dominates; but the cards in Lewis Carroll's novel do not function according to rules of the game made clear in advance, nor are they such that one could hope to reconstitute them *après coup*.

Surely we have some sense of this, if only in a figural way, as Lévi-Strauss records his attempts to systematize their face drawings that in their principles of asymmetry might indeed be said to resemble playing cards.

> These skilful compositions, asymmetrical while still remaining balanced, are begun by starting out from any corner and are carried through to the end without hesitation, erasure, or crossing out [*rature*.] They call upon relatively simple motifs . . . but these were combined in such a manner that each work possesses an original character: of four hundred drawings collected in 1935 I did not observe two that were alike, but since I established the opposite in comparing my collection with one gathered later, it can be deduced that the extraordinarily extensive repertoire of the artists is nevertheless fixed by tradition. Unfortunately it has not been possible either for me or for my successors to penetrate the underlying theory of this indigenous stylistics: the informants give [*livrent*] sev-

eral terms corresponding to the elementary motifs, but they invoke ignorance or forgetfulness in all that relates to the more complex decorations [*décors*]. It may be, in fact, that they proceed on the basis of an empirical ability transmitted from generation to generation or that they are bent on keeping the secret about the mysteries of their art. (212–14F, 187E)

Once again the balance restored by the ethnographer, a symmetry in response to the overall asymmetry of four hundred designs, no two of which were alike for in the relation to another collection identity is found. Thus the patterns may be inscribed as part of an "established tradition," an inventory made of an "ideal *repertoire* that it would always be possible to *reconstitute*" (203F, 178E; emphasis mine). But that reconstitution remains under the aegis of an oblivion, willed or not: the informants claim not to know or perhaps to have forgotten the fundamental theory. The ethnographer must opt indeterminately for an unconscious skill on the part of the artist or an artist who consciously keeps the ethnographer ignorant. One might be able to inventory the individual designs or even those that reappear—without any theoretical understanding: but would one be able, as Lévi-Strauss had proclaimed, to envisage the system, to group them together in the proper "families" (203F, 178E)?

What would it mean, then, to reconstitute this "repertoire" of the Caduveo designs or of all observed customs (for Lévi-Strauss uses the same term for both)? On occasion one has the sense of a race against time: "Only a few very old women seemed to preserve the ancient virtuosity and I was persuaded for a long time that my collection had been gathered together [*réunie*] at the last possible moment" (211F, 185E; see also *SA* 277F, 251E). Lévi-Strauss's structuralist dream as he presents it in the preface to chapter 20 is to "fix" (212–14F, 187E) that which might otherwise crumble in the flood of time, menaced by a certain oblivion, like the anthropologist and his object in chapter 4, like the moments of the sunset in chapter 7.

And yet a repertoire, by definition as well as by etymology, is a guarantee of reproduceability: it is this possibility that haunts Lévi-Strauss as he speaks further of Caduveo art (both in *Tristes Tropiques* and in *Structural Anthropology*). For, despite the nonrepresentational character of the designs, at issue is always not only scientific repeatability but also the manner in which the two halves might double one another as well as the human face they do not duplicate.

We read over and over of the play between symmetry and asymmetry ("skilful compositions, asymmetrical while still remaining balanced" [212F, 187E]) and of other dualisms often claimed in the name of balance.

> The art of the Caduveo is marked by a dualism: that of men and women, the one sculptors, the other painters, the first attached to a representational and naturalistic style . . . while the second devote themselves to a non-representational art. . . . The dualism extends to several levels.
>
> The women practice two styles, equally inspired by the decorative spirit and abstraction. One is angular and geometric, the other curvilinear and free. Most often the compositions are founded on a regular combination of the two styles. (217F, 190E)

And, as Lévi-Strauss continues, so their compositions in general, and so their pottery, and so the face paintings, each related with a back and forth that assures us of a symmetrical harmony of the whole practice. And yet, although he does so in the spirit of symmetry, it is possible to read the extended description that follows in two manners:

> In all the cases the finished work conveys [*traduit*] a concern for balance between other principles which also go in pairs: a design [*décor*] which was originally [*primitivement*] linear is taken up again at the end of the execution in order to be partially transformed into surfaces (by the filling in of certain sections, as we do when we are drawing mechanically [*dessinons machinalement*]); most of the works are based on the alternation of two themes and almost always the figure and the background occupy an approximately equal surface so that it is possible to read the composition in two ways by reversing the groups invited to play one role or the other: each motif can be perceived positively or negatively. Finally the design [*décor*] often respects a double principle of symmetry and asymmetry applied simultaneously which is conveyed [*se traduit*] in the form of contrasting registers. (217–18F, 190–91E)

Are we to understand this as balance or dislocation? Surely something happens to our powers of interpretation, which can read the passage in both ways. For despite the belabored examples of the preceding paragraphs and a topic sentence that insists on balance, Lévi-Strauss proceeds to fill in the details—almost mechanically—without thinking through the implications. If each motif can be perceived positively or negatively, if there is a double principle at work, shall we read the relation between as one of symmetry or asymmetry? And can one ever be certain one has read correctly?

This becomes the overt preoccupation of the lines that follow, or rather—not the reading of Lévi-Strauss's design but that of the Caduveo. Descriptions of such images prove deceptive. The dynamic force of composition comes to belie what one imagined as a stable and static structure.

> Here is a body painting which seems simple (figure 1). It consists of . . . regular fields of which the background is occupied by . . . small charges. . . . This description is deceptive: let us look more closely. It might account for the general appearance once the design has been finished. But the woman who drew it did not begin by tracing undulating ribbons in order to decorate each interstice [*interval*] afterwards with a charge. . . . She worked like a paver constructing successive rows by means of identical elements. Each element is composed of one section of the ribbon formed by the concave part of one band and the convex part of the adjacent band; a tapering field; a charge at the center of the field. These elements overlap each other through dislocation and it is only at the end that the figure finds its stability which confirms and belies all at once the dynamic process according to which it was executed. (218F, 191E)

Through patterns of dislocation and irregularity the final picture tends to obliterate or at least to deny its own execution. The completed drawings of the women are bound to deceive the eye. (Is it by design? for Sanchez Labrador, the first to describe them, insisted that this art was always a matter of deception [214F, 188E].)[30] They give the sense of symmetrical closed figures, of a balance and harmony to which Lévi-Strauss will tellingly return when he seems to close the chapter on the Caduveo.

But here, through the analysis of a particular body painting, Lévi-Strauss goes on to unhinge all he has written of the pervasive dualism that seemed to mark the Caduveo.

> The Caduveo style confronts us then with a whole series of complexities. There is first a dualism that projects itself on successive planes as in a hall of mirrors: men and women, painting and sculpture, representation and abstraction . . . figure and background. But these oppositions are perceived retrospectively [*après coup*]; they have a static character: the dynamics of the art, which is to say the fashion in which the motifs are imagined and executed, cuts this fundamental duality again on all the planes, because the primary themes are first of all disarticulated, then recomposed in secondary themes which makes the fragments borrowed from the preceding ones arise in a provisional unity, and these are juxtaposed in such a

manner that the original (primitive) unity reappears as though by a
conjuring trick [*par un tour de prestidigitation*]. (218F, 191E)

To this too we will return, this cutting of dualities on all planes, this
constitution of unity through a conjuring trick.
    Everything we learn about the arts of the Caduveo women is at
odds with the structuralist program, with the desire to reduce all
"style" to "systems" and to fix these systems at determined positions
in a periodic table of customs (203F, 178E).[31] For when all is said
and done, it is impossible to "penetrate the underlying theory of
[their] stylistics" (212F, 187E); one doesn't know whether to read
figure or background (or even which is which). One is seduced by a
static quality (not unlike that of the periodic table) that belies "the
dynamics of the art," or "the fashion in which [it is] imagined and
executed" (218F, 191E). Lévi-Strauss's table is a static spatial answer
to a temporal dilemma. The dynamics of his text point to the fact
when he juxtaposes the heading paragraph of chapter 20 with long
delvings into the imagination of those he compares to the Queen
of Hearts in *Alice in Wonderland* (203–4F, 177E).
    Under the aegis of a repertoire, of that which has been thor-
oughly rehearsed and is always capable of reconstitution, Lévi-
Strauss might seem to categorize the Caduveo precisely in terms of
their dislocations and to reestablish these dislocations "in the context of traditional institutions" (200F, 176E). This was his solution
to the irregularities of their photographic sessions. While he recognizes in their work "a double principle of symmetry and asymmetry" (217F, 191E), the graphics of the ethnographer are such
that he invites them "to play one role rather than the other," that is,
to play the role of the uncertain, assymetrical object of his observa-
tions, with certainty. As when he confronts the changing slate of the
dusking sky with his own slate, he finds "a language to fix . . . appearances at the same time unstable and rebellious to all effort of
description" (67F, 62E). "At the end of the execution" we cannot
help but feel ourselves in a hall of mirrors in which background
and figure threaten to change places (217–18F, 190–91E).
    The pretensions, if not the results, of Lévi-Strauss's art are quite
other than that of the Caduveo, for he would hope to locate them
in the matrices of a master design, always reconstitutable, while
everything in their intriguing "doubling of representation" rejects
a fixing of its ostensible subject. "The artist improvises on the living
subject, without model, sketch, or point of reference [*point de rep-
ère*]" (212F, 187E),[32] an improvisation without regard to earlier pat-

terns it might duplicate and without regard for the living subject which the artist uses as mere writing slate.

> The face quartered, parted per bend (sliced)—or even parted per bend sinister (cut obliquely)—is then freely decorated with arabesques that do not take into account the placement of the eyes, nose, cheeks, forehead, and chin developing as though on a continuous field. (212F, 187E)

> We have already underlined . . . the dislocation of the subject in elements, that [are then] recomposed according to conventional rules without any relation to nature. (*SA* 278F, 253E)

This disregard for the living subject becomes painfully evident, not only with respect to the Indians but also with respect to the European scientist, when one struggles to translate the first citation: for one must opt either for a vocabulary of unusual violence ("quarter," "slice," "cut") or for the abstract terminology of heraldry to which Lévi-Strauss frequently has recourse ("quartered," "parted per bend," "parted per bend sinister"), a vocabulary of convention singularly oblivious to the contours of the physiognomy.

And so, after all, Lévi-Strauss's text tends to perform with respect to his object the way the graphic art of the Caduveo relates to its object. The entire question of Lévi-Strauss's art is far more complex than we have cared to note until now. There are at least two gestures in the ethnography of *Tristes Tropiques* that must be seen as mutually dislocating. On the one hand, there is that structuralist dream, the great table whose static form and reproduceability is at odds with the Caduveo play between stability and dynamic manner of creation, symmetry of figure and background, and ultimate asymmetry in their ambiguous interpretability. But the grill that Lévi-Strauss proposes shares with Caduveo face design an indifference to mimetic duplication of the object it covers: a periodic table does not imitate the material it organizes. On the other hand, *Tristes Tropiqes* is a travelogue, an autobiography, a stage-by-stage description of the anthropologist's experiences with all the claims to conserving the objects of observation that that entails. And yet it is the content of those descriptions in the case of the Caduveo that questions the concept of description and reproduceability. There is a dynamic relation, then, between the conservative gesture of mimetic description and the content of the descriptions of Caduveo art which obsessively speaks of total, indeed violent, disregard for mimetic art. (Something similar took place in the relation of Lévi-

Strauss's mimetic recording of a sunset, the dynamics of which overwhelmed its frame.)

And it is this indifference (on the part of the natives) to any mimesis and therefore to the surface on which they draw that makes Lévi-Strauss's rich inventory of four hundred designs possible:

> I tried . . . to trace faces on the sheets of paper suggesting to the women to paint them as they would have done on their own face; the success was such that I renounced my maladroit sketches [*croquis*]. Those who drew were in no way disconcerted by the blank pages which demonstrates well the indifference of their art to the natural architecture of the human face. (211F, 185E).

Lévi-Strauss has a good sense of this with regard to the Caduveo, if not with respect to the way it functions or fails to in his own writing.

> [The real face] is no less dislocated by the systematic asymmetry thanks to which its natural harmony is belied to the benefit of the artificial harmony of the painting. But precisely because this painting, rather than representing the image of a deformed face, effectively deforms a true face, the dislocation goes further than previously described. In addition to the decorative value, a subtle element of sadism mixes in, which explains . . . the erotic attraction of the women. (*SA* 279F, 255E)

This is an eroticism which the anthropologist repeatedly touches on with great stylistic delight.[33] If it is easy to locate the erotic object, it is less easy to locate the sadism, which might as well be part and parcel of a textual rhetoric that indifferently reduces the face to a sliced countenance or a heraldic shield.

But alongside this indifference to natural human harmony and architecture is the insistence that such paintings are, in fact, what differentiate the human from the animal. Thus, the Indians spoke of the missionaries' stupidity precisely insofar as they did not paint themselves like the natives: "To be a man it was necessary to be painted; he who remained in the state of nature was not to be distinguished from the beasts" (214F, 188E). The significance of split representation, according to the chapter in *Structural Anthropology,* is a "consequence of the importance . . . ascribed to tatooing" (*SA* 284F, 258E): it arises from the relationship between the plastic element of the human face or body and the graphic (decorative) element (*SA* 288F, 261E). Like the ethnographer, the Caduveo define the human through their graphics, for they too have developed a writing—although it is neither a table nor an autobiography—by means of which the human face gains its significance.

> The design [*décor*], in effect, is *made* for the face but in another sense, the face is predestined for the design because it is only through and by means of the design that it receives its social dignity and its mystic significance. The design is conceived for the face, but the face itself does not exist except through it [the design]. (*SA* 288F, 261E)

> It was necessary either to draw a face [*figure*] exactly and deform the design according to the laws of trompe l'oeil or to respect the individuality of the design and therefore to represent the face [*figure*] as split [*dédoublé*]. One cannot even say that the artist had chosen the second solution, because the alternative never presented itself to her mind. In native thought . . . the design [*décor*] is the face or rather it creates it. It is the design [*lui*] that confers on the face [*lui*] its social being, its human dignity, its spiritual signification. The double representation of the face considered as a graphic process expresses therefore a deeper and more essential doubling—that of the biological "stupid" individual and that of the social personnage which it is its mission to incarnate. (*SA* 285F, 258–59E; see also 290F, 263E)

The Mbaya have their mission linked to a process of incarnation: the Europeans, as we shall see, also have theirs. The Caduveo, it would seem, are untroubled by concepts of deformation, asymmetry, ambiguous reading. Nothing natural, nothing human is distorted or ignored, for they apparently have no illusions—or desires, for that matter—concerning reproduceability or mimetic description. One should reread the passages cited earlier and understand, then, that talk of dislocation of the subject into elements, indifference to natural human architecture, deformation of the true face, must be heard in the voice of the European narrator. The graphics of the Indians confer significance, however mystic, and dignity and are enmeshed in the designation of social order. The face has no existence except through the graphics that create it. They mark the difference, however singularly, between human wisdom and brute stupidity.

If we are to take these passages from "Split Representation in the Arts of Asia and America" at face value, for the Mbaya nothing is lost in this process. The European appearing on the scene, certain that the gesture of painting is a choice to deform, is at least as horrified as intrigued: Lévi-Strauss puts this in theological terms through the figure of the Jesuit missionary Sanchez Labrador:

The missionary appeared alarmed by this contempt for the work of the Creator; why did the natives alter the appearance of the human face?. . . . It's [a question] there "of opposing an artificial ugliness to the graces of Nature."

By their facial paintings . . . the Mbaya were expressing a . . . horror of nature. The native art proclaimed a sovereign contempt for the clay of which we are molded and in this sense it borders on sin. From his Jesuit missionary point of view Sanchez Labrador showed himself singularly perspicacious in sensing [*devinant*] the devil there. He himself underlines the Promethean aspect of this savage art when he describes the technique with which the natives covered their bodies with star shapes. "Thus each Eyiguayegui regards himself as another Telamon who, not only on his shoulders and in his hands, but on all the surface of his body becomes the support of a maladroitly figured universe." Would this be the explanation of the exceptional character of Caduveo art, that by its medium, man refuses to be a reflection of the divine image? (214–15F, 188–89E)

What is so unsettling here—for the missionary Sanchez Labrador and perhaps for the anthropologist? He finds the art of the Mbaya to scorn not only Nature and the human face but that visage as work of the Creator, as the Divine image. From the point of view of the missionary not only is natural grace lost but also divine priority. For the Caduveo do not regard themselves as the image of a divine figure, of a Creator located elsewhere. As Promethean figures who challenge such a concept of theological power, they take it upon themselves, like architectural telamones (those human figures that take the place of columns), to hold up an entablature bearing nothing less than the universe. The Caduveo set themselves up as the locus of a force that only comes about in the form of their graphics, a graphics which at once defines and creates them as human (and god) over and against a biological, stupid individual, as well as over and against a concept of God as Supreme Being outside themselves. For the myth they tell of their origins at once makes Sanchez Labrador's figure of the Creator beside the point and establishes them in a remarkable position of authority:

[They] founded their arrogance on the certitude that they were predestined to command humanity. A myth assured them of it. . . . When the Supreme Being, Gonoenhodi, decided to create human beings, he first drew the Guana from the earth, then the other tribes; to the first he gave agriculture as their share and hunting to the second. The Trickster, who is the other divinity in the native pantheon, saw that the Mbaya had been forgotten at the bottom of the hole and brought them out; but since nothing was left for them, they had the right to the single function that was still available, that of oppressing and exploiting the others. (208F, 182E)

According to myth the Supreme Being, with all the centralization of power and significance such a name implies, may be responsible for bringing the other tribes into existence, but the Caduveo owe their existence to quite another figure who lends a bizarre (a)symmetry to this pantheon of two. Gonoenhodi forgets the Mbaya at the bottom of the hole, and well he might. For as they tell it, their role on earth threatens to replace him. It is rather the Trickster who draws the Caduveo out of the ground like a prestidigitator plucking the last, most spectacular and unexpected object out of his magician's hat, an ultimate irony in a world that seemed to be grounded by the serious logic and necessity of a Supreme Being. All the productive functions have been given away, those of hunting and those of agriculture, all the functions that to someone like Sanchez Labrador make sense, denouncing as he does those "who lose entire days having themselves painted, forgetful of hunting" (214F, 188E). The painting of the Caduveo Indians is inextricably related to their nonproductive role in society. They are left with nothing of utility, nothing functional to do. They are the last laugh of the Trickster ("le Trompeur") in relation to the Supreme Being, playing card figures acting out games that escape the logic of purpose, aligned not with rules but with tricks, deception, illusion, cheating.

The game of these essays is at least a three-way deal—among the natives, the ethnographer, and Sanchez Labrador, who long ago played his hand and left the scene (but who might still maintain some echoes in the second player). The Mbaya, Lévi-Strauss, and the man of God, of course—and this is what leads to all the intricacies and involutions of the text—do not play by the same rules, do not, perhaps, even play the same game. Whereas the missionary anxiously protests the threat to Nature (214–15F, 188–89E), to productive livelihood, to a supreme Creator, the Caduveo, as joke of the supreme Trickster, will go on to create themselves ("to be a man it was necessary to be painted" [214F, 188E], perhaps also to create the universe (215F, 188–89E), while replacing the functions of the Supreme Being in a shocking parody of the Godhead. The ethnographer observes and creates his own graphics—at once a writing "at the last possible moment" (211F, 185E) that hopes to conserve and reproduce the primitive world it records, and also material for a table of customs with less direct mimetic pretensions, but with delusions of reconstitutability and control. And could we not read the Mbaya creation myth with its irreducible joke as an implicit and unintentional ironic commentary on an enterprise in which all societies of the earth are claimed as orderable under the aegis of a Supreme logic?

Where the Caduveo and the anthropologist openly part ways is in a more empirical realm of reproduction (although Lévi-Strauss's last play will be to read one form of reproduction in terms of the other). Sandwiched between his proclamation of the universal chartability of human customs and his narration of the creation myth lies the question of biological reproduction among the Caduveo, last living representatives of the Mbaya-Guaicuru.

> This society showed itself remarkably adverse to the feelings that we consider natural; thus they experienced [*éprouvait*] a lively distaste for procreation. Abortion and infanticide were almost the normal practice [*de façon presque normale*], so that perpetuation of the group was accomplished much more by adoption than by generation, one of the principal aims of warrior expeditions being to procure children. Thus it was calculated at the beginning of the 19th century that barely 10% of the members of the Guaricuru group were blood-related.
>
> When children came to be born, they were not raised by their parents but entrusted to another family, where the parents visited them only at rare intervals; they were kept ritually covered from head to foot with black paint . . . until their fourteenth year, when they were initiated. (206–8F, 180–82E)

One can well understand why Lévi-Strauss would be taken aback by such everyday practice.

Nevertheless, almost everything he has told us about the Caduveo bespeaks such a state of affairs: their hilarious manipulation of that European photographic technology, intended to reproduce the human figure; their refusal to divulge an underlying theory of their stylistics that would permit regeneration of their art; their fascination with a nonrepresentational art that is, in its moment of superimposition on the face, said to first create them as human; their asymmetrically conceived designs that only through a conjuring trick assume the allure of balance and unity, of self-reflection and reproduction; their painting that refuses to double the face but rather seems to dislocate the subject in elements, indifferent to its architecture, to Nature, to the concept of a Creator in whose image mankind might be said to be fashioned; their pantheon of two gods which has all the asymmetry of their designs and in which they align themselves not with the Supreme Being of reasoned generation and production but with the joker in the pack. Almost everything we read, then, is in harmony with their mode of biological reproduction, however shocking, in its refusal of repetition and its abhorrence of identity. It involves the perpetual introduction of something foreign, something unexpected because not generated from, nor traceable to, what came before—a challenge to the predictability in the model of the periodic table, where each new element discovered is alignable because analogous to customs that were there previously.

The ethnographer links the abhorrence of reproduction to the Caduveo disregard for nature in their art: "Through their paintings, as through their custom of abortion and infanticide, the Mbaya expressed the same horror of nature" (215F, 188E). At a critical point a few pages later, he will make the same connection of sociological structure and art, this time with a different agenda. But perhaps what is most disconcerting in all this—although Lévi-Strauss will just note the practice—is that side by side with their destruction of direct progeny, with their obliteration of those born (could it be with the same black paint they use to decorate and create themselves?), not systematically, but often enough to puzzle us and throw us off balance by the nonrepeatability of the first custom, side by side with their outrageous refusal of re-production and repetition is its occasional celebration:

> However, the birth of children of high rank was the occasion for celebrations which were repeated at each stage of growth: weaning, the first steps, participation in games, etc. The heralds would proclaim the titles of the family and prophesy a glorious future for the newly born; another baby born at the same moment was designated to become his brother-in-arms. (208F, 182E)

Joyous celebration of regeneration, doubled in the figure of another born at the same moment, repeated over and over at various stages of growth. Just enough re-production, identity, and symmetry to upset the apparently systematic asymmetry of the usual practice of abortion and infanticide.

Yet the exception does not disprove the rule—or pseudorule— that seems counter to the project of *Tristes Tropiques* and the larger structuralist enterprise. Lévi-Strauss, nevertheless, will find a way to resolve their contradictions or at least to dissimulate their differences. And he does so by asking the question, "What purpose does Caduveo art serve?" (220F, 195E). It is thus under the aegis of purpose that the anthropologist will offer his definitive analysis—an astonishing concept with regard to a people whose creation myth distinguishes them precisely insofar as they have no conventional purpose to fulfill.

Through an "analysis of the social structure," then, Lévi-Strauss will set about accounting for "the original properties of the native art" (220F, 195E):

> The ancient descriptions show them to us paralyzed by their anxiety about saving face [in the case of the Caduveo this turn of phrase has its ironies], about deviating from rank, about marrying beneath their station [*se mésallier*]. . . . Each caste tended to turn in upon itself [*se replier sur elle-même*]. In particular the endogamy of the castes and the multiplication of the nuances of hierarchy must have compromised the possibilities of unions (222F, 195E)

It is to this that Lévi-Strauss will attribute the "paradox" of a people so opposed ("retive à") to procreation that it systematically turns to foreigners and enemies to increase its population rather than risk internal misalliances (222F, 195E).

Let us pause here to underscore that is here, just when the anthropologist is about to propose his master theory about this native art, that we are first led to understand the Caduveo caste system as marital paralysis. We have read of their arrogance with respect to strangers (206F, 180E), to be sure, but more often of an overwhelming eroticism that, far from discouraging marriage, manages to draw spouses from far and wide. "Split Representation" speaks of an erotic attraction that extended beyond the banks of the Paraguay to outlaws ("les hors la loi") and adventurers. That the Caduveo women would appeal to those outside the law would seem to go without saying; that they appeal to those who seek adventure might have resonance for a certain anthropologist:[34] "Several, now grown old and maritally settled among the natives have described to me, while trembling, those adolescent naked bodies completely covered with interlacings and arabesques of a subtle perversity" (*SA,* 280F, 255E). And *Tristes Tropiques* has a similar tale to tell: just eight pages before explaining the native customs of nonreproduction as a reluctance to marry, Lévi-Strauss notes that their erotic painting established the reputation of the women "on both sides of the Paraguay River":

Many half-castes and Indians of other tribes came to settle and to marry at Nalike. The facial and body paintings explain this attraction perhaps; in any case they reenforce it and symbolize it. These delicate and subtle contours as sensitive [*sensibles*] as the lines of the face and which sometimes emphasize [*souligner*] them and sometimes betray them give to the women something delicately provocative. This pictorial surgery grafts art on to the human body. (214F, 188E)

This was an eroticism powerful enough to ensnare even that Jesuit missionary who gets entangled in contradictions when confronted with their art. Sanchez Labrador scorns their ugliness and then "contradicts himself because several lines later he maintains that the most beautiful tapestries could not rival these paintings" (215F, 188E).

The ethnographer who writes of him will also perform an about-face, describing as he does first an allure so phantasmatic that it oversteps all conventional bounds in producing marriage, and then, with subtle perversity, an anxiety so paralyzing that marriage becomes impossible. One might ponder why Lévi-Strauss has to displace his reflections from the astonishing practices of (non)reproduction on the part of the Indian, why in order to close the chapter on the Caduveo his own interpretation of their art takes place in terms of union. The theory Lévi-Strauss proposes, in a style that tellingly slides from cold anthropological notations to impassioned and ecstatic rhetoric, is the following. The Mbaya maintain a sociological structure that divides the society asymmetrically into three endogamous classes. At their extreme borders we find the Guana of Paraguay and the Bororo of the Mato Grosso, with a hierarchical structure almost identical to that of the Caduveo. The significant difference appears as

a division into two moieties of which we know . . . that they cut across [*recoupaient*] the classes. If it was forbidden for the members of different classes to intermarry, the inverse obligation was imposed on the moieties: a man from one moiety was obligated to marry a woman from the other and vice versa. It is therefore fair to say that the asymmetry of the classes finds itself balanced [*équilibrée*] by the symmetry of the moieties. (222F, 195–96E)

It is this lack of a division into moieties that, for Lévi-Strauss, explains the Caduveo's disconcerting relationship to reproduction, a division that he regards as facilitating marital unions. Let us for-

get for the moment that it does not necessarily make sense that re-
ducing one's potential marital partners by half makes union easier.
Let us forget the strange echo of *recouper*, here used to mark a cutting of three classes in the name of union, earlier used to mark a
cutting that revealed the sense of balance in Caduveo art as a conjuring trick (a bit lost in the Weightman translation as "intersects";
see 218F, 191E).

It might seem beside the point to play on such an echo, even in
the name of forgetting—insignificant, after all, since he speaks in
one case of a style of art and in the other of sociological structure.
And yet Lévi-Strauss's point is precisely to claim an analogy between Caduveo design and social structure.

> It is clear that [the system of the Guana and the Bororo] offers on
> the sociological level a structure analogous to that which I have
> brought out on the stylistic level a propos of Caduveo art. We are
> dealing in both instances with a double opposition. In the first case it
> consists primarily in the opposition of a ternary organization to an-
> other which is binary, the one asymmetric and the other symmetric;
> and in the second place in the opposition of social mechanisms
> founded on the one hand on reciprocity and on the other on hier-
> archy. . . . It suffices to consider the plan of a Bororo village . . . to
> see that it is organized like a Caduveo design. (223–24F, 196E)

Everything is in place now for Lévi-Strauss's all-encompassing
theory with respect to the Caduveo—a theory that will situate them
with respect to the neighboring tribes on the one side and the other
of the Paraguay River,[35] with respect to their art and their social
practices, and in a perhaps insidious manner, with respect to the
ethnographer.

There is nothing simple, nothing naive, in what Lévi-Strauss is
about to say: it is one of the richest and most complex moments of
Tristes Tropiques. The overture to that passage, despite its matter-of-
fact tone, still raises more questions than meet the eye. First, what
does it mean to speak of a sociological system with a "structure
analogous to that . . . brought out on the stylistic level" in relation
to a people's art? How are we to imagine the one figuring the other?
Is that figuring through analogy at all akin to the presuppositions
that go to compose a periodic table of customs? Is analogy itself a
binary and reassuring system of reciprocity that hereby assumes a
certain priority? Second, how are we to think the relation of the
asymmetric, ternary, hierarchical system in relation to the symmetrical, binary system of reciprocity? The paragraph that follows does

and does not tell us how to think them. It suggests, or even asserts, that the binary division (the division into moieties which Lévi-Strauss for some reason sees as the panacea for a reluctance to form unions and that reluctance as the explanation for an abhorrence of conventional reproduction) is a solution to the problematic asymmetry of the ternary system.[36]

> Everything takes place as though, faced with a contradiction in their social structure, the Guana and the Bororo had succeeded in resolving it (or in dissimulating it) by what are properly sociological methods. Perhaps they possessed moieties before falling into the Mbaya sphere of influence and the means were thus to be found already at their disposal: perhaps they invented them later. (224F, 196E)

The Guana and Bororo find a sociological solution to a sociological problem; the Mbaya will do otherwise. That aspect of Lévi-Strauss's argument is clear-cut. But less apparent here is the uncertainty with respect to priority, with respect to which came first—the moieties or the classes—and the consequent indecision between resolution and dissimulation, between a true solution to the contradictions of the ternary hierarchy and a dissimulation—a covering over with that which is dissimilar, a trick that gives the illusion of balance to a fundamentally asymmetric predicament.

> This solution was lacking for the Mbaya, either because they were ignorant of it (which is improbable) or rather because it would have been incompatible with their fanaticism. They therefore did not have the chance to resolve their contradictions or at the very least to dissimulate them by means of artificial institutions. But this remedy that they lacked on the social level, or which they forbade themselves to envisage, could not, nevertheless, escape them completely. In an insidious fashion it continued to trouble them. And, since they were not able to become conscious of it and live it, they began to dream it. Not in a direct form which would have clashed up against their prejudices: in a form that was transposed and apparently inoffensive: in their art. (224F, 196–97E)

Art grafted onto the social body as a resolution (or dissimulation); artifice in place of "artificial institutions," what could not be "envisaged" as a social institution literally *envisaged* as art—not directly, but transposed, not consciously, but as a dream, the division into moieties, the line that cuts the three classes, asymmetric design rendered symmetrical. For if the opening paragraph of chapter 20 claims to account for the "dreams and deliriums" of "human society" in general, the closing paragraph will account for the dreams of the Caduveo in particular. It accounts as well to some extent for the text of Lévi-Strauss grafted onto the Mbaya, not consciously, but in a transposed form.

> Because if this *analysis* is *exact,* it will be necessary to *definitively interpret* the graphic art of the Caduveo women, to *explain* its mysterious seduction and its at first sight [*au premier abord*] gratuitous complication as the phantasm of a society which seeks with an unsatiated passion the means of symbolically expressing the institutions that it might have if its interests and its superstitions did not prevent it. (224F, 197E; emphasis mine)

Once again a doubling here, for Lévi-Strauss lays his interpretation on the line. What he dreams of producing is an exact analysis, the definitive interpretation of Mbaya graphic art, to explain and lay bare its complication and above all its "mysterious seduction." He interprets the face and body paintings of the Caduveo women (perhaps it is not too late to underline that more than any other chapter of *Tristes Tropiques* it is always a question here of confronting the *women*) as their passionate phantasm of sexual union allied with harmony, balance, symmetry.

And yet, if the designs of the women are indeed mysteriously seductive, that eroticism is hardly a simple call to symmetry. "On the contrary, one is struck by the rigorous symmetry of the Maori tatooings in contrast with the almost licentious asymmetry of certain Caduveo paintings" (*SA,* 282F, 257E), "the systematic asymmetry thanks to which . . . natural harmony is destroyed" (*SA* 279F, 255E). It is only through a conjuring trick, at the last possible moment, only with the final interpretation, that Lévi-Strauss can appear on the scene, like the Trickster, unlike the latter to produce unity, to (re)instate the harmony and symmetry of an art whose dynamics he has laboriously shown us to deny such tactics (218F, 191E). Does he resolve the problem of asymmetry or dissimulate it—or both? "Adorable civilization where the queens close in on their dream with their make-up: hieroglyphs describing an inaccessible golden age which they celebrate in their ornamentation for lack of a code, and of which they unveil the mysteries at the same time as their nudity" (224F, 197E).

There can be no doubt about Lévi-Strauss's affection for this civilization, at least not here, when he closes in on them with a definitive explanation of their mysterious seduction, when he leaves them dreaming of all the harmonies he earlier dislocated. The Caduveo women have no code, it would seem, to speak directly of their fantasies, no language to fix the articulation of stable symmetries, and so they turn to those hieroglyphs about which the ethnographer has so lengthily written in order to celebrate a "golden age" whose mysteries are unveiled in the wake of their nakedness. Yet what does one see when the Caduveo undress? And does one see more or only differently from when they dress up for the photographer in outlandish costumes that in no way reveal their true traditions. Those young Indian girls—"half-nude . . . with the body patiently decorated with delicate black or blue scrolls which seemed to merge a sheath of precious lace with their skin" (191F, 168E)—continue to wear a veil of lace, even when nude, even when apparently unveiled, even when the ethnographer expects his writing in its moment of exact analysis and definitive interpretation to "explain" or unveil their mysterious seduction.

Whose dream of an inaccessible *"golden* age" then? Is the answer to this question to be found in the ironic echo of the pages that immediately follow, a chapter entitled "Gold and Diamonds" that describes pathetic attempts (surely not on the part of the Caduveo) to catch hold of "miniscule shiny particles [*de menues* parcelles *brillantes*]" (232F, 205E; emphasis mine)? Or shall we return to Lévi-Strauss's earlier reflections on ethnography—to his wanderings through the streets of Lahore and indeed past the gold beaters (44F, 42E)? There, he recognizes himself as an archaeologist of space, trying vainly to reconstitute exoticism with the aid of particles (*parcelles*) and debris in a passage that is the sequel to a moment where the ethnographer speaks of a gold-promising dream that has always slipped through his fingers: "The dream . . . has always slipped through my fingers like elusive quicksilver. Where did it leave me a few shiny particles [*parcelles brillantes*]? At Cuiaba where the soil used to render up nuggets of gold?" (43F, 42E). Is it any wonder that "writing" and sifting gravel for treasure become synonymous at one point in the narration (378F, 329E)?

If the dream of a golden age is Lévi-Strauss's, to reestablish balance in the wake of asymmetry, reproduction in the wake of its aberrations, to find a lost exoticism that cannot be reconstituted, to produce an always reconstitutable table of customs, to enter into union with the natives—it is his graphics, after all, no less double than those of the Caduveo, which also tell the other story: to be like the Indian in the myth is to fail in such endeavors, to see the Caduveo naked is to face a veil of art that displaces the subject it covers, to trace the last golden glimmers of the setting sun is but to see the reconstitution of a celestial landscape in which it is always bound to set again—and never definitively.

The Return

How could we avoid the seductions—and not only because critical convention requires it—of relating the two sections of our reading? The first seven chapters of *Tristes Tropiques* are a struggle to stay the slippage of time or at least to come to terms with it. To come to terms with a realm of fragments that gives no access to an irrecuperable past—that of the primitives, both in their pristine and current states, that of one's own experience—except as debris. Or—and this is the decisive rupture—to imagine that temporal disjunction can be overcome by a master sense available to the scientific eye. It is these two alternatives of which the two geological metaphors speak. It is also of this that the chapter entitled "Sunset" speaks in the disparity between the project of capturing the passing hour of dusk in notes and the written commentary on that enterprise performed by the setting sun.

The chapters on the Caduveo might be envisaged as repeating those two gestures in spatial terms: the graphics of which the anthropologist dreams as a table that might fix the master sense of all human customs and the graphics of the Caduveo that create the human only by displacing the human figure. The doubly drawn central line of the Caduveo face paintings, once as that which seems to organize the balance of an apparently symmetrical design (like the scientifically perceived line of demarcation between two geological strata) and again as the semblance of a symmetry that belies its manner of creation (like the structure that arises from the crumbling ruins of the ethnographer's eye and the object of its gaze).

The dream of time—the illusion of a reproduceable space—slips through one's fingers, even and especially when folding the meditations on Caduveo art back on the theoretical chapters to discover their symmetry, to discover that their parts are superimposable, that the later stages ("étapes franchies") do not destroy but rather verify the validity or contradictions of that which prepared it. More or less, this symmetry and repetition is what Lévi-Strauss posits for all human endeavor. It is in the section entitled "The Return," in a striking passage of the last pages of his closing chapter, that one has the sense of an astonishing temporalization of the periodic table of chapter 20: analogies produced in the course of time; truth as "a progressive dilation of sense but in inverse order and pushed to the point of explosion" (477F, 412E).

And it is here that the discipline of anthropology explodes into "entropology" as Lévi-Strauss reassesses his structuralist enterprise. "The institutions, the manners and the customs that I will have spent my life in inventorying [that is, the entire matter of the periodic table] are a passing efflorescence of a creation in relation to which these institutions possess no sense" (478F, 413E). This is the most radicalized version possible of that architect wiser than Lévi-Strauss's personal history at the origin of the structure formed of the collapse of his eye and his past (45F, 43–44E), for here one finds no architect but only the creation. Paradoxically, the role of the structuralist anthropologist, like that of all mankind, is to work "towards the *disintegration* of an original order and [to precipitate] a powerfully organized matter towards an inertia that is ever greater and which will one day be *definitive*. . . . dissociating thousands of millions of *structures* in order to reduce them to a state no longer susceptible of integration" (478F, 413E; emphasis mine).

And perhaps that explains everything, definitively. In the wake of extended gestures of organization, structuring, and recording which occupy those vast sections of *Tristes Tropiques* to which we have accorded little attention—counterbalanced by seven chapters of remarkable overture, the meditations on the Caduveo, and those on the Nambikwara which Jacques Derrida has read with such revolutionary attention[37]—in the wake of all that comes, with a patient wink of the eye, the calm contemplation of the inevitable catastrophe. And this is a catastrophe so inevitable that Lévi-Strauss can locate his part in it even at the risk of disintegrating all that came before and all that he will afterwards go on to write. It is a question once again of a certain line—how could it be otherwise?—and a certain exchange, of an enterprise which one inevitably imagines as structuring the world but which just as inevitably turns out otherwise. In question is the line, that of the printed word, the line of communication between two interlocutors, and also the line that separates the two:

> Each word exchanged, each printed line establishes a communication between the two interlocutors creating an evenness of level which was characterized before by a split of information [*écart d'information:* dare one translate this as a gap in which form took

place?], therefore by a greater organization. Rather than anthropology, one would have to write "entropology," the name of a discipline dedicated to study, in its highest manifestation, this process of disintegration. (478–79F, 413–14E).

Not only to study it, but also to create it—as time goes on.

2

Poor Timing: The Critical Ford Madox Ford

Wowe much to Ford Madox Ford. How many writers of fiction, after all, have bequeathed their readers such precise accounts of their enterprise? For although Ford began his publishing career with a fairy tale (*The Brown Owl*, 1892), time and time again and to the very end of that career in 1938 (*The March of Literature*), in numerous volumes of literary memoirs and criticism, he recorded not only "the spirit of [his] age"[1] but also a very detailed and (judging from his rhetoric) accurate account of the "school," the "canons" (OI 167, 173), the "techniques" (Te 20) of Impressionism. One can only assume that this was so that "the World [might] have an *aperçu* of [his work] as it is" (*PfL* 207–8). Let us say, no doubt as naively and inefficaciously as Edward Burden in "The Nature of a Crime," that we have come to audit the books.

Perhaps the most critical of Ford's techniques was the "time-shift." For what Ford rejected out of hand was narrative as "chronicle" (OI 174), "pursued chronology" (Te 33), "begin[ning] at the beginning and go[ing] soberly through to the end" (Te 22; see also *TtR* 55). One might wonder, then, if I may be permitted to digress (*IWN* 212), why a number of Ford's readers have set themselves the task of unraveling the complexities of his fiction by laying out the events in the proper chronological sequence.[2] I ask this in all sincerity since I am about to do something analogous, to sedulously try to situate Ford's "point of view" in what one might arrange as the fictional sequence of his authorial positions. Perhaps I wish to find "the inevitable logic of the end" or "to cast light back on the whole affair and, thus, give it its final significance" (*MoL* 579), to

67

show the "conflicting irresolutions ending in a determination" (*HJ* 168). Perhaps not. Ford, after all, was as skeptical about such gestures of resolution (*EN* 17) as he was sometimes in admiration of them.

Speaking of Conrad, and implicitly of himself, Ford wrote that he "found salvation . . . in the sheer attempt to reproduce in words life as it presents itself to the intelligent observer" (*TtR* 46). It was not a matter, then, of simply reproducing life, but of reproducing the presentation of life *to the observer.* And this did not take place as conventional narration but as impressions: "We saw that Life did not narrate, but made impressions on our brains. We in turn, if we wished to produce on you an effect of life, must not narrate but render impressions" (*JC* 194–95). Life makes its impressions on the observer, who in turn wishes to simulate the effect of life by rendering those impressions in writing for the reader. It is a question, then, as so many of Ford's readers could not fail to note, of substituting the impression of consciousness for that of a thing. But is it simply that "it is the subjective side of things that counts"?[3] Is it simply a question of rejecting the temporal sequence of lived events in order to reproduce in linear fashion exactly what goes on in the observer's mind?[4] For such impressions are, of course, to be related according to the technique of time-shift, which dictates a telling in the manner in which forgotten episodes come up in the mind.

> It is in that way that life really presents itself to us: not as a rattling narrative beginning at a hero's birth and progressing to his not very carefully machined yet predestined glory—but dallying backwards and forwards . . . as forgotten episodes came up in the minds of simple narrators. And, if you put your Affair into the mouth of such a narrator your phraseology will be the Real thing (*TtR* 55)

What is this "Real thing" that is promised the aspiring novelist? In the preface to the volume *Joseph Conrad,* where the displacement from life to observer to reader is taken one step further—where Ford, as reader of Conrad, is the writer of a biography who in turn creates a text for us, his readers—Ford dismisses traditional concepts of historical truth for "the truth of the impression as a whole."

> It is the writer's impression of a writer who avowed himself impressionist. Where the writer's memory has proved to be at fault over a detail afterwards out of curiosity looked up, the writer has allowed the fault to remain on the page; but as to the truth of the impression as a whole, the writer believes that no man would care—or dare—to

impugn it. It was that that Joseph Conrad asked for: the task has been accomplished with the most pious scrupulosity. (*JC* vi–vii)

What is this pious scrupulosity in which Ford's trajectory from life to impressions culminates?

In *Memories and Impressions* Ford announces: "I don't really deal in facts; I have for facts a most profound contempt." "This book . . . is full of inaccuracies as to facts, but its accuracy as to impressions is absolute" (*MaI* xviii; see also *PfL* vi). This greater truth in the name of which Ford writes is sincerity, for he dares his reader to "discover . . . any single impression that can be demonstrably proved not sincere on my part" (*MaI* xviii). William Gass writes intelligently of such gestures: "Impressionism, when applied as a method to the memoir, suggests the supremacy of sincerity and standpoint over objective truthfulness and historical fact, and means, in fiction, the rendering of a withdrawn fictive consciousness" (Gass 27).

The key phrase is "fictive consciousness," a consciousness, however, that is hardly restricted, as Gass suggests, to works of so-called imaginative literature.[5] It is as elusive as it is crucial to the critical texts. Almost in the same breath that Ford touts his "pious scrupulosity," he openly announces in *Joseph Conrad* that "a biography . . . should be a novel," "a work of art" (vi), taking with one hand what he gives with the other.

In the essays entitled "On Impressionism," written about the same time as *The Good Soldier*, Ford moves to what one is tempted to think of as the other side of sincerity, to a point of view of "self-consciousness," a term that for Ford was the very mark of true literature. He shifts us here from the truth of impression to the impression of truth (OI 323, 326, 327). "It seems to me that one is an Impressionist because one tries to produce an illusion of reality— or rather the business of Impressionism is to produce that illusion" (OI 323). These, the opening lines of the second essay, are indeed relevant commentary on the first, for every reader of Ford will recognize the voice in the earlier essay:

> The ideal critic . . . is a person who can so handle words that from the first three phrases any intelligent person . . . will know at once the sort of chap that he is dealing with . . . . I don't mean to say that he would necessarily trust his purse, his wife, or his mistress to the Impressionist critic's care. But that is not absolutely necessary. The ambition, however, of my friend the editor was to let his journal *give the impression* of being written by those who could be trusted with the

wives and purses—not, of course, the mistresses, for there would be none—of his readers. (OI 169; emphasis mine).

Can such a passage even pretend to the impression of truth? Ford echoes the voice of John Dowell, citing that narrator's phrases with shattering and wry irony, the voice of John Dowell as he speaks of the "good people" in what should have been their utter knowability (GS 37), and as he bemoans having foolishly trusted his wife to Edward Ashburnham (GS 10–11).[6] The ambition of Ford's editor might be to have the writer give us the impression of being trustworthy, but if we try to piece things together as Dowell suggests, we find that ambition sorely frustrated. Just two pages earlier, also echoing Dowell's voice, pointedly enough in those many moments when Dowell insists on his ignorance (GS 9, 12, 14, 245), Ford writes:

> I don't know; I just write books, and if someone attaches [the] label [of Impressionism] to me I do not much mind.
> I am not claiming any great importance for my work; I daresay it is all right. At any rate, I am a perfectly self-conscious writer; I know exactly how I get my effects, as far as those effects go. Then, if I am in truth an Impressionist, it must follow that a conscientious and exact account of how I myself work will be an account, from the inside, of how Impressionism is reached, produced, or gets its effects.
> (OI 167)

Elsewhere we have seen Ford elaborate a sequential creation myth for Impressionism[7] the truth of which, although not factual, was absolutely guaranteed by such moral categories as sincerity and pious scrupulosity. In his essays "On Impressionism" the parodic renderings of Dowell's voice turn all that on its end. By the very act of parody, apparent sincerity gives way to an evident lust for mastery: in the specific echoes of a narrator who avows his total blindness, even that mastery dissolves. At what, then, does it all work out? I have laid out the linearity in the implicit temporal tale of Ford's theory of Impressionism neither to reveal him as a hypocrite[8] nor to claim him, as he seems to, an author in perfect control of his illusions.

Impressionism begins, after all, less in memory than where memory fails.[9] This forgetting is constitutive of the way in which the Impressionist is called on to write: nothing must be rendered whole and especially not speech (OI 174–75; Te 23, 35). Language cannot be repeated and must therefore be conjured up as though half-forgotten. In a different sense the author, too, must be forgotten, absolutely suppressed (*TtR* 138; *MoL* 840–41) in a gesture of "self-abandonment" (*TtR* 70), his language becoming so transparent as to transport the reader into the rendered scene. "The language is again so low-keyed, so of the vernacular, so just, so fluid that when you read you have again no sense of reading" (*MoL* 845). "The author is invisible and almost unnoticeable and . . . his attempt has been, above all, to make you see" (*MoL* 841).

And yet, let us dwell on the "almost," for every once in a while what Ford makes us see is the *almost* in the unnoticeability of the author. Perhaps this will explain why he frequently called down upon himself the label, awarded more or less politely, of an outrageous liar.[10] He claimed, for example, to have met Byron. And there is the even more infamous "impression" that he "heard Thomas Carlyle tell how at Weimar he borrowed an apron from a waiter and served tea [coffee a few pages later] to Goethe and Schiller" (*MaI* xv–xvi). Ford was publicly ridiculed for this by "a distinguished critic" (ibid.)—nevertheless a critic who couldn't read. The story of Carlyle meeting Goethe, like that of Ford meeting Byron, emphatically ironizes the chronological reasoning Ford dismissed both as a content for fiction-telling and as a last word on literary methodology. It is an outrageous but obvious chronological joke,[11] also a joke about chronology and about memory per se. It takes only the barest rudiments of literary history combined with some small ability to read to see that. For Ford juxtaposes alongside this chronological impossibility a tale of his father's "positively extraordinary" memory (*MaI* 46). He links the two episodes with the witty connective: "I presume I should not remember half so vividly the story of Carlyle and the author of 'Wilhelm Meister' if my father had not subsequently frequently jogged my memory upon the point" (*MaI* 46).

In such moments—and they are plentiful—Ford solicits from his reader what he claims above all to avert—those doltish phrases of disbelief placed in the voice of an incredulous reader: "Hullo, this fellow is faking this" (*OI* 174; see also *MoL* 842). Must we not see, then, that side by side with his calls for realism, a certain transparency, texts written in the service of memory and history (Ford's titles and subtitles alone seem to call for this), side by side are thrusts bound to surreptitiously blast us out of our absorption in such fictions of methodology?

Or is it, rather, that "a lie is a figurative truth" (*NC* 66), as the narrator of *The Nature of a Crime* tells us. With this excuse we could

explain (away) the complication of Ford's lies, as he does, by insisting that they tell the truth, the by far greater truth, of his impressions, *figuratively* (*MaI* xvi–xvii). A lie is a figure for truth. The narrator of the early story, on the other hand, is writing to recount
long years of fraud and deception. He has stolen from the trust of
Edward Burden and plans to silence his own narrative voice, by
suicide, to preempt being exposed. For Burden has announced his
intention to audit the books. By his own admission the speaker of
the phrase is a "charlatan," a "gambler," and a "poet." It makes good
sense, then, to read it again: "A lie is a figurative truth." Perhaps all
truths, once figured, are lies; perhaps all truths are lies is a reading
equally as viable as "all lies are truths." [12]

The narrator of *The Nature of a Crime* has more to say: "For a lie
is a figurative truth—and it is the poet who is master of these illusions" (*NC* 66). The assertion is that the poet, at least, is master of
the illusions of lies and figural truths. Perhaps keeping this in mind
as Ford parodies Dowell could set matters straight. Yet the certainty
implied by this control is no doubt also an illusion. For the speaker
repeatedly equates such deceptive activities as his own with being a
poet. It is difficult to say just where we stand. The "illusions" referred to are just as likely the two complementary, contradictory
readings we have found in that first phrase—in which case no mastery is possible at all. Moreover, if the first phrase is (doubly) true,
we have absolutely no way of knowing how to read the second, as
truth or lie. We go forward, we go back; there is always another way
of looking at the matter.

Let me juxtapose alongside this predicament a number of enigmatic passages, assertions, situations. I do this less to arrive at a
definitive resolution than to see if they might not galvanize the affair (*MoL* 804).

Once again the essays "On Impressionism," with Ford belaboring
the possibilities of simultaneous or superimposed emotions:

> Indeed, I suppose that Impressionism exists to render those queer
> effects of real life that are like so many views seen through bright
> glass—through glass so bright that whilst you perceive through it a
> landscape or a backyard, you are aware that, on its surface, it reflects
> a face of a person behind you. For the whole of life is really like that;
> we are almost always in one place with our minds somewhere quite
> other. (OI 174)

Impressionism here is not that which above all makes you see, from
the point of view of a particular controlling "ego" (OI 167), as

through a glass clearly; it is a force of what Ford calls "vibration," inconspicuous deflections, tossing you through the glass to the scenes in question, only to make you aware that behind you is another pair of eyes. What one sees, moreover, is not quite a self-reflection, but the reflection of a face which could at once be an other watching the narrator or a figure for one's mind that at the same time is "almost always somewhere quite other." (Such an image could begin to account for Ford's parody of Dowell in "On Impressionism.")

One last reflection on Impressionism, one last image of the Impressionist: "The main canon of the doctrine of Impressionism had been this: The artist must aim at the absolute suppression of himself in his rendering of his Subject" (*TtR* 138). To clarify this suppression of the author, Ford, as Impressionist, speaks to his readers and offers us the following figure:

> Let me . . . repeat this formula in another image. . . . Is the Reader, then, conversant with the Theory of Podmore's Brother? . . . Podmore's Brother was accustomed to perform certain tricks on members of the public whilst so holding their attentions that they were quite unconscious of his actions. He talked so brilliantly that whilst his tongue moved his hands attracted no attention. It is not a very difficult trick to perform. . . . If the Reader will give a box of matches to a friend and then begin to talk really enthrallingly, he will be able to take the box of matches from his friend's hands without his friend being in the least conscious that the matches have gone. Closing his discourse, he will be able to say to his friend: "Where are the matches?"—and the friend will not have any idea of their whereabouts. . . . It is a trick worth performing—the tongue deceiving the eye . . .
>
> It is a trick worth performing—because it is the Trick of Impressionism—the Impressionist writer or painter telling his story with such impressiveness that the Reader or the Observer will forget that the Impressionist is using pen or brush; just as your supposititious Friend, lost in your conversation, forgets that you take the matches from his hands . . . (*TtR* 138–39)

Everything and nothing works here. This is the image offered for the author who suppresses himself or herself, who writes a language so fluid that you have no sense of reading, for the author's language disappears and the reader is aware only of the action rendered. Yet the image is of a prestidigitator who so calls attention to his brilliant *talk* that "the tongue deceiv[es] the eye," and you remain unaware of the action. Ford, too, it would seem, enjoys performing certain tricks on members of his audience, interchanging the role of language and action in his figurative truth, interchanging, moreover, prestidigitator and audience, for in the passage above the trick is said to be in the hands of the Reader who is in turn to pull it off on one of his or her friends, behind their backs so to speak. Surely this has something to do with a theory that apparently cannot be ascribed to a fixed identity, but is shifted to the *brother* of someone named Podmore.

Impressionism is not only, then, the exercise of an implicitly linear temporal order that culminates in "making you see," as Ford liked to put it (*MoL* 841), or even in a failure to make you see. It must also be viewed as a "shimmering" (*JC* 204), also as a vibratory reality in which "the mind passes . . . perpetually backwards and forwards between the apparent aspect of things and the essentials of life" (*HJ* 153). We have seen dislocations, variously, in a disintegration of the unities both of narrative perspective and of the object rendered, in the uncontrollable interrelations of truth, lie, and figure, in the shuttlecocking among author, narrator, and reader. This is a shifting juxtaposition in which the unpredictable takes place, a nonsequential and almost unnoticeable (because not literal) explosion.[13]

What, though, of the matches? How can we cast light back on the whole affair with that particular image, "a lightning flash . . . thrown back over the whole story" (*MoL* 580)? For it is the matches that are the point of the surreptitious struggle and the blind spot of the audience in the long figure for Impressionism above. As an excuse for commentary, and to bring about the "progression d'effet," I close by juxtaposing a passage from *Memories and Impressions*. If Ford had had the positively extraordinary memory of his father, we would claim that these lines must have played in his memory while writing *Thus to Revisit*. As Ford moves, in the passage below, to shed light on the scene, I leave it to the reader to weigh the contradictory implications of Madox Brown's two utterances: the question that expresses apparent alarm about a certain explosion and the exclamation which, taken literally, is a call for that very blast.

> Lady Burne-Jones . . . whispered to me, unheard by Madox Brown, that I should light the studio gas, and I was striking a match when I was appalled to hear Madox Brown shout, in tones of extreme violence and of apparent alarm:
> "Damn and *blast* it all, Fordie! Do you want us all *blown* into the next world?" (*MaI* 8; emphasis mine)

3

The (too)
Good Soldier,
"a real story":
Ford Madox Ford's
The Good Soldier

For a lie is a figurative truth—
and it is the poet who is master of
these illusions.

> —Joseph Conrad and Ford Madox Hueffer,
> *The Nature of a Crime*

Tristes Tropiques begins by juxtaposing the dilemmas of recuperating the past with the otherness of the other. It ends by linking the passage of time to communication with the reader in an entropological lurch toward disaster. *The Good Soldier* too is a struggle to record the past, and as with Lévi-Strauss that reach across time becomes caught in the intricacies of a meditation on representation. If Lévi-Strauss feels inevitably distanced from the natives of South America, the narrator of Ford's novel sets out to recuperate the past as intimacy with the other: the unproblematic knowability of both characters and readers would seem to be a given. For this reason it would have been more in the spirit of things to communicate what follows personally. It is that fictive theater that I will enact here, however bizarre it may be for a critical text. As the reader will come to understand, it is this stance that Ford's fiction forces us to assume if we are to understand how his narrative plays out. For in Ford's novel it is a question of taking others in—into the narrator's confidence, that is. But can I reasonably hope to inspire the same trust in my readers as John Dowell of *The Good Soldier* inspires in his? I offer you his bid to the reader's imagination:

> So I shall just imagine myself for a fortnight or so at one side of the fireplace of a country cottage, with a sympathetic soul opposite me. And I shall go on talking, in a low voice while the sea sounds in the distance and overhead the great black flood of wind polishes the bright stars. From time to time we shall get up to go to the door and look out at the great moon and say: "Why, it is nearly as bright as in Provence!" (12)[1]

You see, don't you, what it would take to have a heart-to-heart talk—about this text, itself so concerned with affairs of the heart. In order to have confidence in what I am about to say—you see—it is merely a matter of closing your eyes to the reality at hand. It is perhaps not too soon to admit that the room in which you sit is unlikely to resemble a country cottage. And it is only fair to remind you—for I want to be as honest as "the situation" permits, now that we are on intimate terms—that nine years of extreme intimacy with the Ashburnhams left John Dowell as blind to what they were about as anyone could be. This is the way he opens his story:

> This is the saddest story I have ever heard. We had known the Ashburnhams for nine seasons of the town of Nauheim with an extreme intimacy—or, rather, with an acquaintanceship as loose and easy and yet as close as a good glove's with your hand. My wife and I knew Captain and Mrs. Ashburnham as well as it was possible to know anybody, and yet, in another sense, we knew nothing at all about them. This is, I believe, a state of things only possible with English people of whom, till today, when I sit down to puzzle out what I know of this sad affair, I knew nothing whatever. (3)

To be sure, Dowell is the most straightforward character of the novel, and past ignorance offers no ground for present mistrust. No narrative could be more insistent on "puzzling out" the past (3), as Dowell puts it, on "piec[ing] together afterwards" (109), just as I hope to piece together for you the broken threads of the text at hand. And if that text forgets to put the pieces in their proper places, if it now and again creates false impressions, if the path of the narrative which ultimately promises to bring us out of the labyrinth occasionally seems less than straightforward, doesn't this paradoxically authenticate the reality of the tale?

> I have, I am aware, told this story in a very rambling way so that it may be difficult for anyone to find his path through what may be a sort of maze. I cannot help it. I have stuck to my idea of being in a country cottage with a silent listener, hearing between the gusts of the wind and amidst the noises of the distant sea the story as it comes. And, when one discusses an affair—a long, sad affair—one goes back, one goes forward. One remembers points that one has forgotten and one explains them all the more minutely since one recognizes that one has forgotten to mention them in their proper places and that one may have given, by omitting them, a false impression. I console myself with thinking that this is a real story and that, after all, real stories are probably told best in the way a person telling a story would tell them. They will then seem most real. (183)

There would seem to be nothing amazing in taking this line of argumentation. Certainly Dowell's roundabout way of saying things approximates the involuted ramblings of human thought far better than a linear narration. What we have before us is the impressionistic experiencing of Dowell's past and therefore not only a "real story" but one that justly "seems most real" (183).[2] Isn't that the point Dowell is making? Perhaps. But the other point he immediately gets to is Maisie Maidan's death. This point, at least, has found its proper place. The passage continues as follows:

> At any rate, I think I have brought my story up to the date of Maisie Maidan's death. I mean that I have explained everything that went before it from the several points of view that were necessary—from Leonora's, from Edward's, and, to some extent, from my own. You have the facts for the trouble of finding them; you have the points of view as far as I could ascertain or put them. (183–84)

We are compelled to be amazed after all. For just after Dowell admits that "it may be difficult for anyone to find his path through what may be a sort of maze," we arrive at Maisie Maidan's death, the death of the maiden of the maze. Are we not, as readers of the text, very much like Maisie, lost in a labyrinth from which we can never escape? Are we not brought to a country cottage far away from all that is familiar—just as Maisie was brought to Germany all the way from Chitral—in order to be entangled in a maze of illusions and conjecture? At the last moment, in fact, Maisie finally reads the scene correctly. In this, her triumphant moment of interpretation, when she has finally gotten to the heart of the matter,[3] when she has understood the intrigues of Nauheim, just as she is packing her portmanteau and preparing her exit, she finally succumbs to her heart and dies:

> [Leonora] had not cared to look round Maisie's rooms at first. Now, as soon as she came in, she perceived, sticking out beyond the bed, a small pair of feet in high-heeled shoes. Maisie had died in the effort to strap up a great portmanteau. She had died so grotesquely that her little body had fallen forward into the trunk, and it had closed upon her, like the jaws of a gigantic alligator. The key was in her hand. (75–76)

"The key was in her hand." Could this be our key to the interpretation of the text? If so, it remains closed within that which it would presume to open. How could it be otherwise? For if Dowell's narrative promises "the facts for the trouble of finding them," it nonetheless lures us into the comfort of blind alleys:

> Somewhere between Nice and Bordighera provided yearly winter quarters for us, and Nauheim always received us from July to September. You will gather from this statement that one of us had, as the saying is, a "heart," and, from the statement that my wife is dead, that she was the sufferer.
> Captain Ashburnham also had a heart. . . . The reason for his heart was, approximately, polo, or too much hard sportsmanship in his youth. The reason for poor Florence's broken years was a storm at sea upon our first crossing to Europe. (4)

The facts are indeed troublesome to find here, since what we "will gather" can only be what Dowell strews in our path—the misinformation that Florence had heart trouble and died of it—that Edward too had a heart. To be sure, both Florence and Edward committed suicide because they "had, as the saying is, a 'heart' "[4] in another sense, but this play on words renders Dowell's statement accurate only at the price of questioning the univocity of his tale.

And question it one should.[5] Not only does the narrative mislead us, but as it "goes forward" (183) it doubles back on itself with a violence usually camouflaged in better circles. If the intimacy of the Ashburnhams and the Dowells is like a tranquil "minuet de la cour" (6), one page later "it was a prison—a prison full of screaming hysterics, tied down so that they might not outsound the rolling of our carriage wheels." (7). If Edward and Leonora are the "model couple" (8), "perfectly wealthy" (9), "honest" (8), "the real thing" (8–9), perfectly devoted, one page later they are endlessly poor, endlessly acting, and (in a scene that recalls *Madame Bovary*), we find Leonora ready to commit adultery in the back of a carriage. As the narrative rolls along in this manner, we begin to suspect that the text itself is a kind of adulterer, continually turning from the straight line of narration in which it might remain true to what it said before. It promiscuously betrays not only itself, but also us, its intimates,[6] enticed as we are to a two-week honeymoon in a country cottage only to find that our own text is unfaithful.

This proves all the more amazing since the reader has taken it for granted that Dowell was one of the "good people." It was a given proposition. "Indeed, you may take it that what characterized our relationship was an atmosphere of taking everything for granted. The given proposition was that we were all 'good people' " (34). What does it signify to be among this elite? "You meet a man or a woman and, from tiny and intimate sounds, from the slightest of movements, you know at once whether you are concerned with good people or with those who won't do. You know, that is to say, whether they will go rigidly through the whole programme from the underdone beef to the Anglicanism" (37). As the concept is introduced, it appears an appropriate subject for epistemological and semiological ecstasy. "Good people" are immediately recognizable, immediately predictable, and the two-word rubric is permanently linked to a fixed catalogue of significations. Yet as Dowell continues, the phrase becomes less a vehicle for intimate understanding than a guarantee of mere acquaintance, indeed less a guarantee of acquaintance than an aggressive refusal of comprehension.[7] "But the inconvenient—well, hang it all, I will say it—the damnable nuisance of the whole thing is, that with all the taking for granted, you never really get an inch deeper than the things I have catalogued" (37).

The moral of the story is that the "good people" are those who are "too good to be true" (9). Or is this saying too much? For the narrative as I have cited it spoke not of falsehood but only of a resistance to penetration. Yet how else can one explain that Florence's maiden aunts are unable to warn Dowell that their niece, as they thought, was a harlot? Unable to speak directly, their most impassioned pleas are a wide deviation from the truth:

> You see, the two poor maiden ladies were in agonies—and they could not say one single thing direct. They would almost wring their

hands and ask if I had considered such a thing as different tempera-
ments. I assure you they were almost affectionate, concerned for me
even, as if Florence were too bright for my solid and serious vir-
tues. . . .
    . . . And they carried their protests to extraordinary lengths, for
them. . . .
    They even, almost, said that marriage was a sacrament; but nei-
ther Miss Florence nor Miss Emily could quite bring herself to utter
the word. And they almost brought themselves to say that Florence's
early life had been characterized by flirtations—something of that
sort. (81)

They were too good to be truthful. Perhaps even this is saying
too little. With each definition one gives to the phrase "good
people," it is as though the text retorts, "That's too good to be true."
It retaliates with an abrupt escalation of the term, always radically
shifting its definition. Consider, for example, that other event that
occurs on the date of Maisie Maidan's death. The Dowells and the
Ashburnhams have traveled to Marburg, where Florence has
staged her first open assault on Edward's heart by insulting Leonora's religion and nationality. Leonora, who reads the scene immediately, reacts with an impassioned horror that even Dowell does
not fail to sense. Being one of the "good people," however, she displaces the crux of the matter, the question of the impending affair,
with the same figural language that Florence has used. She voices
her warning to Dowell as follows: " 'Don't you know,' she said, in
her clear hard voice, 'don't you know that I'm an Irish Catholic?' "
(46). The blank whiteness of a chapter break marks the end of this
phrase and also marks the obliteration of its meaning that Dowell,
himself one of the "good people," performs. As chapter 5 opens he
writes, "Those words gave me the greatest relief that I have ever
had in my life" (46). And as if even this denunciation from Leonora
is too violent to take at face value, Dowell goes on to displace her
meaning yet further:

    Yes, I remember thinking at the time that it was almost as if Leonora
    were saying, through me, to Florence:
    "You may outrage me as you will; you may take all that I person-
    ally possess, but do not you dare to say one single thing in view of
    the situation that that will set up—against the faith that makes me
    become the doormat for your feet."
    But obviously, as I saw it, that could not be her meaning. Good
    people, be they ever so diverse in creed, do not threaten each other.
    So that I read Leonora's words to mean just no more than:

> "It would be better if Florence said nothing at all against my co-religionists, because it is a point that I am touchy about." (68–69)

"Good people," then, not only deviate from the truth like the aunts Hurlbird; they camouflage its violence with metaphor, saying something utterly different from what they mean, like Leonora, or purposely disfigure it, like Dowell.[8]

Even systematic distortion and misinterpretation may not be the text's final word on the "good people." It nevertheless explains why one of the key passages in the novel should be the moment when Florence rounds a screen in the hotel corridor to find a certain scene of entanglement. It is a scene in which language has been silenced—"There was not a single word spoken" (53)—a scene in which violence has left only the barest of traces, the red mark on Maisie Maidan's cheek where Leonora has slapped her. In this, the only instance of literal violence in the text, Leonora has forgotten to act with the repressive decorum of a good person. She immediately attempts to cover her tracks.

> And there was not a work spoken. You see, under those four eyes—her own and Mrs. Maidan's—Leonora could just let herself go as far as to box Mrs. Maidan's ears. But the moment a stranger came along she pulled herself wonderfully up. She was at first silent and then, the moment the key was disengaged by Florence, she was in a state to say: "So awkward of me . . . I was just trying to put the comb straight in Mrs. Maidan's hair. . . ." (53)

Dowell marks this scene as a pivotal point, for it was at this moment that Florence became intimate with Leonora and began to gain control. "Leonora behaved better in a sense. She just boxed Mrs. Maidan's ears—yes, she hit her, in an uncontrollable access of rage, a hard blow on the side of the cheek, in the corridor of the hotel, outside Edward's room. It was that, you know, that accounted for the sudden, odd intimacy that sprang up between Florence and Mrs. Ashburnham (52). "At any rate that was how Florence got to know her" (53).

Florence knows to interpret the signs just as we as "good" readers of the text must learn to read its traces. Let us begin by reading one that is left there specifically for us. What is it after all that entangled Leonora in Maisie's hair but the gold key that hung from her wrist and about which Dowell has already written:

> Certain women's lines guide your eyes to their necks, their eyelashes, their lips, their breasts. But Leonora's seemed to conduct your gaze

always to her wrist. And the wrist was at its best in a black or a dog-skin glove and there was always a gold circlet with a little chain supporting a very small golden key to a dispatch box. Perhaps it was that in which she locked up her heart and her feelings. (32)

Like Maisie's (and our) key, it is caught within the very labyrinth from which it would hope to provide an escape. For it is, of course, precisely by disengaging it as she does that Florence becomes the next point of entanglement.

As I am sure you see, then, this scene entangles more than meets the eye. The violence here is demarcated by the silent trace, that almost perfect expression which expresses almost nothing.[9] The silence quickly gives way first to the rhetorical screen of the "good people" and then to that fateful moment of Leonora's compromise when she openly begins to indulge herself in intercourse:

> She opened the door of Ashburnham's room quite ostentatiously, so that Florence should hear her address Edward in terms of intimacy and liking. "Edward," she called. But there was no Edward there.
>
> You understand that there was no Edward there. It was then, for the only time of her career, that Leonora really compromised herself—she exclaimed: "How frightful! . . . Poor little Maisie! . . ." (53)

This movement from silence to talk will prove significant for the text as a whole. The lapse into communication takes place at the juncture marked by the scene in the corridor and the trip to Marburg:

> If there was a fine point about Leonora it was that she was proud and that she was silent. But that pride and that silence broke when she made that extraordinary outburst, in the shadowy room that contained the Protest. (184)
>
> That was really a calamity for Leonora, because, once started, there was no stopping the talking. She tried to stop—but it was not to be done. . . .
>
> I don't in the least blame Leonora for her coarseness to Florence. . . . But I do blame her for giving way to what was in the end a desire for communicativeness. (192)

As Dowell would have it, however, these "nine years of uninterrupted tranquillity" from the death of Maisie Maidan to the death of Florence "were characterized by an extraordinary want of any communicativeness" (34) between the Ashburnhams and the Dowells, between Edward and Leonora, who "never spoke a word to each other in private" (8), and of course between Dowell and Florence. Dowell's entire role as nurse to Florence was, as he understood it, to restrain her intercourse because she "had, as the saying is, a 'heart' " (4).

> For do you understand my whole attentions, my whole endeavors were to keep poor dear Florence on to topics like the finds at Gnossos and the mental spirituality of Walter Pater. I had to keep her at it, you understand, or she might die. For I was solemnly informed that if she became excited over anything or if her emotions were really stirred her little heart might cease to beat. For twelve years I had to watch every word that any person uttered in any conversation and I had to head it off what the English call "things"—off love, poverty, crime, religion, and the rest of it. (15–16)

It is strange that the only function of the novel's narrator is to silence all reference to love, poverty, crime, and religion, the very subject matter of the text; for what is *The Good Soldier* about if not love, the poverty of the Ashburnhams, the crime of adultery, and questions of Protestant and Catholic religion? One wonders if Dowell's habit of "heading off" rhetorical violence, the violence of rhetoric, hasn't been difficult to break. "You cannot, you see, have acted as a nurse to a person for twelve years without wishing to go on nursing her" (70–71).

Dowell's imposition of censorship functions as something of a joke, of course: silence does not repress Florence's emotions but merely deforms her discourse. There is perhaps a certain shrewdness in the gesture after all, however, for the violence of *The Good Soldier* takes place, not in the outburst of sexual passion, but in that of talk. Language operates in this tale less by way of expressing passion than by creating it. It creates the greatest passion of Dowell's life, for example, and the only real passion of Edward's.

> The odd thing is that what sticks out in my recollection of the rest of that evening was Leonora's saying:
> "Of course you might marry her," and when I asked whom, she answered:
> "The girl."
> Now that is to me a very amazing thing—amazing for the light of possibilities that it casts into the human heart. For I had never had the slightest conscious idea of marrying the girl; I never had the slightest idea even of caring for her. (103)

> And in speaking to [Nancy] on that night, [Edward] wasn't, I am
> convinced, committing a baseness. It was as if his passion for her
> hadn't existed; as if the very words that he spoke, without knowing
> that he spoke them, created the passion as they went along. Before
> he spoke, there was nothing; afterwards, it was the integral fact of
> his life. (116)

Language, the talk of desire, does not mediate an already existing passion but, rather, generates it. And it's not simply that language generates passion: the fatal driving passion of the tale becomes this desire for talk, the "desire for communicativeness"
(192). However Dowell may condemn it in Leonora, it is certainly
his single passion, determined as he is to create the text as a space
for a fortnight of intimate conversation. Isn't it Edward's talk that
drives Maisie to her death and Florence to suicide, and isn't it the
talk at Branshaw Teleragh that ultimately brings Edward to suicide
and drives Nancy to madness? Before we reach this point, let us
make a detour by way of Marburg to retrace the path of this lapse
into talk.

This journey, you understand, turns the relationship of the four
completely on its end. The upheaval is not merely the result of Leonora's outburst (her displaced announcement that she is Irish Catholic). Dowell writes of this entire day: "I was aware of something
treacherous, something frightful, something evil in the day. I can't
define it and can't find a simile for it" (44). What is it on this journey
that is treacherous and indefinable, treacherous perhaps because it
is that for which no simile can be found? If we can offer no definitive answer to this question, we might begin by noting that the entire journey rides on Florence's seemingly insignificant chatter.
And not only Florence's, for Dowell, in turn, chooses this moment
of his story to ramble on rather aimlessly, to interject the single gay,
descriptive, and apparently irrelevant interlude of the novel. It is
here when we are most thrown off guard that Dowell's narrative
operates as an inexorably precise, almost mechanical, if ultimately
problematic, allegory.

> Why, I remember on that afternoon I saw a brown cow hitch its
> horns under the stomach of a black and white animal and the black
> and white one was thrown right into the middle of a narrow stream.
> I burst out laughing. But Florence was imparting information so
> hard and Leonora was listening so intently that no one noticed me.
> As for me, I was pleased to be off duty; I was pleased to think that
> Florence for the moment was indubitably out of mischief—because

she was talking about Ludwig the Courageous (I think it was Ludwig
the Courageous but I am not an historian), about Ludwig the Courageous of Hessen, who wanted to have three wives at once and pa-
tronized Luther—something like that!—I was so relieved to be off
duty, because she couldn't possibly be doing anything to excite herself or set her poor heart a-fluttering—that the incident of the cow
was a real joy to me. . . . [I]t does look very funny, you know, to see a
black and white cow land on its back in the middle of a stream. It is
so just exactly what one doesn't expect of a cow. (42)

This is exactly what one doesn't expect of a text; and yet it is there
for us in black and white.[10] Three times, we are told, it is the "black
and white" that is turned on its end. This passage that talks of Florence imparting information and history, that itself appears an in-
formative if pointless moment of personal history, has a certain
hitch. It is just about this time, while the narrator is "off duty," that
Maisie Maidan is thrown into the middle of a portmanteau, with
her feet in the air, like the black and white cow. It is the same moment in which Florence is maneuvering to toss Leonora aside:

> And we went up winding corkscrew staircases and through the Rit-
> tersaal, the great painted hall where the Reformer and his friends
> met for the first time under the protection of the gentleman that
> had three wives at once and formed an alliance with the gentleman
> that had six wives, one after the other (I'm not really interested in
> these facts but they have a bearing on my story). (43)

These facts *are* Dowell's story. For who is the "gentleman that had
six wives, one after another," if not Edward Ashburnham, whose
love affairs and flirtations (you have the facts for the trouble of
finding them) are just about to number six at this point in the tale:
Leonora, the servant girl of the Kilsyte case, the Grand Duke's mis-
tress, Mrs. Basil, Maisie, and Florence. And who is "the gentleman
that had three wives at once," under whose protection the Reformer and the man with six wives meet, if not the protective Dowell, who in the course of the novel admits to having loved Leonora
(32), Maisie Maidan (51), and Nancy Rufford at one and the same
time.[11] And who is the Reformer, if not Florence, who, we have just
been told, "was at that time engaged in educating Captain Ashburnham" (39).

Her method of education is by way of a certain text: "You see, in
the archives of the Schloss in that city there was a document which
Florence thought would finally give her the chance to educate the

whole lot of us together" (40). This text which holds such promise of enlightenment documents the entire problematic of the trip to Marburg—Florence's coded monologue, Dowell's narration of that monologue, and the lapse into talk in general. It does this less by way of what it says than by way of its unlikely appearance. "She was pointing at a piece of paper, like the half-sheet of a letter with some faint pencil scrawls that might have been a jotting of the amounts we were spending during the day. . . . 'There it is—the Protest.' . . . 'Don't you know that is why we were all called Protestants? That is the pencil draft of the Protest they drew up' " (44). Florence points the finger at a scrap of paper, the original draft of the Protest, the point of rupture between Catholics and Protestants, and between Leonora and Edward, of course. She never bothers to elaborate on its content. It resembles the "half-sheet of a letter with some faint pencil scrawls" and thereby claims the same insignificant innocence as the chatter of Florence and the conversational recordings of Dowell. Unlike the all too clear letter Maisie presently writes, the Protest is a study in illegibility. It forewarns us that the shift into talk will not fulfill a promise of revelation but will produce a text all the more demanding of interpretation.

All the more demanding of interpretation because Protestantism functions in *The Good Soldier* as the destruction of an established code, the moral code of the marriage sacrament. This is the maddening lesson that Nancy will learn at Branshaw Teleragh:

> "I thought," Nancy said, "I never imagined. . . . Aren't marriages sacraments? Aren't they indissoluble? I thought you were married . . . and . . ." She was sobbing. "I thought you were married or not married as you are alive or dead."
> "That," Leonora said, "is the law of the church. It is not the law of the land. . . ."
> "Oh, yes," Nancy said, "the Brands are Protestants."
> She felt a sudden safeness descend upon her, and for an hour or so her mind was at rest. It seemed to her idiotic not to have remembered Henry VIII and the basis upon which Protestantism rests. (220–21)

The Protest makes possible polygamy and divorce, having three wives at once or six wives one after another. It challenges the law of the church, which insists on the indissoluble one-to-one relationship between man and wife and implicitly between sacramental text and meaning.[12]

It is this challenge that takes place as they enter the "large old chamber, full of presses" in which that document is to be found.

> [Florence] told the tired, bored custodian what shutters to open; so that the bright sunlight streamed in palpable shafts into the dim old chamber. She explained that this was Luther's bedroom and that just where the sunlight fell had stood his bed. As a matter of fact, I believe that she was wrong and that Luther only stopped, as it were, for lunch, in order to evade pursuit. But, no doubt, it would have been his bedroom if he could have been persuaded to stop the night. (43–44)

It is the sunlight, of course, that is palpable, and not the bed of Luther that Florence passionately strives to evoke. Unlike her reformer counterpart, Florence has no desire to "evade pursuit." She could well—this is her point—she could well be "persuaded to stop the night." "And then," the passage continues, "in spite of the protest of the custodian, she threw open another shutter and came tripping back to a large glass case" (44). The custodian, who was tired and bored only a few lines back, seems to recognize the potency of those "palpable shafts" of sunlight that create beds where only printing presses stood before. He raises a "protest" as a reminder of the significance of the term, for Florence is about to illuminate *the* Protest, which is to say, as we have seen, that Florence is out to re-form it.

> She continued, looking up into Captain Ashburnham's eyes: "It's because of that piece of paper that you're honest, sober, industrious, provident, and clean-lived. If it weren't for that piece of paper you'd be like the Irish or the Italians or the Poles, but particularly the Irish. . . ."
> And she laid one finger upon Captain Ashburnham's wrist. (44)

It is indeed hard to put one's finger on what is happening here. As Dowell puts it two lines later, "I can't define it and can't find a simile for it," and it is now, you remember, that Leonora is driven to her "desire for communicativeness." The indefinability and the lapse into communication both revolve around Florence's reading of "the Protest" by means of a certain mode of discourse in which literal and figural language prove mutually exclusive. It is because of that piece of paper, she insists, that Edward is sober, industrious, provident, and clean-lived. Edward, of course, is none of these: he nearly drinks himself to death, is indolent, cannot control his excessive expenditures, and is heading rapidly for his sixth affair. If Florence inverts each of his characteristics, she does so, it would seem, out of ignorance. What she means by saying that Edward is clean-lived is that she wishes he weren't,[13] for the reformer wishes to go to bed with the "gentleman that had six wives, one after the other." She lays her hand on Edward's wrist, then, by way of saying, "This is my body."

What does it mean to say "This is my body" in the Castle of Marburg while pointing at a manuscript signed, we are told, by Martin Luther, Martin Bucer, and Zwingli (44)? Dowell and Florence have been "imparting information so hard" (42) that one is tempted to remain "off duty" (42). In rejecting a literal reading of their narrations, one is tempted, that is, simply to fix upon the limited mechanical allegory of Dowell's black and white cow as Maisie Maidan or Leonora[14] and of Florence's Reformer, Henry VIII, and Ludwig the Courageous as figures for Florence, Edward, and Dowell. But let us shuttle back from the figurative to the historical, as the document in question demands in order to restore to it its proper name. It is thus, paradoxically enough, that the black and white is turned truly on its end.

The fact of the matter is that the "piece of paper" Florence insists on calling "the Protest" can be none other than the Articles of Marburg signed in the Castle of Marburg in October 1529 by Luther, Bucer, Zwingli, and seven others.[15] "I don't really deal in facts; — [you understand. Along with Ford Madox Ford] I have for facts a most profound contempt."[16] It is not that "I'm . . . really interested in these facts but they have a bearing on my story" (43). Those articles, history tells us, are the result of several days of vertiginous argument between Luther and Zwingli as to the reading of the phrase "This is my body."[17] Throughout the talks on the interpretation of these words, Luther insists that he "cannot understand them in any other way than according to their literal meaning."[18] For him, the proper interpretation of the sacrament means "The body is present in the bread" (*LW* 30). Zwingli and Oecolampadius, however, regard the bread of the sacrament only as a spiritual remembrance of the body of Christ. They read the phrase "This is my body" as figurative speech: "In such cases [Oecolampadius explains], words have a different meaning from what they say" (*LW* 37). It is precisely this difference that Luther will not accept. "A metaphor," he says, "abolishes the content altogether: e.g., as when you understand 'body' as 'the figure of a body,' . . . Your figure of speech does away with the kernel and leaves the shell" (*LW* 30–31).

In this shell and kernel game of the colloquy one wonders indeed where the kernel is to be found. The critical problem at hand, it would seem, continually shifts from the question of the phrase "This is my body" to the status of the sacramental bread as either literally or figuratively the body of Christ, as equivalent to the body or merely a sign for it. The shift permits a repeated repression of the role of the phrase itself in the context of the argument.[19] Significantly enough, none of the interlocutors at Marburg pronounces the phrase, presupposing it to function *either* literally *or* figuratively *in that context.* When Luther writes "Hoc est corpus meum" on the table top, he does not expect "the body [to be] present bodily in the word" (*LW* 25), nor does the Swiss contingent read here a figural representation. "This is my body" is, rather, the verbal contrivance that fabricates the discord between the literal and the figurative: it is the locus of rupture and operates altogether differently from the linguistic machines that Luther and Zwingli attempt to construct. These latter would guarantee the presence of Christ's body, the one literally or immediately, the other figuratively or mediately. Their complicity, you will perceive, is all but manifest. The phrase "This is my body," however, is the kernel that cracks the shell: it generates days (and even years) of unending talk in which neither language as literal nor as figurative expression can gain the upper hand. "This is my body" generates the disparity between the two and their ultimate indecidability: "And talk!" (201), the passion for talk.

"Is all this digression or isn't it digression?" (14). I have given you the historical facts necessary for the interpretation of this passage, for here as elsewhere in Ford, it is a question of how one reads history and whether one can retell it. I regret it provides "no current to draw things along to a swift and inevitable end" (164). For if I earlier gave the impression that Dowell might be deciphered by shuttling from a literal to a figural reading, you will gather that this is no longer possible. His narration is governed by the same passion for talk as the Marburg Colloquy, in which the literal and figurative remain perpetually in conflict.

We begin at least to have some sense of why this scene takes place coincident with the shift into talk and why it is precisely this for which Dowell can find no definition and no simile. The talk in which Florence, Leonora, Edward, and later Nancy are about to indulge themselves is language denying the operations both of literal and figural adequation. It is not the answer to the camouflage of silence. It does not release those once repressed passions in a violent wave of expression. The violence is not on the side of that which is expressed but is the force of language itself, language as the force of refusal:

> What had happened was just hell. Leonora had spoken to Nancy; Nancy had spoken to Edward; Edward had spoken to Leonora— and they had talked and talked. And talked. . . . You have to imagine my beautiful Nancy appearing suddenly to Edward, rising up at the foot of his bed. . . . You have to imagine her, a silent, a no doubt agonized figure, like a spectre, suddenly offering herself to him—to save his reason! And you have to imagine his frantic refusal—and talk. And talk! (201)

The more they talk the worse it gets. As the orgiastic exchanges become increasingly exaggerated, Dowell's narrative searches more and more desperately for the appropriate simile, for the key that will enable him to ground this violence in a "real world" counterpart:

> Those two women pursued that poor devil and flayed the skin off him *as if* they had done it with whips. I tell you his mind bled almost visibly. I seem to see him stand, naked to the waist, his forearms shielding his eyes, and flesh hanging from him in rags. I tell you that is *no exaggeration* of what I feel. It was *as if* Leonora and Nancy banded themselves together to do execution, for the sake of humanity, upon the body of a man who was at their disposal. They were *like* a couple of Sioux who had got hold of an Apache and had him well tied to a stake. I tell you there was no end to the tortures they inflicted upon him.
> Night after night he would hear them talking; talking; maddened, sweating, seeking oblivion in drink, he would lie there and hear the voices going on and on. (239; emphasis mine)

But what if the "situation" excludes the possibility of tying it down? What if the flaying, whipping, bleeding, and execution are inadequate to fix that which takes place—in a figure that is "as if," that is "like," that is "no exaggeration"? What if there is indeed "no end," if the voices will insist on "going on and on"? Isn't that what Dowell must finally concede? Isn't this the unimaginable hell of a narrator who can no longer say what he wishes except through the oblique admission that it exceeds his powers of definition and simile, except by a comparative that renounces finding an equivalent violent enough to express the state of affairs? "It was a most amazing business, and I think it would have been *better* in the eyes of God if they had all attempted to gouge out each other's eyes with carving knives. But they were 'good people' " (249; emphasis mine).

You will forgive me if I have made another detour, if I have shuttlecocked once again to the question of the narrative. This going back and forth cannot be avoided, for it is not only the so-called "Protest," Florence's description of it, and the shift to talk, but also storytelling, and especially Dowell's, that is at stake here. The fidelity between narrative text and its signification is menaced at the very moment when the language of its characters becomes most frenzied. The violence generated by the repressive force of their talk is carried over into Dowell's attempts at description where the same refusal of definitional similitude takes place. From the very beginning, Dowell has more or less intimated to us that it could not be otherwise. Just a few pages into his tale, he writes about the relationship between stories told and the reality behind them:

> For, as I've said, what do I know even of the smoking-room? Fellows come in and tell the most extraordinarily gross stories—so gross that they will positively give you a pain. And yet they'd be offended if you suggested that they weren't the sort of person you could trust your wife alone with. And very likely they'd be quite properly offended. . . . Then, if they so delight in the narration, how is it possible that they can be offended—and properly offended—at the suggestion that they might make attempts upon your wife's honour? Or again: Edward Ashburnham was the cleanest-looking sort of chap. . . . And he never more than once or twice in all the nine years of my knowing him told a story that couldn't have gone into the columns of the *Field*. . . . You would have said that he was exactly the sort of chap that you could have trusted your wife with. And I trusted mine—and it was madness. (10–11)

As paradoxical as the situation may seem here, we are provided with a rather simple key to interpretation. Those who tell gross stories are unlikely to live them: those who are offended by gross stories are not to be trusted. The relationship between textual statement and meaning is merely a matter of inversion. But there is a noncoherence added to the notation of this hermeneutic formula, and that noncoherence is Dowell.

> And yet again you have me. If poor Edward was dangerous because of the chastity of his expressions—and they say that is always the hall-mark of a libertine—what about myself? For I solemnly avow that not only have I never so much as hinted at an impropriety

in my conversation in the whole of my days; and more than that, I will vouch for the cleanness of my thoughts and the absolute chastity of my life. At what, then, does it all work out? Is the whole thing a folly and a mockery? (11–12)

Dowell insists on the coherence between his textual and sexual chastities and with that gesture indeed makes a mockery of all hermeneutic consistency.[20]

It is here—and certainly it is no coincidence—that Dowell invites us to a fortnight of conversation in the country cottage of his imagination. It is just here, after the insistence on a coherence between story and history has disrupted the formula for exegesis, that Dowell will set the scene for his narration as one in which the intimacy between storyteller and auditor should guarantee its historical validity. Of these two passages, "I can't make out which of them was right. I leave it to you" (246).

You will understand, no doubt, that I have to leave all critical judgment to you. For if the talk of the "good people"—Edward, Leonora, and Nancy—was more violent than the gouging of each other's eyes because it refused the expression of passion, if Dowell's talk in turn is invaded by the violent force of nonadequation, if Dowell repeatedly admits his own ignorance, how am I to find the facts? "I don't know; I don't know" (9). How successfully can I piece together the past of Dowell in the fragments from a narrator who never noticed that his wife was living with her lover in his own apartment, who was thirteen years a devoted nurse to a heart patient who didn't have a heart, from a narrator for whom all memories are fragments to begin with?

> Florence got all she wanted out of one look at a place. She had the seeing eye.
> I haven't, unfortunately, so that the world is full of places to which I want to return. . . . Not one of them did we see more than once, so that the whole world for me is like spots of colour in an immense canvas. Perhaps if it weren't so I should have something to catch hold of now.
> Is all this digression or isn't it digression? Again I don't know.
> You, the listener, sit opposite me. But you are so silent. You don't tell me anything. (14)

Perhaps this is because you are "good people." "Good people,"; if you remember, are always silent, even when they talk. No, doubtless you have your reason. Silence is the logical response to a call for critical judgment in the context of this novel. Yours is certainly the silence of perfectly normal reason.

Indeed, the novel leaves us, the living, with only two alternatives between which we are "tossed backwards and forwards" (253)—the perfectly normal reason you have chosen and madness:

> Nancy was a splendid creature but she had about her a touch of madness. Society does not need individuals with touches of madness about them. So Edward and Nancy found themselves steam-rolled out and Leonora survives, the perfectly normal type. (238)
>
> Well, that is the end of the story. . . . The villains—for obviously Edward and the girl were villains—have been punished by suicide and madness. The heroine—the perfectly normal, virtuous, and slightly deceitful heroine—has become the happy wife of a perfectly normal, virtuous and slightly deceitful husband. (252)

But not only the perfectly normal, also the mad—you see, don't you?—can be quite reasonable. As Dowell comes upon her in Ceylon, Nancy is uttering the most reasonable words of the entire novel. It is, at least, a very rare moment when Dowell will insist on the category of reason.

> I have visited Asia, to see, in Ceylon, in a darkened room, my poor girl, sitting motionless, with her wonderful hair about her, looking at me with eyes that did not see me, and saying distinctly: "*Credo in unum Deum Omnipotentem. . . . Credo in unum Deum Omnipotentem.*" Those are the only reasonable words she uttered; those are the only words, it appears, that she ever will utter. I suppose that they are reasonable words; it must be extraordinarily reasonable for her, if she can say that she believes in an Omnipotent Deity. (234)

There is, however, her other declaration, and it is that other assertion, surely, that is the sign of her hopeless condition; for rather than a grounding in theological stability, it concerns the perpetual shift between possibilities.

> Well, yesterday at lunch she said suddenly:
> "Shuttlecocks!"
> And she repeated the word "shuttlecocks" three times. I know what was passing in her mind, if she can be said to have a mind, for Leonora has told me that, once, the poor girl said she felt like a shuttlecock being tossed backwards and forwards between the violent personalities of Edward and his wife. . . . And the odd thing was that Edward himself considered that those two women used *him* like

> a shuttlecock. . . . And Leonora also imagined that Edward and
> Nancy picked her up and threw her down as suited their purely va-
> garant moods. So there you have the pretty picture. (252–53)

If the same word passed in the mind of the perfectly normal Leonora, it cannot simply be "shuttlecocks" that marks the madness of
Nancy but rather the endless back and forth between "shuttlecocks" and the Omnipotent Deity. This is what robs the pretty picture of its meaning.

> Then she will say that she believes in an Omnipotent Deity or she
> will utter the one word "shuttlecocks," perhaps. It is very extraordi-
> nary to see the perfect flush of health on her cheeks, to see the lustre
> of her coiled black hair, the poise of the head upon the neck, the
> grace of the white hands—and to think that it all means nothing—
> that it is a picture without a meaning. (254)

And now I'm sure you finally have a clear insight into our amazing predicament. I have played the role of the omnipotent narrator, for according to our epigraph, this figure is promised the mastery of the illusions of figurative truth, and who can resist the
illusion of mastery? And yet, since we are now on intimate terms, I
felt obligated to make clear to you my readers just where we stand,
to shuttle back to my role as reader and to make you see that the
reader of *The Good Soldier* is tossed back and forth between possibilities. For if we started with Maisie Maidan as the figure of Dowell's
auditor—caught as she is at the very center of the text just at the
moment of perfect understanding—the other figure of the listener
(and, I suppose, reader) is, of course, Nancy. "They haven't restored her reason. She is, I am aware, sitting in the hall, [just the
distance of eye to text] from where I am now . . ." (236).

4

Fictional Histories: Lessing's *Laocoön*

The merest glance at a reproduction of the famous statue of Laocoön tells us that it is a question of three figures in a rather critical situation. Laocoön, whose words of warning about the Trojan horse meet with disdain, is punished, Virgil tells us, along with his two sons for "having . . . profaned the sacred image" (*Aeneid,* bk. 2, p. 40).[1] The three figures are bound together by a common adversary: it entangles their limbs, trips them up, while at the same time directing its viperous fangs at well-chosen points of the anatomy. To place Lessing in perspective, only a small displacement is necessary. This moving situation that we observe is also that of Lessing's *Laocoön,* for what is this essay about if not an attack on three figures, one major and two now minor. The textual situation of the "Essay on the Limits of Painting and Poetry" evolves as a polemic against Winckelmann's *Gedanken über die Nachahmung der griechischen Werke,* Spence's *Polymetis,* and Caylus's *Tableaux tirés de l'Iliade, de l'Odysée d'Homère et de l'Énèiade de Virgil.*

What does it mean to confront a polemical text? To what end does one read it? Lessing himself comes to terms with this in 1769, several years after completing the *Laocoön,* in the preface to a text entitled "How the Ancients Portrayed Death" ("Wie die Alten den Tod gebildet.") The later essay was written as an attack on the classical philologist Klotz,[2] who had entered into an elaborate struggle with the Berliners Lessing and Herder. Klotz's preface to the *Abhandlungen* of Caylus had refuted an assertion in the *Laocoön* about the manner in which the ancients represented death. Lessing opens his counterattack with a commentary on the nature of polemics: "I would not like it if this inquiry were to be judged according to that which gave it occasion. Its occasion is so despicable that only the manner in which I have used it can excuse that I wanted to use it at all."[3]

If Lessing asks that his work not be judged by that which gave it occasion, this is not to say that he is offended by the violence of polemics. What Lessing finds despicable is not the state of struggle but rather the content of Klotz's preface; in fact, Lessing chides his readers for being overly sensitive to polemics, for finding them a little too revolting.

> This is not to say that I don't consider our present-day public a little too disgusted by everything that is called and resembles polemics. It seems to wish to forget that it owes thanks for the explanation [*Aufklärung*] of so many important points to pure contradiction, and that human beings would still not be agreed about anything in the world if they had never quarreled about anything in the world. (Lachmann 11:3)

What the public wishes to forget, what it tries to repress, is that it is precisely through contradiction that elucidation is made possible. Enlightenment is grounded in contradiction, and the German term *Streitschrift* (polemics) must be read literally as a writing or text (*Schrift*) with a struggle inscribed at its point of inception.

But doesn't Lessing suggest that having words with someone is the means to an ultimate accord? If so, what would such an accord imply, and what would be its relation to truth?

> But truth, it is said, gains so seldom in the process. — So seldom? It may be that truth has never yet been determined through struggle [*Streit*]. Struggle has nourished the spirit of investigation, has kept prejudice [*Vorurteil*] and authority [*Ansehen*] in a *constant* state of shakenness [*Erschütterung*]: in short, it has prevented un-truth from fixing itself in the place of truth. (Lachmann 11:3; italics mine)

By means of the polemic, truth profits or improves (*gewinnt* as an intransitive verb). It never definitively triumphs, but it becomes a better opponent by repeatedly preventing untruth from taking its place. It maintains its enemies (and itself) in a state of perpetual shakenness, and these enemies are the forces of authority and pre-judgment.

If any truth can be said to arise from the polemics of Lessing's *Laocoön*, then, it can hardly be truth in any fixed, conventional sense of the term—which is to say, it cannot be said to be truth as fixed, sense, or term. The truth of the polemic is a perpetually increasing force of text as struggle (*Streitschrift*), such that neither truth nor untruth is ever constituted or determined.[4]

How, then, are we to explain the frame of the *Laocoön* Section 1 opens with a gloss and long citation from Winckelmann's *Thoughts about the Imitation of the Greek Works (Gedanken über die Nachahmung der Griechischen Werke)* of 1755.

> Herr Winckelmann places the general, preeminent characteristics of the Greek masterpieces of painting and sculpture in a noble simplicity and quiet grandeur, both in posture as well as in expression. "Just as the depth of the sea," he says, "remains still at all times, however much the surface might still rage, so, amidst all the passions, the expression in the figures of the Greeks shows a great and calm soul."

> This soul portrays itself in the face of the Laocoön—and not only in the face—under the most violent suffering . . . Laocoön suffers, but he suffers like the Philoctetes of Sophocles: his misery pierces our very soul; but we would wish to be able to endure misery like this great man. (6G, 7E)[5]

It is the content of this passage that becomes the point of departure of the polemic, for Lessing accuses Winckelmann of failing to distinguish appropriately between the arts of sculpture and poesy.

Chapters 1–25 of the *Laocoön* are written as though Winckelmann had never written a further word on the subject—when in chapter 26, almost at the end of the essay, the reader abruptly comes upon the following:

> Herr Winckelmann's "History of the Art of the Ancients" has appeared. I dare not take another step without having read this work. To reason speciously simply from general concepts about art can lead us astray—to caprices that, sooner or later, to our shame we would find refuted in the works of art. The ancients, too, knew the bonds that connect painting and poesy with one another and they will not have drawn them closer together than was advantageous for both. What their artists did will teach me what artists in general should do; and there where such a man carries forward the torch of history, speculation can boldly follow after. (156G, 138E)

Lessing almost breathlessly announces the appearance of Winckelmann's *History*. We have the sense that Lessing's essay has indeed been something of a critical stroll[6] and that he has just stumbled across an object in his path. This object is placed there, he tells us, less to trip him up than to prevent him from being misled into the byways of capricious ideas. To be sure, this promise of guidance radiates not from any theoretical enlightenment Winckelmann may have to offer, but rather from Lessing's expectation of finding there the "works of art" themselves and "what their [the ancients'] artists did." Winckelmann is thus heralded as the "man [who] carries forward the torch of history" so that Lessing's theoretical speculation may boldly follow.

This holding aloft of Winckelmann's torch of history is apt to blind us to another torch of history, the light that might illuminate the history of the writing of the *Laocoön.* Implicit in Lessing's apparent praise of Winckelmann in the opening paragraph of chapter 26 is a historical relationship of his *Laocoön* to the 1755 *Thoughts about the Imitation of the Greek Works* and the later *History of the Art of the Ancients* that is entirely fictional.[7]

Lessing began making preliminary drafts of his essay at the beginning of the decade, but the manuscript was not completed and published until Easter of 1766. When Winckelmann's *History* appeared in December of 1763, Lessing had, in all probability, just completed the first two sections of a brief preliminary sketch.[8] In the third section of that draft, Lessing goes on to note that Winckelmann's *History* makes precisely those distinctions between sculpture and poesy on which he himself had planned to elaborate: "Herr Winck. himself recognized, in his *Hist. of Art* that the sculptor had been bound to this repose because of the beauty that was to be retained and that this was no law for the poet."[9]

Why, then, in the *Laocoön* do we read well over one hundred pages that suggest ignorance of Winckelmann's new text and posture? Why is the frame of the *Laocoön* a frame-up that purposely fabricates the historical facts of its own production while in the same breath claiming to follow "the torch of history"? With the manuscript cited above as well as other textual evidence, Lessing made certain that literary historians would be able to read his ruse clearly.[10] It is hardly, then, that Lessing copies Winckelmann and tries to cover his traces,[11] but rather that he wishes to establish contradiction as his polemical point of departure. What is crucial here is not whether it was Winckelmann or Lessing who first delineated the borderline of differentiation between poetry and painting. What is crucial in the *Laocoön* is not the fact of an original discovery of truth but the way in which the difference between Lessing and his adversary is elaborated. By setting up a polemical framework that can be immediately recognized as historically fictional, the *Lao-*

coön tells us that *actual* historical priorities are not at stake but rather the very concept of historical priority so thoroughly ironized throughout the text.[12]

Nowhere is this more evident than in the passage that follows the pseudohistorical pronouncement at the opening of chapter 26:

> One tends to leaf through an important work before beginning to read it seriously. My curiosity was, above all, to know the author's opinion about the Laocoön—indeed not concerning the artistry about which he had already expressed himself, but rather about its age. Whom does he side with in this matter? Those to whom it seems that Virgil had the group before his eyes? Or those who would have it that the artist's work followed that of the poet? (156G, 138E)

Lessing's curiosity, he admits, leads him from the path of a serious reading. What fascinates him above all is to know whether Winckelmann sides with those who see Virgil copying the statue or those who see the sculptors copying Virgil.[13] This question of who copied whom follows directly upon, and is parallel to, the implicit question raised in the chapter's opening paragraph, in which Lessing had just established the fiction that Winckelmann followed Lessing rather than Lessing following, and perhaps copying, Winckelmann. Throughout the chapters to come, Virgil becomes metaphorical for Lessing as the sculptors are metaphorical for Winckelmann. Only this displacement could explain the histrionic vehemence with which Lessing defends his assumed position.[14]

Such concerns as who copied whom sidestep the actual issues of the *History*, since Winckelmann remains silent on these matters.

> It is very much in keeping with my taste that he is entirely silent about an imitation on the part of the one or the other. Where is the absolute necessity of it? It is not at all impossible that the similarities between the poetic painting and the work of art that I drew into consideration above, are incidental rather than deliberate similarities; and that, far from one serving as the model for the other, they both need not have had a common model. (156G, 138E)

Fundamental similarities between two works need not imply imitation; it goes without saying that the same would be true for the relationship between the *Laocoön* and Winckelmann's *History*.[15]

If the question of model and historical priority are, momentarily, pushed to the side, if there is no absolute necessity to such questions, the author of the *Laocoön* seems compelled, nevertheless, to reinstate them. "If [Winckelmann] too had been dazzled by the

semblance of such an imitation, then he would have been obliged
to declare himself in favor of those who believe that the poet had
the statue before his eyes" (156–57G, 138E). To be sure, imitation
in this context is a brilliant illusion, calculated to dazzle. At least
doubly so—for with the same flash of wit, Lessing at once tells us
that Winckelmann was not blinded by the semblance of such imitation, and yet proceeds as though he had been. The next two chapters are written in light of this fantasized position for Winckelmann
in a nonexistent dispute. With a telltale pettiness of tone and ted-
ium of style not to be found elsewhere in the essay, Lessing argues
for an inverse order of events. That is to say, he argues for Virgil's
historical priority with respect to the sculptors and, metaphorically,
for his own with respect to Winckelmann.

It is not only the open declaration of ruse, but also the rhetoric
of his polemic that bedazzles the reader. A few pages later Lessing
bases his argument on a reading of a passage from Pliny that begins
as follows.

> Beyond these, there are not many sculptors of high repute, for in
> the case of several works of very great excellence, the number of art-
> ists that have been engaged upon them has proved a considerable
> obstacle to the fame of each, no individual being able to engross the
> whole of the credit, and it being impossible to award it in due pro-
> portion to the names of the several artists combined. Such is the case
> of the Laocoön, for example. (234E)

One cannot avoid being struck by the way in which Pliny's passage
mirrors the problematic of Lessing's relationship to Winckelmann.
The fame of the individual is menaced when several artists have
worked on the same project, for it is neither possible to attribute
that fame to the identity of a single subject, nor to make each one
equally or equitably nameable. The example Pliny chooses is the
sculpture of Laocoön, but his words could apply as well to the discursive text of the same name. The authority behind the *Laocoön*
cannot be attributed to Lessing alone, nor can it be successfully located in a multiplicity of subjects—say, Lessing and Winckelmann.
The *Laocoön* refuses to be controlled by either of these gestures that
would locate its origin in the figure of a subject.

Pliny's passage continues:

> Such is the case of the Laocoön, for example, in the palace of the
> Emperor Titus. . . . This group was made in concert by three emi-
> nent artists—Agesander, Polydorus, and Athenodorus, natives of

Rhodes. In a similar manner [*similiter*] also the palaces of the Caesars in the Palatium have been filled with the most splendid statuary, the work of Craterus in conjunction with Pythodorus, of Polydeuces and Hermolaus, and of another Pythodorus with Artemon (234–35E)

Lessing proposes to draw his conclusions about Pliny's text from the way in which the whole passage hangs together (from the "Zusammenhange der ganzen Stelle" [159G]). Everything turns on the word *similiter* ("in a similar manner") and the particular twist that Lessing will give to this term.[16]

An elaborate proof places the artists whose names follow the *similiter* in the late period. From there, Lessing jumps back to the artists before the pivotal term: the *similiter*, he insists, is temporal, an expression of the historical contemporaneity of the two groups.

> But if it is thus beyond all doubt that Craterus and Pythodorus, Polydectes and Hermolaus, along with the others, lived at the time of the emperors it seems to me that one can also ascribe no other period to those artists from whom Pliny passes over to these by means of a *similiter*. And those are the masters of the Laocoön. Consider now: if Agesander, Polydorus, and Athenodorus were such old masters as Herr Winckelmann takes them to be, how improper it would seem for an author for whom precision of expression is no trifling matter if he were forced to leap [*springen*] from them to the very latest masters—to make this leap [*Sprung*] with [the words] "in the same way"? (160–61G, 142–43E)

With this praise for Pliny as a writer for whom "precision of expression is no trifling matter," with derision for the text that would make such a spring, Lessing's text itself makes something of a confessional leap.

> But it will be objected that this "similiter" does not refer to the connection with regard to period but refers to another circumstance which these masters, who with respect to time were so dissimilar, would have had in common with one another. Pliny it will be said, was speaking of those artists who worked together and because of this collaboration remained more unknown than they deserved. For, since no single individual could claim for himself alone the honor of the work done in common, and since it would have been too tedious to name all those who had taken part each time, . . . their names would all have been neglected. This, says Pliny, happened to the masters of the Laocoön, this happened to so many other masters whom the emperors engaged for their palaces. (161G, 143E)

If, as the passage suggests, this is the reading on which most anyone would insist, there has indeed been a trifling with precision of
expression, a "violence [done] to the natural interpretation of an
unfalsified textual passage," as Lessing had put it a few lines earlier
(160G, 142E). He has shifted the basis on which the terms of the
comparison were said to be similar.

What is the point of all this? Certainly neither precision of
expression nor the natural interpretation of unfalsified passages—
but just as certainly not the opposite of these. The point is not to
read Lessing's *Laocoön* as a text with a point to make in his (fictional)
polemic with Winckelmann about a dating of the statue. It is,
rather, a text with a *"Sprung"* to make, a discontinuity among several models of reading, each as disconcerting as the next.

If we are to take Lessing at his word, the choice seems a simple
one—between his own proper reading and a misinterpretation (although for all to see, Lessing reverses the polarities of his labels in
midstream, in the name of an objecting, if unimaginative reader):[17]

—Misread, Pliny tells us of the inevitable loss of the identity of the individual at the origin of the work of art where there has been a multiplicity of artists. He tells us of this loss at the begin-ning of the passage, gives the case of the Laocoön group as an ·example, and, following the *sim-iliter,* reiterates the problem for the artists of the Palatium.	—Properly read, by Lessing (but with an insistence on critical precision that leads to a later confession of strategical ruse), this same passage is interpreted for us as presenting an abrupt break in logical continuity, when Lessing insists that the last part of Pliny's passage has to do with the historical placement of the making of the statue.

Yet the opening of chapter 26 made it more than obvious that it
is not these two readings that are at stake, but rather Lessing's apparent self-interest in their metaphorical implications. The choice,
then, is not between a proper and an improper reading, but between two readings that are already transfigurations of these. As
we have seen, the metaphorical reverberations of the so-called misreading would be devastating to the authority of Lessing's text. If
similiter means "in the same manner," Lessing's authorial presence
is menaced. If *similiter* is read temporally, then historical priority is
reinstated for Virgil as for Lessing. The metaphorical implications
of the second reading would extricate Lessing from his dilemma
because if the artists in Pliny's passage are contemporaneous, then

the statue of the Laocoön group was made in the late period. And if the statue was made later, then Virgil's *Aeneid* preceded its making and his text was conceivably the model for the sculpture. In the framework of Lessing's analogies, then, Lessing preceded Winckelmann, the writing of the *Laocoön* preceded the publication of the *History*, and Lessing's authority with respect to the former text is guaranteed.

Nor is it simply a matter of these particular historical priorities. What the so-called proper reading of the text defends are the concepts of history, authorship, subject, and originality, among others. The fundamentals of metaphysics are ostensibly saved, yet only with a simultaneous questioning of the metaphysical status of Pliny's text, its ability to maintain the logical sequence of its argument and to simply say what it means, to talk of ancient sculpture rather than talking figuratively of Lessing's status as a writer. Lessing's disfigurative mode of reading, then, is totally at odds with the principles he wishes to draw from the text. It is at odds as well with the mode of imitation at stake in the relationships of Virgil and the sculptors and of Lessing and Winckelmann, in which the constitutive elements of these works become their contents, one work copying the literal contents of the other.

Nowhere is such a reductionist reading for referent performed as more beside the point than here. We have already seen that there are no proper and improper interpretations, not only because Lessing designates both readings as both, but also because each of these polemical positions is metaphorical for something else. We might take the cue and read Lessing for the mode of his text's articulation rather than for its content. Implicit in all this is a particular structure of figuration based on a series of controlled substitutions: Lessing and Winckelmann for the sculptors of the Laocoön group in the first (improper) reading and Lessing for Virgil, Winckelmann for those same artists, in Lessing's reading. This structure of coded, limited figuration is dependent on the same series of concepts seemingly saved by Lessing's temporal reading of *similiter*. Yet what does this passage perform if not the impossibility of such control of figuration? The point is that the pivotal point of the argument (the *similiter*) will not hold still. The very crux of analogizing cannot be fixed so that it is impossible to determine definitively the basis on which two things are compared. The principle of analogy floats about in an argument that ostensibly manages to guarantee those concepts on which controlled figuration is based.[18] At the same time that "precision of expression" is lost, one loses the distinction between proper reading and "violence done to . . . natural interpretation" (160G, 142E).

Lessing begins with a polemic about a historical fact, an argument in which language would be referential in the simplest of manners. This admittedly fictional polemic, however, does not mean what it says, but becomes metaphorical for the historical priority and originality of Lessing and for a string of other metaphysical concepts as well. And yet, this new polemic based on limited figuration ends up disintegrated by the force of its own expression, for *similiter* performs the indeterminacy of the force of analogy. And there is, of course, no "begins with," "becomes," and "ends up," for the so-called beginning and middle are predicated on repressing the mode of operation of figural language.

If the concepts of temporal priority, originality, and conventional constructs of figuration are menaced or, more accurately, in Lessing's terms, "kept in a constant state of shakenness," what can this mean for the *Laocoön* as a whole, a text that represents itself as a treatise on the nature of imitation?[19] Should we regard the polemical framework as an embarrassing aberration and look rather to chapters 1–25 for the real content of what Lessing wished to say? Chapter 1 opens, as we saw, with a long citation from Winckelmann about the beauty of the surface in Greek art. In chapter 2, Lessing goes on to "establish that among the ancients beauty was the supreme law of the visual arts" (14G, 15E). By the end of the essay, the subject matter is quite the opposite. Chapter 23 is about ugliness in poetry, chapter 24 about ugliness in painting, and chapter 25 concerns the disgusting.

As Lessing moves from the beautiful to the ugly to the disgusting (keeping in mind his insistence in the *Laocoön*, here and there, on good taste),[20] we might well question the effect of these final passages of the essay proper. "The harmonious effect of many parts which produces beauty can be destroyed by a single improper part. But the object does not thereby become ugly. Ugliness, too, demands a number of improper parts which we also must be able to take in at a glance if we are to feel the opposite of that which beauty makes us feel" (139G, 121E). What if these passages operate as a litany of the ugly exaggerated into the repulsive? What if chapters 23, 24, and 25 are the "several improper parts" that push the text toward a culmination in the repulsive, destroy the harmonious interaction of its parts, and point toward a transformation of the whole, even if (or perhaps because) we cannot take them in at a single glance? To begin with, not only has the subject matter reversed itself, but the roles of poetry and painting in relation to that which they represent are also totally transformed—not without a certain logic of reversal, to be sure. Poetry, as the opening chapters insist, is unable to represent physical beauty without destroying its effect because of language's temporality of successive enumeration. For this very reason, however, ugliness may be an appropriate subject for poetry.

> Is not the effect of ugliness impeded by the successive enumeration of its elements just as much as the effect of beauty is thwarted by a similar enumeration of its elements?
> Of course it is; but therein lies Homer's justification. Precisely because ugliness becomes in the poet's description a less offensive manifestation of physical imperfection and, as it were, ceases to be ugly in its effect, it becomes usable for the poet. (139G, 121E).

Here as elsewhere, Lessing's concern is with the effect (*Wirkung*) of the work of art. Yet for the first time in the *Laocoön* the new economy of imitation is openly one of expending the effect of the original object rather than reproducing it. In the name of protecting the sensitive reader from a potentially distasteful experience, the successive temporality of language is used, not to preserve its object, but to dissipate it.

But where does this dissipation lead? For as long as we remain in a poetics of the ugly, everything takes place within a systematic of reversal, in the name of preserving both the author's control and the reader's delicate feelings. Once we are caught up in the aesthetics of the disgusting, however, it is the structural rules of imitation that are dissipated, and with them the integrity of object, author, and reader alike.

The disgusting is broached with a gesture of ventriloquism. The etymology of that term—a speaking from the stomach—is hardly irrelevant. Lessing throws up his voice from the depths of his stomach in order to have Moses Mendelssohn speak for him in the opening passage of chapter 24.

> A perceptive critic has already noted this fact about disgust. "Representations [*Vorstellungen*] of fear, of sadness, of terror, of pity, etc., can only arouse dislike [*Unlust*] insofar as we hold the evil to be real. Through the memory [*Erinnerung*] that it is an artificial deceit [*künst-*

licher Betrug], these can be resolved [*aufgelöst*] into pleasant sensations. The repugnant sensation of disgust, however, results by dint
of the law of imagination [*Einbildungskraft*] [operating] on the mere
representation [*Vorstellung*] in the soul, whether or not the object is
held as real. What good does it therefore do the offended mind,
however much the art of imitation betrays itself? Its dislike arose,
not from the supposition that the evil was real, but from the mere
representation of it, and this [representation] is really there. Sensations [*Empfindungen*] of disgust are therefore always Nature, never
imitation [*Nachahmung*]." (143G, 126E)

We can transform the dislike or negative desire [*Unlust*] aroused
by certain representations by remembering that they are mere illusions. Implicit in Mendelssohn's strategy for self-defense is a tripartite scheme in which reality, imitation, and mind can be maintained,
when necessary, as three separate realms. We are offended by representations of fear, sadness, terror, and pity only insofar as we
hold them to be real evils. Through an act of memory, an internalization (*Er-innerung*) or withdrawal into the soul or mind, we remind ourselves that reality and its imitations do not coincide with
one another, nor do they coincide with our innermost spirit. The
sensation of disgust, however, obeys the law of the imagination,
Ein-bildungs-kraft in German, which, literally rendered, suggests a
power of internal imaging. Representation in the case of disgust is
not an imitation external to the mind of a reality which is in turn
external to the representation. The tripartite structure collapses. It
is no longer a question of whether or not the object is real (*wirklich*)
but only of the reality of the representation which is *really* (*wirklich*)
there, there in the mind. This is why the "sensations of disgust are
. . . always Nature, never imitation," which is to say that imitation
falls out as the middle term that protected the mind from the reality of evil. Nature is no longer a space outside the mind but coincident with it.

This ventriloquism is really disgusting, for such stomach talk,
such placing of Lessing's words in Mendelssohn's mouth (or is it the
other way around? because it will never be certain who is regurgi-
tating whom here), such stomach talk does nothing short of upsetting and repudiating the very logic of mimesis on which the entire
Laocoön was predicated. Let us keep these general implications of
the disgusting in mind—Mendelssohn has told us that there is no
other place to keep them—lest we become bogged down by the
particular tidbits of the pages that follow. For the effect on the
reader of chapter 25—and, as we know, Lessing is principally con-

cerned with effect—the effect of chapter 25 is to make her forget the general for the particular, to become morally enraged and physically disgusted in the belief that the evil is real. Yet what the reader ultimately is force-fed is thought for food and that is even harder to keep down than . . .

Than what? for we are all too eagerly jumping ahead. Lessing begins the chapter with a long quotation from Klotz, who rejects the disgusting as that in which the soul can recognize no pleasure whatsoever. "Perfectly correct" (147G, 130E), Lessing adds, and immediately thereafter, as though he had forgotten both the words of Mendelssohn and of Klotz, he goes on to describe its place in the imitative arts.

> Moreover, the disgusting relates to imitation in precisely the same manner as the ugly. Indeed, since its unpleasant effect is the more violent, it is even less capable than the ugly of becoming in and of itself an object for either painting or poetry. Only because the disgusting is likewise greatly softened through verbal expression, did I trust myself nevertheless to maintain that the poet might use at least a few disgusting features as an ingredient for those same mixed feelings. (148G, 132E).

The disgusting will serve as an ingredient? What can Lessing be cooking up for us?

Although he insists that the disgusting per se is improper as the subject matter for poetry, he offers us no less than eight examples of how it may be used to produce mixed sensations. We read of a weasel defecating into Socrates' mouth,[21] of noses from which discharge flows, of "long nails protruding beyond the fingers" "that tear the flesh from the cheeks so that the blood streams to the ground" (150G, 133E), of a heap of "torn rags full of blood and pus" (151G, 134E), of "hair dripping with grease" (149G, 133E), and finally of the flaying of Marsyas in which his "skin cracked from his body in one wound" (151G, 230E).

At each turn, with each example, Lessing reminds us that the disgusting is in its proper place. But is it? Is the disgusting—here is the real question—is the disgusting in its proper place in Lessing's text? Why does he insist on piling up example after example? Why does he gorge himself on the disgusting? Why does he delight in serving up these morsels, or rather, ramming them down our throats?

In Lessing's own words, "[The critic] must know what effect he wishes to thus bring about and it is necessary that he weigh his words according to this effect" (Lachmann 10:436). He seems to understand quite well that his reader may have had his fill already. At a crucial juncture of chapter 25 we read the following:

> But who does not also feel that the disgusting is here in its proper place? It makes the terrible horrible, and the horrible is not altogether displeasing even in nature, so long as our compassion is engaged. And how much less so in imitation? I do not want to pile up the examples, and yet I must note the following—that there is a type of the terrible to which the path stands open for the poet almost exclusively by way of the disgusting. It is the dreadfulness of hunger. (151G, 134–35E)

The path to hunger is open to the poet only if he passes by way of the disgusting. It is, you remember, here that the path of Lessing's *Laocoön* will almost immediately come to an end, for in the next chapters, as Lessing has written, he does not dare to go one step farther. To reach the culmination point of Lessing's essay in what we too will provisionally call "hunger," we must pass by another list of excessive examples. The path includes Ugolino, a father tempted to set his teeth into his own offspring; Eresichthon, driven to sustain his own body by devouring it (152G, 136E); and a text in which the hunger "is no real, present hunger" (153G, 136E) but rather the subject of a prophecy made void by a play on words. The allusions to self-consuming texts and points of origin smack of something more than artless examples of the disgusting. But let us not move too abruptly. Lessing concludes his discussion by writing: "In the footnote I wish to cite another passage from the play by Beaumont and Fletcher that might have served in place of all the other examples if I had not been forced to recognize it as a little too exaggerated" (153G, 137E). An example to replace all other examples is truly irresistible for any reader. For two entire pages, through the mouths of Beaumont and Fletcher, Lessing speaks of eating suppositories, wens, and poultices previously used on wounds.

What is the effect of this slightly exaggerated text? It is hardly matter to whet the appetite of the reader. For here Lessing has reached the heights of bad taste he so often rails against. Not to mince words, the effect is plainly nauseating.[22] And this is Lessing's point, for he has said a few pages earlier with regard to the sensations of disgust and their relations to our sense of sight: "The more delicate the temperament is, the more we will feel of those agitations in our body that precede vomiting. Only that these agitations [caused by objects to the sense of sight] subside again very quickly, and a real vomiting can scarcely result" (148G, 131E).

Yet our peptic distress is merely and above all symptomatic of a certain crisis of mimesis that hunger exemplifies, for if these examples of the disgusting turn our stomachs, they also turn the gestures of imitation inside out.

> It is the dreadfulness of hunger. Even in ordinary life we express the most extreme hunger in no other fashion than by telling of all the unnutritious, unwholesome, and especially disgusting things with which the stomach must needs be satisfied. Since imitation can arouse nothing of the feeling of hunger itself in us, it resorts to arousing another unpleasant feeling which, in the case of starvation, we recognize as the lesser evil. It seeks to arouse this feeling so that from our aversion to it we may conclude how strong that other aversion must be under the influence of which we would happily forget the present one. (151–52G, 135E).

The mechanics of this remedy to a shortcoming in the mimetic arts are as wounding to that concept as Mendelssohn's treatment of the disgusting. Hunger is a lack in the system of mimesis, for no imitation can arouse it in the reader. It is itself a lack, an absence that cannot be represented. Rather than present that which is less than nothing, the writer chooses to represent something. It happens to be the very thing that would still that hunger. He represents hunger by that which would sate it, and as if this disruption in the logic of representation were not enough, he thereby arouses in the reader a feeling that is the very opposite of satiety and of the desperate desire to take in food.

Nor is it simply a question of literal vomit, which is, after all, here as well as in Lessing's text, a rather distasteful subject matter. Lessing's treatise on the mode of imitation culminates with a structure of imitation that, rather than fulfilling the promise of coincidence with a presence, systematically evacuates that possibility. In the ideal workings of the tripartite mimetic system, at least as Lessing describes it elsewhere in the *Laocoön*, the reader is taken in by the object portrayed[23] as the representation reproduces reality and arouses a similar effect in the mind of the reader. In the case of hunger, there is also an inescapable collapse of the barriers between reader and object, but the representation is the inverse of that which it should represent and the effect on the reader is to make him as different from the figure imitated as possible. The formal gestures of this new mimesis are at once total identity and total alterity, an obliteration of the difference between sameness and otherness.[24]

In a sense we have been circling round the problem in the *Laocoön* proper, for if we started from the outer frame and the questionable question of polemics, and then spiraled around to the inner frame, the extremes of the beautiful and the disgusting, we have left untouched the very center and substance in Lessing's argument, those many chapters in between whose provisions seem far more digestible. If Lessing's historical facts were fabrications, if a polemic seemingly fixated on its own literal content gave way to the unfixable ground of figural language, if the semiotics of hunger and the disgusting upset both conventional expectations and Lessing's rules of literary representation, aren't the central chapters based on the proper demarcation between painting and poesy argued according to more traditional mimetic structures?

They are premised on the critic's possession of what Lessing at one point calls "the power of differentiation [*Unterscheidungskraft*]" (63G). It is this power that Spence, the target of the polemic in chapter 8, lacks, for he fails to distinguish properly between the arts: "That poesy is the broader art, that there are beauties at her command that painting cannot attain . . . —to this he seems to have given no thought and, therefore, the slightest differences that he notices among the ancient poets and artists disconcert him" (61G, 50E).

There are modes of representation appropriate to each medium, Lessing tells us. Yet in this context whether he is declaiming on the proper way to represent the gods, the muses, or the invisible, or on the proper relationship of ancient statuary to beauty, another figure seems inevitably to cast its double shadow and this is the distinction between representing the thing itself on the one hand and signifying through abstraction, analogy, or symbols, on the other. And once this distinction insinuates itself, simple difference cannot hold—neither in the works about which Lessing speaks nor in Lessing's work itself.

What, then, makes poesy the broader art, as Lessing would have it above? What beauties are exclusively at its command? What are the limits of painting and poesy that Spence fails to take into account? The painter's figures are limited by the necessity of recognizability. "The gods and spiritual beings as the artist presents them, are not fully the same ones that the poet needs. For the artist they are personified abstractions which must always maintain a similar characterization if they are to be recognizable. For the poet, on the other hand, they are real, acting beings who, beyond their general character, possess other attributes and emotions" (63G, 52E). Here, then, begins that distinction between painting and poesy that is so exemplary of many other passages in Lessing's text. One of the arts is real, the other bound to the necessity of the arbitrary. Thus, the gods of poesy are "real, acting beings," while the artist can create only "personified abstractions which must always maintain a similar characterization."

Because of this distinction, the poet is allowed more than the sculptor and painter: the "more" specifically forbidden to the artist is the figure of contradiction.

> An altogether angry Venus, a Venus driven by revenge and fury is a true *contradiction* for the sculptor; for Love as Love is never angry, never vengeful. To the poet, on the other hand, Venus is, to be sure, also Love, but she is the Goddess of Love who beyond this characteristic has her own individuality, and consequently, she must be just as capable of the impulses of aversion as of inclination . . .
>
> It is indeed true that the artist . . . can introduce Venus . . . outside her character as a really acting being just as well as the poet. But then her actions must at least not *contradict* her character. (63–64G, 53E; emphasis mine)

Nor is the contradiction to be understood simply as a potential conflict between action and character, a conflict in the nature of that which is portrayed. Contradiction is to be taken literally, for it is performed at the level of the verbal utterance. Literature alone is able to describe by means of the negative, to say what is, by saying what is not. "The poet alone can perform the feat of describing with negative characteristics and through a mixing of these negative and positive characteristics, bringing two appearances into one. No longer the gracious Venus, no longer is her hair fastened with golden clasps, no azure robe floats about her, without her belt" (65G, 54E).

If poesy speaks through negation and contradiction, if Lessing denies painting this particular mode of internal discrepancy, this is hardly to say, as we have already seen, that the visual arts offer an unproblematic and direct reproduction. In chapter 8, the artist's creations are called "personified abstractions," and in chapter 10 Lessing insists on the significance of their allegorical symbols. For the poet, the name and action suffice to characterize the figure, but painting is in need of the conventional array of attributes.

If the poet personifies abstractions, they are sufficiently characterized through their names and through that which he has them do.
The artist lacks these means. He must therefore add symbols to
his personified abstractions, through which they become recognizable. These symbols make them into allegorical figures because they
are something other and mean something other. (72–73G, 60E).

The artist must add emblems to his personified abstractions, emblems that are different from that which they portray, emblems—
however naturally represented—that signify something other than
that which they represent. The poetic attributes distinguish themselves from the allegorical in that the former supposedly "signify
the thing itself," the latter, "merely something analogous" (74G,
61E).[25]

But what can it mean to insist here that the poet says "the thing
itself" or represents real beings, if the reader has also been in-
structed on poetry's privilege of speaking through negation and
contradiction? Moreover, and more tellingly, the opening lines of
this chapter are a rather bizarre example of the writer—in this case
Lessing—inevitably signifying something else at the very moment
of apparent polemic clarity. The attack on Spence opens with that
author's astonishment about the poet's reluctance to describe the
muses: " 'As to the Muses in general,' he says, 'it is still strange that
the poets are so sparing in their descriptions, far more sparing than
one would expect in the case of Goddesses to whom they have such
a great obligation' " (71G, 59E). For Spence, it is a question of describing the source of poetic inspiration, a question of the writer's
account of his own production. Lessing proves his point by citing a
poetic nondescription of Urania, the muse of astronomy.

> The artist, in order to make [her domain] . . . recognizable, must
> have her point to a celestial globe with a wand, this wand, this celes-
> tial globe, this, her position, are the letters out of which he lets us
> assemble the name Urania. But when the poet wants to say: Urania
> had long ago foreseen his death in the stars . . . why should he, out
> of respect for the painter, add to it, Urania, her wand in hand, her
> celestial globe before her. Would it not be as though a person who is
> permitted and able to speak out loud were, nevertheless, at the same
> time to make use of those signs which the dumb in the Turkish ser-
> aglio, because of a lack of voice, invented among themselves? (72G,
> 59E)

Spence's concern is the muse as the origin of the poet's production,
but Lessing chooses an example that radically alters her signifi-

cance. If the artist gives us emblems out of which we must assemble the name Urania, how are we to piece together what it is that Lessing's text is saying? How are we to read this passage, and can we simply read it as saying "the thing itself"? If the writer, as Lessing tells us, claims power to directly name the goddess, she, in turn, as he does so, names him in a manner that is anything but benign. Urania, in the citation chosen from Statius, hardly stands as the source of poetic creation. Her function is, rather, to read, to read the text of the stars, and predict the future. And what she reads, what she assembles by piecing together the positions of the heavenly bodies is not poetic creation but death, the death of the poet, a death she predicts well before his actual demise. It is as though Lessing, who could, or would, speak literally, were also, for lack of the voice to declare it openly, inventing a silent language of signs to insist on a hidden, ever-present threat to the origin and authority of the writerly voice that he openly declares to be literal and transparent.[26]

Perhaps this threat to the authority of the word becomes clearer in chapter 12, where it is a question of the visible and the invisible. Caylus is accused of offering poor advice to the artist on how to depict those scenes in Homer where the visible and the invisible take place side by side. "This difference cannot be indicated by painting, in which all is visible—and visible in only one way" (81G, 66E). Certainly this makes sense, for how could art be supposed to mark the disappearance of its own medium? The painting that attempts to represent visible and invisible events on the same canvas necessarily results in that which is "confused, incomprehensible, and contradictory" (82G, 66E).

But the error of the artist faced with such a predicament is not merely that of taking on the apparently contradictory task of making visible the invisible, representing the obliteration of representation. His gravest error is one of misreading (and all of the *Laocoön*, after all, is more or less a lesson about misreading). Only this can explain the artist's (and Caylus's) solution to the problem of painting the invisible.

> The means that painting uses to give us to understand that this or that must be regarded as invisible in its compositions is a thin cloud in which it covers it from the side of the other people taking part in the picture. This cloud seems to be borrowed from Homer himself. For when in the tumult of battle one of the more important heroes gets into a danger from which none other than a divine power can

save him, the poet has the protecting deity envelop him in a thick
mist or in night and thus lead him away. . . . And this mist, this
cloud, Caylus will never forget to recommend heartily to the artist
when he outlines for him a painting of such occurrences. Who, however, does not see that for the poet the wrapping up in mist and
night is supposed to be nothing more than a poetic figure of speech
for making invisible? It has always astonished me to find this poetic
expression made into something real [*realisieret*] and to find a real
cloud introduced into the painting. (85G, 68E)

The poet's use of the cloud is a literary figure and therefore signifies something other than what it says. Yet Caylus takes the poetic
manner of speaking literally and insists on seeing an actual cloud
on the canvas.

> That was not the intention of the poet. That means going beyond
> the limits of painting; for this cloud is here a true hieroglyph, a
> mere symbolical sign that does not make the rescued hero invisible
> but, rather, calls to the spectators: you must imagine to yourselves
> that he is invisible. It is here no better than the little scrolls covered
> with writing that issue from the mouths of people in old Gothic
> paintings. (86G, 68–69E)

The problem is twofold. On the one hand, the poet did not intend
to have a "cloud" signify a cloud. Instead, Homer used this term as
a poetic figure of speech for rendering invisible. On the other
hand, if it is within the domain of poetry to say one thing by saying
another, it exceeds the limits of this kind of painting to present
hieroglyphic or symbolic signs that tell the spectator to imagine
something other than that which is literally given. This is like the
written labels added to the mouths of Gothic figures: this is the
written word, and with it the realm of the arbitrary sign invades
that of painting.

What has happened to that insistence on the poetic text dealing
with the thing itself, or, for that matter, the matter-of-fact accept-
ance that painting must often use the arbitrary sign? It is not simply
a matter of poetry, too, signifying by means of an allegorical figuration. The particular figures that are at issue in chapter 12 (veil-
ing, clouding, striking blind) and Lessing's manner of linking them
to the "intention of the poet" can hardly be dismissed as purely
insignificant. They operate as an indirect commentary on the nature of literary language in general.

If painting must not represent the effacement of its own figures,
it seems to go without saying that poetry should. For it is practically

unthinkable to Lessing that anyone would "*not* see that . . . mist and night is . . . a poetic figure of speech for making invisible" (85G, 68E; emphasis mine). But what is it exactly that this Everyreader sees? She sees that she does not see what she thinks she sees (or rather does not read what she seems to read), that she does not see a cloud. This power of figural language as deliteralization is bound up with an act of reading that places the reader in a position not entirely unlike that of the more passive observer in those scenes from Homer.

> Achilles did not see an actual mist, and the entire artifice with which the gods rendered something invisible did not consist of the mist, but rather, in its being carried off swiftly. Only in order to indicate at the same time that the abduction took place so swiftly that no human eye could follow the abducted body does the poet veil it first in mist. It is not because instead of the abducted body one sees a mist, but because we think of that which is in a mist as not visible. Therefore, he turns it around sometimes, and instead of making the object invisible, he has the subject struck with blindness. . . . In actuality, however, the eyes of Achilles are as little darkened here as there the abducted hero is wrapped in mist. Rather, the poet merely adds the one thing or the other in order to make the extreme swiftness of the abduction, which we call disappearing, more perceptible [*sinnlicher*]. (86G, 69E)

Lessing's exemplary reader is, however, in a sense, struck blind, for she is forced to understand that literary language or figuration, rather than making substance palpable, makes the "disappearing" of substance "more perceptible." Whereas Caylus's spectator sees what it is that is hidden behind the cloud, sees what it is not given to the spectators *in* the painting to see, Lessing's reader sees that there is nothing to see behind the cloud, and not even a cloud itself. The reading of poetic expressions brings about this loss of perception.

The cloud in Lessing's somewhat cloudy and indirect passage operates then as the figure of figuration: the particular image of the cloud marks not only the disappearance of the hero but also the disappearance of the cloud, for the process of reading any poetic figure is to make both the figure and that which it apparently figures disappear. To that extent, all figures perform what the cloud represents, a making invisible, a making "disappearing more perceptible" (86G, 69E).[27]

If chapter 12 has reversed earlier distinctions, if it might lead us to believe that all this belongs to the realm of the literary alone, and that the visual arts are those which should keep its spectators to the natural and literal presence, we have only to look at chapter 2, which discusses imitation in painting and sculpture. Here, Lessing "wishes merely to establish that beauty was the highest law of the plastic arts for the ancients"(14G, 15E). In this the arts are said to differ from the sciences, for the purpose of the latter is truth, while the purpose of the arts is pleasure (just what strange pleasures, we are about to see). For this reason, Lessing defends the right of the lawgiver "to determine what kind of pleasure and how much of each kind he will permit" (13G, 14E). As so often in Lessing, it is a question of the effect the work of art produces that requires particularly careful scrutiny: "The plastic arts in particular . . . are capable of an effect that requires the closer supervision of the law. If beautiful men rendered beautiful statues, these in turn had an effect back on them, and the state owed its thanks for beautiful men to beautiful statues. With us, the delicate imaginative power of the mothers seems to express itself only in monsters" (13G, 14E).[28]

The logic of the imitative chain seems to be one of cause and effect. Human beauty resulted in the artistic beauty of the statuary, and the beauty of the work of art was responsible, in turn, for producing beautiful men.[29] It is the last sentence of the paragraph that begins to suggest just how art begets human beauty. In modern times the delicate imagination of mothers, we are told, expresses itself in monsters—a reference, no doubt, to the opening pages of the chapter, in which contemporary art is criticized for its willingness to paint almost anyone, regardless of the lack of beauty in the subject. Thus, when the delicate, impressionable mother-to-be contemplates a work that is "as deformed as possible" (11G, 12E), the chain of mimetic reproduction results in offspring that bear the mark of her encounter.

Lessing goes on to draw conclusions about how such encounters must have operated in ancient times. "From this point of view I believe I catch sight of something true in certain old stories" (13G, 14E). One expects here a parallel narration of pregnant women regarding the beautiful forms of ancient sculpture, with an appropriate, inverse effect. Yet something is awry in the logical continuity of the passage that follows.

> From this point of view I believe I catch sight of something true in certain old stories that are directly dismissed as lies. The mothers of Aristomenes, Aristodamas, Alexander the Great, Scipio, Augustus,

and Galerius all dreamed during pregnancy that they had relations with a serpent. The serpent was a sign of the deity; and the beautiful statues and paintings of a Bacchus, an Apollo, a Mercury, a Hercules were seldom lacking a serpent. The honest women had feasted their eyes by day on the god, and the confusing dream awakened the image of the animal. Thus I save the dream and abandon the explanation that the pride of their sons and the impudence of the flatterer made of it. For there must indeed be a cause for the fact that the marriage-breaking fantasy was always a serpent.

But I am getting off my track. (13–14G, 14–15E)

Every time Lessing gets off the track, we should know we are on to something. It is when he seems to lose control of his prose, whenever it seems to go somewhere he hadn't really intended, that the text is really saying something. The passage begins by salvaging a law-breaking fantasy that threatens not only the relationship of man and wife but, more significantly, that between imitated and imitation. Lessing implies that modern mothers procreate by a process of incorporating the image (once again, a realization of the term *Ein-bildung*) and later expressing it: "With us, the delicate imaginative power of the mothers seems to express itself only in monsters." Yet the relationship among mothers, image (statue), and expression (offspring) in ancient times breaks the rules set down for procreation through mimesis. Another kind of fantasy is at play.

The pregnant women all dream of intercourse with a snake. Lessing explains that those objects of libidinous desire, the representations of Bacchus, Apollo, and Mercury (the gods of intoxication, poetry, and message-bearing), were rarely to be found without a snake (*Schlange*). From a certain point of view, this is reassuring, no doubt. "The serpent was a sign of the deity," and it was this that might seem to explain the displacement of the god by the snake in the fantasy of the woman—a system of metonymic or metaphoric substitution, a detour, not quite like the linear reproduction earlier suggested. Yet this creates any number of complications. If Lessing gets sidetracked here, it has something to do with this shift from the deity to its sign. The snake functions not merely as a metonymic signifier for the godhead, nor merely as a jocular metaphor for the phallus. It is impossible to read of snakes in the *Laocoön* without reading them in the context of the myth. In Lessing's passage the monstrous qualities of modern art are placed in opposition to the beauty of ancient statuary, yet the snakes operate in the *Aeneid* precisely as the monstrous (bk. 2, p. 39 [Humphries trans.]) and thus turn the logic of Lessing's contrast on its tail. Chapter 2 may represent them as the phantasmatic origin of beautiful children, but in Virgil as well as elsewhere in the *Laocoön* they are "child-eaters"(35G, 35E). Nor is it that they devour in Virgil what they might seem to father in Lessing's passage, in a literal sense. The snake appears in chapter 2 as a minor quirk explained away in an otherwise simplistic scene of linear imitation. Yet Virgil's scenario is a complex drama that questions the kind of signification seemingly presupposed by Lessing. In the tale told by Aeneas, Laocoön warns his countrymen not to take the wooden horse for what it seems to be.

> "Let me tell you,
> Either the Greeks are hiding in this monster,
> Or it's some trick of war, a spy, or engine,
> To come down on the city. Tricky business
> Is hiding in it. Do not trust it, Trojans,
> Do not believe this horse. Whatever it may be,
> I fear the Greeks even when bringing presents."
> With that, he hurled the great spear at the side
> With all the strength he had. It fastened, trembling,
> And the struck womb rang hollow, a moaning sound.
> He had driven us, almost, to let the light in
> With the point of steel, to probe, to tear, but something,
> Got in his way. . . .
> *(Aeneid,* bk. 2, p. 33 [Humphries trans.])

Laocoön speaks the truth, insisting that some delusion is taking place. The womb of the horse (for here, as in Lessing, it is the space of reproduction that is in question) hides something far less benign than its wondrous exterior would suggest. Laocoön almost drives the Trojans to open up the image, "to probe" the lie of their literal interpretation. Soon thereafter Laocoön is punished by the serpents, or so the Trojans read the scene, for having "profaned the sacred image" (bk. 2, p. 40). The snakes in Virgil's text, therefore, are monsters sent to silence the voice that would speak the truth[30] about any deceptively simplistic system of representation—about metonymic continuity between the snake and god or between the outside and inside, about metaphoric stability in substituting serpent for phallus, etc.

To be sure, in Lessing's second chapter, the serpent does not represent the god by resembling him, but operates as a conventional, unproblematic, metonymic substitute, "a sign for the deity." What is it, however, that Lessing actually wishes to save? The same Virgilian themes of truth and lie are at play in Lessing's passage. Lessing claims to see something true in those stories that others have tossed aside as lies. Yet, what he saves thereby (and this he proclaims openly) is not something called truth, but the dream. The dream is the force of confusion ("der verwirrende Traum") that "awakened the image of the animal" in place of that of the god. It is the force that confuses the deity and its sign rather than allowing the one to unproblematically substitute for the other. The dream awakens the image of the serpent which in Lessing's chapter 2 may be metaphorical simplicity itself but which in Virgil's passage about Laocoön represents a repression of the true involutions in figural language. We begin to understand the grounds on which "there must indeed be a cause for the fact that the marriage-breaking fantasy was always a serpent."

It should be clear by now in the *Laocoön* that no place is reserved for either poesy or the visual arts in which the one or the other might truly represent "the thing itself." The game of the "power of differentiation" between the two art forms that governs so many of Lessing's straightforward assertions changes its ground rules arbitrarily from passage to passage. Thus the *Laocoön* performs at the level of discursive argumentation the same refusal to say what it seems to say (to say the thing itself) that takes place for all modes of art. But if saying the thing itself is impossible, finding a language of controlled allegorical or metaphorical substitution is equally at variance with the experience of Lessing's text. When Lessing seems most intent on declaring the self-evidence of the metaphorical, something else takes place that is more like all the hypothetical forms of double talk that Lessing's similes reject along the way: like the scrolls that issue from the mouths in Gothic works of art to say again, differently, what the painting doesn't quite make clear, like the language of the dumb in the seraglio used alongside the spoken voice, a silent echo that cannot help but distract the observer. Thus, although the cloud in Homer is said to function as an absolutely transparent figure for invisibility, Lessing's text gets off its track by insisting on the making perceptible of the disappearance of substance. Although the serpent on the statues of divine figures is said to simply substitute for the deity in the fantasies of pregnant women, it awakens instead a confusion between metaphor and its referent echoing the hollow reverberations of the Trojan horse's womb.[31]

All of the *Laocoön* is not only a lesson on reading the arts, then, but also a lesson on reading its own critical performance. An exemplary passage in this regard is chapter 16, in which Lessing's commentary on literary language includes a moment of literary interpretation. Chapter 16 is the best known of the essay, for it is to this passage that scholars have always turned for the kernel of the argument, an argument so succinct and so clearly reasoned (punctuated as it is by if-then's and consequently's) that a simple citation has seemed to substitute for interpretation.[32]

> I reason thus: if it is true that in its imitations painting uses completely different means or signs than does Poesy, the former, namely, figures and colors in space, the latter, however, articulated tones in time; if, uncontestably, signs must have a comfortable relationship to the signified, then signs that are ordered next to one another [in space] can express only objects that exist next to one another or whose parts are next to one another, and signs that follow one after another can express only objects that follow one after another or whose parts follow one after another.
> Objects that exist next to one another . . . are called bodies. Consequently, bodies along with their visible characteristics are the proper objects of painting.
> Objects that follow one after another are called, in general, actions. Consequently, actions are the proper object of Poesy. (94–95G, 78E)

When Lessing finishes what he himself calls this "dry chain of conclusions" (95G, 79E), he turns to a stylistic analysis of his model poet, Homer, in order to illustrate the progressive nature of the literary description. Given that it is not appropriate for signs that follow one another to describe a fixed object existing in space, what is it that Homer must do if he wishes to give us a detailed view of a single object? "He knows, through countless artifices, to place this single object in a series of moments—in each of which it looks different. . . . For example, if Homer wishes to let us see the chariot of Juno, then Hebe must put it together before our eyes, piece by piece" (96G, 80E). "With the poet . . . we see being formed [*entstehen*] what, with the painter, we can only see as [already] formed [*entstanden*]" (100G, 84E). We see Homer "dispersing this image in a kind of history of the object" (100G, 83E). But before we blindly accept the blind poet's conclusions, we should follow the succession of Lessing's arguments as he reads and comments on two passages from the *Iliad* in which the history of a scepter is narrated.

What does Homer care how far he leaves the painter behind him? Instead of a picture he gives us the history/story of the scepter: first it is the work of Vulcan; now it glitters in the hands of Jupiter; now it marks the dignity of Mercury; now it is the staff of command of the warlike Pelops, now the shepherd's staff of the peaceful Atreus, etc.

.   .   .   .   [citation from Homer]

Thus I finally know this scepter better than if the painter could lay it before my eyes or if a second Vulcan could deliver it into my hands. (98G, 81E)

Why is a scepter in the hand worth less than a scepter in Homer? For the history of the scepter is not only better than the painting: it is also better than having a second Vulcan place it in our hands. It seems to be a question of "know[ing] this scepter better" than if the thing itself were in our grasp. What is it we will know? Or is it perhaps that we learn to know that a scepter in the hand, the scepter as thing, in terms of this passage, is not worth all that much, either in terms of knowledge or in terms of power? What Homer actually tells us in this history is that

> Powerful Agamemnon
> stood up holding the sceptre Hephaistos had wrought him
>   carefully.
> Hephaistos gave it to Zeus the king, the son of Kronos,
> and Zeus in turn gave it to the courier Argeïphontes,
> and lord Hermes gave it to Pelops, driver of horses,
> and Pelops again gave it to Atreus, the shepherd of the people.
> Atreus dying left it to Thyestes of the rich flocks,
> and Thyestes left it in turn to Agamemnon to carry
> and to be lord of many islands and over all Argos.
>   (2.100–108)[33]

What is it that we learn about Homer's scepter that makes it better than the thing itself? Before we interpret this passage, let us read Lessing's interpretation, for ours is, necessarily, a reading of his.

> Thus I finally know this scepter better than if the painter could lay it before my eyes or than if a second Vulcan could deliver it into my hands. It would not astonish me if I were to find that one of the ancient commentators of Homer had admired this passage as the most perfect allegory of the origin, the progress, the strengthening,

and ultimate hereditary succession of royal power among men. I
would, of course, smile. (98G, 81–82E)

Why would Lessing smile? He seems to do so so rarely. Where is the
joke? For it is not just that the passage is rich, nor is it simply that
the history of the scepter, according to Lessing, would conflate the
concepts of poesy as both the ultimate thing itself (better than the
thing in the hand) and allegorical sign. What makes Lessing smile
is the following hypothetical, allegorical interpretation of Homer's
passage.

> I would indeed smile if I read that he who had made [*gearbeitet*]
> the scepter, Vulcan, as fire, as that which is the most indispensable to
> man for his preservation, indicated an end to those needs which in-
> duced primitive man to subjugate himself to an individual—that the
> first king, a son of time had been a venerable ancient, who wished to
> share his power [*Macht*] with an eloquent, clever man, with a Mer-
> cury, or to give it over entirely to him—that the clever orator, at a
> time when the young state was threatened by external enemies had
> relinquished his supreme might [*Gewalt*] to the bravest warrior—
> that the bravest warrior, after he had subdued the enemies and se-
> cured the realm, had been able to play it into the hands of his son,
> who, as a peace-loving regent, as a benevolent shepherd of his
> people, had acquainted them with prosperity and superabundance,
> through which, after his death, the way was paved for the richest of
> his relatives to appropriate for himself by presents and bribes that
> which until now trust had bestowed and merit had considered more
> a burden than an honor, and to secure it permanently ever after for
> his family as though it were a bought property. I would smile; never-
> theless, my respect for the poet to whom so much can be lent would
> be strengthened.—But this is off my track. (98–99G, 82E; Greek
> phrases eliminated in my translation)

Lessing has gotten off the track again in more senses than one.
He has lost the sense of his own authority. This interpretation is
surely not "the most perfect allegory of the origin, the progress, the
strengthening, and ultimate hereditary succession of royal power
among men," as Lessing previously insisted. This is at least one reason to smile on reading this passage. What takes place in the longer
commentary just cited is a decided decadence in the successive
handing down of power, a decadence worth tracing. Let us mark
out before we do so just what the stakes are. The object at hand is a
scepter, an ornamental symbol of authority, so that both the concepts of authority and of the ornamental symbolic are in question.

In terms of Lessing's sixteenth chapter we have also to consider the potentially triple narrative at play: Homer's passage that follows the temporal movement of an object, the insistence on the allegorical thrust within this narration, and Lessing's own more elaborate commentary that he adds to it. What takes place for the scepter inevitably says something about a temporal narrative or history of an object, about allegorical literary language, and about critical commentary.

But before we get carried away by the figural implications, let us return first to the passage itself. According to Lessing's reading (a reading that he hypothetically dislocates to the authorship of "one of the ancient commentators of Homer"), the original moment of producing the scepter, emblem of authority, is, remarkably enough, allied with a liberation from a unique center of authority. Vulcan, as fire, figures as the means for primitive man to free himself from such a subjugation. Here there is a break of sorts in Lessing's paraphrase, for whereas Homer tells his reader that Vulcan "*gave* [the scepter] to Zeus the king" (emphasis mine), Lessing refuses to trace this passage, and rightly so. If Lessing's allegorical reading of Homer associates Vulcan with a disinterested dispersal of Power, it is the Zeus figure as "the first king" that establishes the concept of sovereign power. The commentary severs the link with Vulcan and underscores instead another line of heredity, that of Zeus to his father Kronos. Although Homer names Zeus directly, Lessing's allegory, in fact, simply calls him "the first king, a son of time," establishing sovereign authority and temporal differentiation in the same moment of rupture. From this point on, it is not the ornamental scepter that is passed along, as Homer's text, read literally, would have it, but the supreme power and authority it symbolizes. (This is what the allegorical interpretation uncovers.) When the first king wishes to share his power, it is with an orator, a man characterized by the language he wields in order to achieve a desired end.[34] This Mercury, in turn, passes his power to a warrior who secures the authority of the realm by eliminating all threats from the outside. All nobility in the handing on of authority appears lost now, for the man of war manipulates, "play[s]," his power into the hands of his son. The son, in turn, prepares the way for transforming that authority, no longer menaced from without, into a force with all the characteristics of property. His relatives then complete the transformation such that power is bought and secured in exchange for other property.

So much takes place in this palimpsest of multiple readings that one does not know where to begin. Homer's sparse lines are the pretext for Lessing to speak of an allegory of origin, continuation, and strengthening of power. This synopsis of an allegorical reading would, of course, exactly parallel the claim that Homer's delineation of an object's origin and formation through time is better than the thing itself. The allegorical reading is therefore allegorical in turn for the power (or failure) of language to "express" its "object" (94G, 78E), to strengthen its power by means of a "kind of history" (100G, 83E). The more elaborate interpretation makes Lessing smile (although he wrote it) and us as well, for it blatantly belies the optimism of the first. What takes place in this reading is not merely a weakening in the quality of power through suggestions of moral decadence but a number of specific gestures that cannot be insignificant. At the scepter's origin, in fire, the sovereign power is annulled. In Lessing's chronicle, it is only in time (Kronos) that sovereign power is introduced and with it: an interested language used to convince, an elimination of external threats as well as an enriching of internal plenitude (prosperity), so that power ultimately acquires the characteristics of a property or thing. If in Homer the thing operates as a figure (the scepter is an ornamental emblem of power), in Lessing's chronicle the emblematic quality is lost, and power, as it is handed down, becomes a thing. This reification marks the de-allegorization of the scepter (power). To this extent one might understand why the thingified power is better than a scepter delivered into one's hands by a second Vulcan, for the scepter in the hands of fire marked a liberation from authority. The power as property at which Lessing ends up could be seen to guarantee a palpable, manipulable value of sorts, but it also tells the story of an allegorical reading that obliterates the nature of the scepter at its origin. The allegorical reading at once lends (*leihen*) the scepter its value as thing and robs it of its original (non)value.

Things cannot be otherwise because allegorical authority in time should be a dispersal of the authority the scepter has when Vulcan creates it at the original moment of the story. Since that authority is entirely negative, the allegorical and temporal evolution of power can only speak of it in terms of that which it is not—as positive, tangible power. The allegorical reading lays out in time that which was posited for the scepter to begin with. It performs the rupture in the authority of the explication such that that power is given substance and given as substance.

What has taken place in the course of this reading—and the passage insists on this twice—is a certain smiling. It is as if no commentary can be written without immediately distancing the commentator from his interpretation. No sooner has Lessing written his commentary, or, more precisely, even before his commentary appears in the text, he is already distanced from it, and in the position of an ironical reader or of a reader who ascribes that commentary to an other—the hypothetical ancient commentator. Homer's text about the scepter as emblem of authority generates a textual problematic of origin and authority parallel to that of its own subject matter. All this takes place under the aegis of allegorical explication. Allegory, explication, and time (or *Geschichte*) are forces that operate with a similar unthinkable undertow, guaranteeing a distance from the authority they at the same time promise. Thus, Lessing here dramatizes the fundamental and unavoidable error of another order of so-called allegorical reading that might pretend to uncover or reveal that of which the allegory is an emblem. Lessing's hypothetical reading tells the tale, not of the emblem, the scepter, but of the power it symbolizes. Yet the scepter operates not only as an allegorical figure of power, but also as the irrepressible power of allegory; and any attempt to unveil its referent, any attempt to eliminate the ornamental allegorical force in favor of substance, becomes inevitably caught up in an allegory of allegory— and is doomed therefore to impotence in the very moment that the scepter's power becomes most substantial.

The failure of such a reading becomes more decisive in the passage that immediately follows, a passage that handles a scepter of another kind. Here, it is a question of Achilles' scepter, a scepter that the hero not so incidentally swears by, as though it could guarantee the authority of his words and grant value where it has been denied. "Even when Achilles swears by his scepter to avenge the scorn with which Agamemnon treated him, Homer gives us the history of this scepter" (99G, 82E). The history of this scepter is too blatant to be entirely misread. Perhaps this is why Lessing limits himself to a slightly distorting paraphrase.

> But I will tell you this and swear a great oath upon it:
> in the name of this sceptre, which never again will bear leaf nor
> branch, now that it has left behind the cut stump in the mountains,
> nor shall it ever blossom again, since the bronze blade stripped
> bark and leafage, and now at last the sons of the Achaians
> carry it in their hands in state when they administer
> the justice of Zeus. And this shall be a great oath before you. . . .
> (1.233–39)

The origin of this symbol of authority is a violent moment of rupture. Its history tells of its organic sterility, its refusal to connect with either past or future history, a history that belies the premises of continuity that Lessing's allegorical commentary lent to the history of Agamemnon's scepter. It is here that Lessing parts with his artifice of insisting that the historical mode is Homer's "artifice to make us dwell with a simple thing" (99G, 82E), for it is that which rather questions the very category. Perhaps this is why Lessing goes on to say: "Homer was not so much concerned with describing two staffs of differing material and figure as with making for us a palpable image of the difference of power of which these staffs were signs. . . . This was really the disparity in which Agamemnon and Achilles found themselves [separated] from one another" (99–100G, 83E).

What concerned Homer was not the description of the staffs. Nor did the scepters even operate as objects open to conventional description, as matter and form. Nor were these scepters symbols of power, as any dictionary might indicate—but rather of disparity of power, of a difference between.

The questions and questionings of authority, origin, formation, and history were critical to the matter in the framework of the *Laocoön*. Now here at its very core, they once again would seem to play a central role. Lessing reads in Homer a double history of the sign of power and designates the model moment in the model literary text as the image of signs of a difference of authority. What can this signify? Perhaps the only question to be asked is, How does this signify? a question adequately answerable in turn only with a *similiter*.

It operates in a manner similar to (which is not to say identical to) Lessing's polemical maneuvers. At least, here as before, authority, history, and origin as fixed structures are dissolved. They were ultimately dissolved in the name of a *similiter*, which is no name at all, but both the basis for and ungrounding of that which we call interpretation. At the crucial theoretical moment of the *Laocoön*, it is once again a question of figural language or what Lessing calls allegory. This figurality of the literary text is inextricably bound to the question of its commentary. The double allegorical reading that Lessing offers up and that forces us to read him, in turn, allegorically proved allegory to be anything but an unveiling of meaning. This takes place in a manner similar to Lessing's corrective about Caylus's misreadings of Homer's image of the cloud. For there also, reading the literary figure appropriately made disappearing (rather than substance) more perceptible.

In a sense, any reading could go on like this forever, for it seeks at this point to describe the source of its own authority and production, the muse of its own commentary. Let us just say that, if I have clouded over Lessing's text with the result of making it disappear, substantially, as fixed and recognizable truth, nevertheless, I have saved something in it, "the disconcerting dream" (14G, 15E). I may smile, but am nevertheless strengthened in my respect for the writer to whom so much can be lent.

5

The Monstrosity of Translation: Walter Benjamin's "The Task of the Translator"

Darin besteht das eigentliche Kunst-
geheimnis des Meisters, daß er den
Stoff durch die Form vertilgt.
(Therein lies the real secret of art of
the master—that he obliterates the
subject matter through the form)

—Schiller, cited by Benjamin in
"Zwei Gedichte von Friedrich Hölderlin"

In 1923, when Walter Benjamin published his translations of Baudelaire's "Tableaux parisiens," he prefaced them with a short essay entitled "Die Aufgabe des Übersetzers."[1] Was this intended to unfold for us the nature of the difficult task that claimed so many years of Benjamin's life? Does it signify an unprecedented consideration for the understanding of his readers—for those to whom the reading of lyric poetry would present difficulties? No less than the introductory poem of Baudelaire's *The Flowers of Evil* ("Au lecteur"), the opening lines of Benjamin's essay close the gates abruptly on such illusions of brotherly concern. "The poem to the reader closes with the apostrophe: 'Hypocritical reader,—my likeness,—my brother!'" The situation turns out to be more productive if one reformulates it and says: "[Benjamin] . . . has written an [essay] . . . that, from the beginning, had little expectation of an immediate public success" (from "Über einige Motive bei Baudelaire," 1, pt. 2:607). "Nowhere does consideration for the perceiver with respect to a work of art or an art form prove fruitful for their understanding. . . . For no poem is intended [*gilt*] for the reader, no image for the beholder, no symphony for the audience" (4, pt. 1:9).

What Benjamin's essay performs (and in this it is exemplary among his works) is an act of translation. It is, to begin with, a translation of "translation," which then rapidly demands an equally violent translation of every term promising the key to its definition. "Die Aufgabe des Übersetzers" dislocates definitions rather than establishing them because, itself an uncanny translation of sorts, its concern is not the readers' comprehension nor is its essence communication.

> Is a translation intended [*gilt*] for the readers who do not understand the original?. . . . What does a piece of writing 'say'? What does it communicate? Very little to him who understands it. The essential is not communication, not assertion. . . . If [the translation] were aimed at the reader, the original would have to be also. If the original does not exist for him, how could the translation be understood in this respect? (4, pt. 1:9)[2]

> (Gilt eine Übersetzung den Lesern, die das Original nicht verstehen?. . . . Was 'sagt' denn eine Dichtung? Was teilt sie mit? Sehr wenig dem, der sie versteht. Ihr Wesentliches ist nicht Mitteilung, nicht Aussage. . . . Wäre [die Übersetzung] aber für den Leser bestimmt, so müßte es auch das Original sein. Besteht das Original nicht um dessentwillen, wie ließe sich dann die Übersetzung aus dieser Beziehung verstehen?)

If, one by one, once familiar words become incomprehensibly foreign, if they relentlessly turn on their past, traditional ("althergebrachte," "herkömmliche") meanings, if the essay systematically roots itself in that past only to shift the very ground it stands on, this, after all, is the way in which translation functions. For Benjamin, translation does not transform an original foreign language into one we may call our own, but rather, renders radically foreign that language we believe to be ours. Benjamin cites Rudolf Pannwitz:

> Our translations, even the best ones, proceed from a false grounding: they wish to germanize Hindi, Greek, and English instead of

hindicizing, grecizing, and anglicizing German. They have a much
more significant respect for their own linguistic usage than for the
spirit of the foreign work . . . the fundamental error of the translator is that he holds fast to the incidental state of his own language
instead of letting it be violently moved by the foreign. (20)

(Unsre übertragungen auch die besten gehn von einem falschen
grundsatz aus sie wollen das indische griechische englische verdeut-
schen anstatt das deutsche zu verindischen vergriechischen vereng-
lischen. sie haben eine viel bedeutendere ehrfurcht vor den eigenen
sprachgebräuchen als vor dem geiste des fremden werks . . . der
grundsäztliche irrtum des urbertragenden ist dass er den zufälligen
stand der eigen sprache festhält anstatt sie durch die fremde sprache gewaltig bewegen zu lassen.)

This invasion of the foreign is perhaps merely prescriptive for
other translations, for the initial attack on his audience immediately gives way to a more amicable rhetoric of life, kinship, harmony, fidelity, religion, and nature. As in Baudelaire, where the
wounds inflicted by "Au lecteur" are soon to be soothed by the balm
of "Correspondances," so in Benjamin's essay it would seem we find
ourselves again on native soil. (Benjamin's essay could well be read
as an ironical commentary on the traditional reading of "Correspondances" in "Über einige Motive bei Baudelaire" [1, pt. 2:638–
48], where Benjamin reinterprets the "correspondences" as a temporal displacement bound to the "essentially distant," the "inap-
proachability" of the cult image).[3]
    In the metaphorical climate that now sets in, translations seem to
promise the organic temporality of plant life: they blossom forth
from the original as a continuation of that former "life"[4]–as a
"transplant," a "ripening," a germination of the original "seed." But
for all this apparently abundant flourishing, at no point does translation relate organically to the text that temporally precedes it. On
this point Benjamin is as ironical as he is deceptive. The "Entfaltung" ("unfolding," 11)[5] that the life of the original achieves in
translation never quite brings its seeds to flower. Translation denies
the linear law of nature in order to practice the rule of textuality. If
the original "cannot reach . . . [the realm of linguistic fulfillment]
root and branch" ("mit Stumpf und Stiel," 15; italics mine), this figure
of speech, metaphorical for completion in both German and English, must also be taken in its "fully unmetaphorical reality" (11).
Nowhere in the essay does translation develop into the future

promised by the germ ("keimhaft," 12), the kernel ("Kern," 15), the seed ("Samen," 17).

> More precisely, this essential kernel is definable as that in translation which, in its turn, is untranslatable. . . . Unlike the poetic word of the original, it is not translatable because the relationship of content to language is completely different in the original and the translation. If language and content constitute a certain unity in the original, like fruit and rind, the language of translation envelops its contents in vast folds like an emperor's robes. For this language signifies a loftier language than its own and therefore remains nonadequate, violent, and foreign with respect to its own content. (15)

> (Genauer läßt sich dieser wesenhafte Kern als dasjenige bestimmen, was an ihr selbst nicht wiederum übersetzbar ist. . . . Es ist nicht übertragbar wie das Dichterwort des Originals, weil das Verhältnis des Gehalts zur Sprache völlig verschieden ist in Original und Übersetzung. Bilden nämlich diese im ersten eine gewisse Einheit wie Frucht und Schale, so umgibt die Sprache der Übersetzung ihren Gehalt wie ein Königsmantel in weiten Falten. Denn sie bedeutet eine höhere Sprache als sie ist und bleibt dadurch ihrem eigenen Gehalt gegenüber unangemessen, gewaltig und fremd.

The natural metaphors for translation produce the opposite of organic fruition. The "Nachreife" (literally, "after-ripeness," 12 and 13) hardly completes the maturing process of the original, but rather, withers the fruit of meaning. The "unfolding" of the original paradoxically results in a proliferation of abundant folds that violently camouflage the content while maintaining it as nonadequate otherness. No further germination is possible: "This brokenness prevents any [further] translation, and at the same time makes it superfluous" (15).

The *Ver*-pflanzung ("transplant," 15) of the original bespeaks far less the temporally continuous life of the plant than a displacement of its ground:

> This task of ripening the seed of pure language in translation seems never to be solvable, to be definable in no solution. For is not the ground pulled out from under such a language if the restitution of meaning [*Sinnes*] ceases to be decisive? And indeed nothing else—to turn the phrase negatively—is the significance of all the foregoing. (17)

> (Ja, diese Aufgabe: in der Übersetzung den Samen reiner Sprache zur Reife zu bringen, scheint niemals lösbar, in keiner Lösung be-

stimmbar. Denn wird einer solchen nicht der Boden entzogen, wenn die Wiedergabe des Sinnes aufhört, maßgebend zu sein? Und nichts anderes ist ja—negativ gewendet—die Meinung alles Vorstehenden.)

With this negative turn of the phrase, Benjamin defines translation as undefinable. The unfixable task of translation is to purify the original of meaning: only poor translations seek to restore it (9). This is why translations are themselves untranslatable: "Translations on the other hand show themselves to be untranslatable—not because of the heaviness, but because of the all too fleeting manner in which meaning [*Sinn*] attaches to them" ("Übersetzungen dagegen erweisen sich unübersetzbar nicht wegen der Schwere, sondern wegen der allzu großen Flüchtigkeit, mit welcher der Sinn an ihnen haftet," 20).

The relation between translation and original, then, although "seemingly tangible," is always on the verge of eluding understanding (11). And eluding of understanding (*Erkenntnis*) is precisely what translation performs (*darstellt*). Benjamin insists on the verb *darstellen*, as opposed to *herstellen* or *offenbaren* (12), for translation neither presents nor reveals a contents.[6] It touches on the meaning of the original only by way of marking its independence, its freedom—literally—to go off on a tangent: the point it chooses remains irrelevant.

> What meaning [*Sinn*] remains of significance in the relation between translation and original can be grasped in a simile. Just as a tangent touches the circle fleetingly and only at one point, and just as it is the touching and not the particular point that dictates the law according to which it takes off on its straight trajectory further into infinity, so translation touches the original fleetingly and only at an infinitely small point of meaning in order to . . . follow its own trajectory. (19–20)

> (Was hiernach für das Verhältnis von Übersetzung und Original an Bedeutung dem Sinn verbleibt, läßt sich in einem Vergleich fassen. Wie die Tangente den Kreis flüchtig und nur in einem Punkte berührt und wie ihr wohl diese Berührung, nicht aber der Punkt, das Gesetz vorschreibt, nach dem sie weiter ins Unendliche ihre gerade Bahn zieht, so berührt die Übersetzung flüchtig und nur in dem unendlich kleinen Punkte des Sinnes das Original, um . . . ihre eigenste Bahn zu verfolgen.)

Certainly, it is its own trajectory that "Die Aufgabe des Übersetzers" follows when touching on such terms as *fidelity, literality,* and *kinship.* These it translates from a familiar German to another that hardly seems germane. But that, after all, is the point. Nowhere is this unfamiliarity more intensely sensed than when the essay turns to the familial relations between languages. The "kinship" Benjamin sets out to describe gathers much of its strangeness from the discrepancy between his mode of defining and his ultimate intention of definition. If we are made at all familiar with the notion of kinship, it is by learning what kinship is not. Kinship between languages is not similarity (12, 13), nor can it guarantee the preservation, in translation, of the original's form and sense. Benjamin touches fleetingly here on a point of epistemological concern.

> In order to grasp the genuine relation between original and translation, we must set up a deliberation whose design is completely analogous to the train of thought in which a critique of cognition demonstrates the impossibility of a mimetic theory. [*And tangentially the impossibility of traditional epistemology.*] If it is shown here that there could be no objectivity in knowledge—not even a claim to it—if it consisted in duplication of the real, then it can be proven here that no translation would be possible if it strove with its total being for similarity with the original. (12)

> (Um das echte Verhältnis zwischen Original und Übersetzung zu erfassen, ist eine Erwägung anzustellen, deren Absicht durchaus den Gedankengängen analog ist, in denen die Erkenntniskritik die Unmöglichkeit einer Abbildtheorie zu erweisen hat. Wird dort gezeigt, daß es in der Erkenntnis keine Objektivität und sogar nicht einmal den Anspruch darauf geben könnte, wenn sie in Abbildern des Wirklichen bestünde, so ist hier erweisbar, daß keine Übersetzung möglich wäre, wenn sie Ähnlichkeit mit dem Original ihrem letzten Wesen nach anstreben würde.)

This explains why kinship may only be defined negatively. The kinship between languages generates their *difference:* on what basis could translation claim to duplicate the original if no language, however original, in turn guarantees the objective reality of that which it names?

For all this insistence on kinship as differentiation, kinship sets forth a certain sameness as well. The elusive nature of this sameness presents particular difficulties to the English translator. In the long passage that speaks of this sameness, Harry Zohn remains far less "true" to the original, far less "literal" than the text demands. This is because he maintains a significant respect for his own linguistic usage, and traditionally, that is to his credit. Understandably then, his translation results in phrases such as "the same thing," "the same object," where the German speaks neither of objects nor things. In an admittedly germanized English, the passage would read as follows:

> All suprahistorical kinship of languages rests in the fact that in every one of them as a whole . . . one and the same is meant [*gemeint*], which, however, is not reachable by any one of them, but only by the totality of their mutually supplementing intentions—pure language. While, namely, all individual elements of foreign languages—the words, sentences, contexts—exclude one another, these languages supplement one another in their intentions. To grasp this law, one of the fundamental laws of the philosophy of language, is to differentiate what is meant [*das Gemeinte*] from the manner of meaning [*die Art des Meinens*] in the intention. In "Brot" and "pain" what is meant is indeed the same; the manner of meaning it, on the other hand, is not. . . . While in this way the manner of meaning in these two words is in conflict, it supplements itself in both languages from which they are derived. The manner of meaning in them supplements itself into what is meant. In the individual, unsupplemented languages, what is meant is never found in relative independence, as in individual words or sentences; rather, it is grasped in a constant state of change until it is able to step forward from the harmony of all those manners of meaning as pure language (13–14)

> (Alle überhistorische Verwandtschaft der Sprachen [beruht] darin, daß in ihrer jeder als ganzer . . . eines und zwar dasselbe gemeint ist, das dennoch keiner einzelnen von ihnen, sondern nur der Allheit ihrer einander ergänzenden Intentionen erreichbar ist: die reine Sprache. Während nämlich alle einzelnen Elemente, die Wörter, Sätze, Zusammenhänge von fremden Sprachen sich ausschließen, ergänzen diese Sprachen sich in ihren Intentionen selbst. Dieses Gesetz, eines der grundlegenden der Sprachphilosophie, genau zu fassen, ist in der Intention vom Gemeinten die Art des Meinens zu unterscheiden. In "Brot" und "pain" ist das Gemeinte zwar dasselbe, die Art, es zu meinen, dagegen nicht. . . . Während dergestalt die Art des Meinens in diesen beiden Wörtern einander widerstrebt, ergänzt sie sich in den beiden Sprachen, denen sie entstammen. Und zwar ergänzt sich in ihnen die Art des Meinens zum Gemeinten. Bei den einzelnen, den unergänzten Sprachen nämlich ist ihr Gemeintes niemals in relativer Selbständigkeit anzutreffen, wie bei den einzelnen Wörtern oder Sätzen, sondern vielmehr in stetem Wandel begriffen, bis es aus der Harmonie all jener Arten des Meinens als die reine Sprache herauszutreten vermag.)

What is meant in *Brot* and *pain* is "the same," but this is not to say that they mean the same *thing*. The same that is meant is "pure language." Benjamin states this quite literally at the beginning and end of the passage, but a hunger for substance could well allow us to forget it. What is meant by "pure language"? Certainly not the materialization of truth in the form of a supreme language. Benjamin sets this temptation aside with a passage from the "Crise de vers" (17). He displaces his own text with the foreignness of Mallarmé's in which the latter insists on the insurmountable disparity between languages. The "pure language" of the lengthy citation above does not signify the apotheosis of an ultimate language (even at the end of history) but signifies, rather, that which is purely language—nothing but language. "What is meant" is never something to be found independently of language nor even independently in language, in a single word or phrase, but arises instead from the mutual differentiation of the various manners of meaning. There is not quite so much difference as one might suspect then, between "kinship" as sameness and "kinship" defined as differentiation, for each generates the other, in language, indefinitely.

In a sense, one could argue, the kinship of language as here defined says nothing after all. If so, the translation of Benjamin has been rendered with the great fidelity the essay requires. For the translator's task of "fidelity" (*Treue*) calls for an emancipation from all sense of communication (19), a regaining of pure language. The "one and the same" which is meant in pure language means nothing.

> To win back pure language formed in the flux of language is the violent and single power of translation. In this pure language— which no longer means anything and no longer expresses anything, but which, as expressionless and productive word, is that which is meant in all languages—all communication, all meaning, and all intention ultimately meet with a stratum in which they are destined to extinction. (19)

> (Die reine Sprache gestaltet der Sprachbewegung zurückzugewinnen, ist das gewaltige und einzige Vermögen der Übersetzung. In dieser reinen Sprache, die nichts mehr meint und nichts mehr ausdrückt, sondern als ausdruckloses und schöpferisches Wort das in allen Sprachen Gemeinte ist, trifft endlich alle Mitteilung, aller Sinn und alle Intention auf eine Schicht, in der sie zu erlöschen bestimmt sind.)

This productive word which renders meaning extinct is that of literality (*Wörtlichkeit*). In the text of translation, the word replaces sentence and proposition as the fundamental element (18). The result is a teratogenesis instead of conventional, natural reproduction, in which the limbs of the progeny are dismembered, all syntax dismantled.

> Literality thoroughly overthrows all reproduction of meaning with regard to the syntax and threatens directly to lead to incomprehensibility. In the eyes of the nineteenth century, Hölderlin's translations of Sophocles were monstrous examples of such literality. . . . [T]he demand for literality is no offspring of an interest in maintaining meaning. (17–18)

> (Gar die Wörtlichkeit hinsichtlich der Syntax wirft jede Sinneswiedergabe vollends über den Haufen und droht geradenwegs ins Unverständliche zu führen. Dem neunzehnten Jahrhundert standen Hölderlins Sophokles-Übersetzungen als monströse Beispiele solcher Wörtlichkeit vor Augen. . . . [D]ie Forderung der Wörtlichkeit [ist] unableitbar aus dem Interesse der Erhaltung des Sinnes.)

The demand is Benjamin's for it is this monstrosity that he praises above all as the most perfect of all translations. Hölderlin's translations are touched upon at three other points in the essay and always spoken of as exemplary.[7]

This exaction of literality, the passage continues, must not be understood as an interest in meaning, but "aus triftigeren Zusammenhängen" (18). Must it be understood, then, "in a more meaningful context," as Zohn's translation insists (Z 78)? Or is the contextuality of original and translation such that this phrase too must be taken literally. The linking together of the two would then be *triftig* in its etymological sense—from *treffen*—as striking, fragmentary. This is certainly the point if not the tone of the simile that follows.

> Just as fragments of a vessel, in order to be articulated together, must follow one another in the smallest detail but need not resemble one another, so, instead of making itself similar to the meaning [*Sinn*] of the original, the translation must rather, lovingly and in detail, in its own language, form itself according to the manner of meaning [*Art des Meinens*] of the original, to make both recognizable as the broken part of a greater language, just as fragments are the broken part of a vessel. (18)

> (Wie nämlich Scherben eines Gefäßes, um sich zusammenfügen zu lassen, in den kleinsten Einzelheiten einander zu folgen, doch nicht

so zu gleichen haben, so muß, anstatt dem Sinn des Originals sich ähnlich zu machen, die Übersetzung liebend vielmehr und bis ins Einzelne hinein dessen Art des Meinens in der eigenen Sprache sich anbilden, um so beide wie Scherben als Bruchstück eines Gefäßes, als Bruchstück einer größeren Sprache erkennbar zu machen.)

In the literal translation above,[8] the passage leaves things incomplete. With the joining together of translation and original, language remains a *Bruchstück*. Such is the mode of Benjamin's articulation despite its apparent reference to organic growth, kinship, sameness, fidelity. (And it is after all both that of Baroque allegory, with its insistence on the ruin [in *Ursprung des deutschen Trauerspiels,* "Allegorie und Trauerspiel"], and also the vision of the "angel of history" in the "Theses on the Philosophy of History" [IX].)[9]

Perhaps this helps account for the involuted formulation— translation must awaken from its own language the original's echo. This is not to say that translation, in coming after, echoes the original. Translation relates to the original as to pure language—in a way that the original, so laden with its apparent content, is rarely deemed to function.

> In this lies a characteristic of translation totally different from that of poetic works, since the intention of the latter is never towards language as such, its totality, but rather solely and directly towards definitive linguistic coherences of content. Translation, however, does not view itself as does poetry as in the inner forest of language, but rather as outside it, opposite it; and, without entering, it calls into the original, into that single place where, in each case, the echo is able to give in its own language the resonance of a work in a foreign tongue. (16)

> (Hierin liegt ein vom Dichtwerk durchaus unterscheidender Zug der Übersetzung, weil dessen Intention niemals auf die Sprache als solche, ihre Totalität, geht, sondern allein unmittelbar auf bestimmte sprachliche Gehaltszusammenhänge. Die Übersetzung aber sieht sich nicht wie die Dichtung gleichsam im innern Bergwald der Sprache selbst, sondern außerhalb desselben, ihm gegenüber und ohne ihn zu betreten ruft sie das Original hinein, an demjenigen einzigen Orte hinein, wo jeweils das Echo in der eigenen den Widerhall eines Werkes der fremden Sprache zu geben vermag.)

To locate the source of these reverberations is not an easy matter. Though, logically, the original should originate the call, Benjamin's formulation leaves this task to translation.

There is an unmistakable echo here of a German saying that both amplifies and clarifies the predicament: "Wie man in den Wald hineinruft, so schallt's heraus" ("As one calls into the forest, so it will resound"). Translation's call into the forest of language is not a repetition of the original but the awakening of an echo of itself. This signifies its disregard for traditional temporal priorities as well as for coherence of content, for the sound that returns is its own tongue become foreign. Just as the vase of translation built unlike fragment on unlike fragment only to achieve a final fragmentation, so the echo of translation elicits only fragments of language, distorted into a disquieting foreignness.

But who pieces the vase together? Who sounds the echo? Which is to say, who writes the text of translation? Or are these questions that necessarily lose their meaning in the context of the essay? By now it is evident that when Benjamin speaks of "translation," he does not mean translation, for it has never ceased to acquire other, foreign meanings. One is tempted to read "translation" as a metaphor for criticism, to offer the answer that the critic writes translations. How else to explain the following:

> Translation transplants therefore the original into a more insofar as—ironically—conclusive language realm, since it cannot be displaced from it through further translation. . . . The word 'ironically' does not recall thoughts of the romantics in vain. They above others possessed insight into the life of works of which translation is the highest testimony. To be sure, they did not recognize translation as such, but turned their entire attention to criticism. (15)

> (Übersetzung verpflanzt also das Original in einen wenigstens insofern—ironisch—endgültigeren Sprachbereich, als es aus diesem durch keinerlei Übertragung mehr zu versetzen ist. . . . Nicht umsonst mag hier das Wort 'ironisch' an Gedankengänge der Romantiker erinnern. Diese haben vor andern Einsicht in das Leben der Werke besessen, von welchem die Übersetzung eine höchste Bezeugung ist. Freilich haben sie diese als solche kaum erkannt, vielmehr ihre ganze Aufmerksamkeit der Kritik zugewendet.)

Translation may indeed be metaphorical for criticism,[10] but the critical text is inexorably bound to a certain irony. That irony dislocates the syntax of Benjamin's phrase above as well as the tentative solution to the question "who writes," in which our own critical distance was not ironical enough.

"Translatability," which we might also call the critical text within, is a potential of the work itself.

> Translatability belongs to certain works essentially—which is not to say that their translation is essential to them, but rather that a certain significance dwelling within the originals expresses itself in their translatability. (10)
>
> (Übersetzbarkeit eignet gewissen Werken wesentlich—das heißt nicht, ihre Übersetzung ist wesentlich für sie selbst, sondern will besagen, daß eine bestimmte Bedeutung, die den Originalen innewohnt, sich in ihrer Übersetzbarkeit äußere.)

This, then, is the text-ness of the text or a criticism without critic. From the very beginning, the essay dismisses the necessity of a translator for translation.

> Certain relational concepts maintain their good, perhaps best sense . . . when they are not a priori exclusively referred to man. In this way one might speak of an unforgettable life or moment even if all men had forgotten it. When, namely, its essence demands not to be forgotten, then that predicate would not correspond to something false, but rather to a demand which does not correspond to man, and would at the same time include a reference to a realm to which it does correspond—to a remembrance of God. (10)
>
> (Gewisse Relationsbegriffe [behalten] ihren guten, ja vielleicht besten Sinn . . . wenn sie nicht von vorne herein ausschileßlich auf den Menschen bezogen werden. So dürfte von einem unvergeßlichen Leben oder Augenblick gesprochen werden, auch wenn alle Menschen sie vergessen hätten. Wenn nämlich deren Wesen es forderte, nicht vergessen zu werden, so würde jenes Prädikat nichts Falsches, sondern nur eine Forderung, der Menschen nicht entsprechen, und zugleich auch wohl den Verweis auf einen Bereich enthalten, in dem ihr entsprochen wäre: auf ein Gedenken Gottes.)

The translatability of the text excludes the realm of man and with him the translator, the figure to which Benjamin's essay is devoted. The "Aufgabe" of the translator is less his task than his surrender: he is "aufgegeben," given up, abandoned. This is its initial irony.

Yet no sooner is the figure of man abandoned than another appears to offer itself. At the beginning and the end Benjamin turns to the realm of the theological, which seems to redeem this monstrous loss (if also, in a sense, to cause it). This is the way, in the essay's closing paragraph, he writes of Hölderlin's translations— the most perfect of their kind. The overwhelming danger they create may only be contained by the Holy Script.

Because of this there lives in [Hölderlin's translations] above all the monstrous and originary danger of all translation—that the gates of a language so expanded and controlled may fall shut and enclose the translator in silence. The Sophocles translations were Hölderlin's last work. In them meaning plunges from abyss to abyss, until it threatens to lose itself in the bottomless depths of language. But there is a halt [*Halten*]. However, no text guarantees it but the holy text. (21)

(Eben darum wohnt in ihnen vor andern die ungeheure und ursprüngliche Gefahr aller Übersetzung: daß die Tore einer so erweiterten und durchwalteten Sprache zufallen und den Übersetzer ins Schweigen schließen. Die Sophokles-Übersetzungen waren Hölderlins letztes Werk. In ihnen stürzt der Sinn von Abgrund zu Abgrund, bis er droht in bodenlosen Sprachtiefen sich zu verlieren. Aber es gibt ein Halten. Es gewährt es jedoch kein Text außer dem heiligen.)

What is it exactly that the Holy Scripture vouchsafes? Is it really a halt to the precipitous loss of meaning, or must we translate *Halten* rather as a holding and retaining of that loss? For in the Holy Scriptures meaning no longer separates language and revelation. The holy text is totally literal, in Benjamin's sense of the word, which is to say, because no meaning stands behind its language, because language and revelation coincide absolutely, it is as absolutely meaningless as an original may be.

However, no text guarantees it but the holy text, in which meaning has ceased to be a watershed for the flow of language and the flow of revelation. Where a text belongs to a truth or doctrine immediately, without the mediation of meaning, in its literalness of true language—that text is absolutely translatable. . . . Such boundless trust with respect to it is demanded from the translation that just as in this [holy text] language and revelation are united without tension, so in the translation, literality and freedom must join in the form of the interlinear version. For to some degree, all great writings—but above all the Holy Scriptures—contain their virtual translation between the lines.(21)

(Es gewährt es jedoch kein Text außer dem heiligen, in dem der Sinn aufgehört hat, die Wasserscheide für die strömende Sprache und die strömende Offenbarung zu sein. Wo der Text unmittelbar, ohne vermittelnden Sinn, in seiner Wörtlichkeit der wahren Sprache, der Wahrheit oder der Lehre angehört, ist er übersetzbar schlechthin. . . . Ihm gegenüber ist so grenzenloses Vertrauen von der Übersetzung gefordert, daß spannungslos wie in jenem Sprache und Offenbarung so in dieser Wörtlichkeit und Freiheit in Gestalt der Interlinearversion sich vereinigen müssen. Denn in irgendeinem Grade enthalten alle großen Schriften, im höchsten aber die heiligen, zwischen den Zeilen ihre virtuelle Übersetzung.)

And what of Benjamin's "between the lines," for from the beginning, we recognized this essay as a translation of sorts. Between the lines of German, he has slipped in a phrase from the original of the Holy Writ. It apparently speaks of the beginning of linear time and coincidently, therefore, posits both the origins of language and the condition of temporality which makes a conventional concept of translation possible. ἐν ἀρχῇ ἦν ὁ λόγοϑ (18). These are the opening words of the Gospel According to John, and the text to which Benjamin's clearly refers when it speaks of the Holy Scriptures. "Die Aufgabe des Übersetzers" serves as a translation for the following lines which are given below in an interlinear, literal translation from Luther's version of the text.

1. Im   Anfang   war das Wort, und das Wort war beig Gott
1. In the beginning was the word, and the word was with God

   und Gott war das Wort.
   and God was the word.

2. Dasselbige   war im   Anfang   bei Gott.
2. The same (the word) was in the beginning with God.

3. Alle Dinge sind durch   dasselbige gemacht und ohne
3. All things are through the same   made   and without

   dasselbige ist nichts   gemacht, was   gemacht ist.
   the same   is nothing made   which made   is.

This is the final irony.

6

The Metaphor of Temporality: Paul de Man's Rousseau Essays and "The Rhetoric of Temporality"

> And to read is to understand, to
> question, to know, to forget, to erase,
> to deface, to repeat—that is to say,
> the endless prosopopoeia by which
> the dead are made to have a face and
> a voice which tells the allegory of
> their demise and allows us to apos-
> trophize them in our turn. No de-
> gree of knowledge can ever stop this
> madness, for it is the madness of
> words.
>
> —"Shelley Disfigured"

There is no way to say adequately what the significance of de Man might be. It could not be otherwise, for he himself linked death to the impossibility of defining man as pres- ence and with man's perpetual transgression of his own sense of self as totalized. And given that the transgression is perpetual, it took no literal death to both upset and set the task, that of reading the man, which is to say, of writing about him.

"We write," as the essay entitled "Allegory" reminds us, "in order to forget our foreknowledge of the total opacity of [de Man's] words . . . or, perhaps worse, because we do not know whether . . . [his writings] have or do not have to be understood" ("Allegory," 203).[1] Let us forget, then, both this foreknowledge and this ignorance and the constant warning against the mystification of adopting a privileged viewpoint forever unable to understand its own genealogy. For the question that this reading will first raise is apparently one of origins and teleology: how does de Man's critical narrative move in the second part of *Allegories of Reading,* the essays on Rousseau? How does it move from the first chapter, "Metaphor," to the last, entitled "Excuses"; how does it cross the borders from one essay to the next; and do the provisional syntheses that take place along the way mark a genuine progression in our understanding of Rousseau's text and de Man's?

There is much in these texts that would lead us to believe so. Almost all of the essays begin with a reference to the conclusions reached by the previous reading, giving us, at the very least, a parodic sense of traditional critical progress. Within the essays there are constant reminders of what we have learned earlier in such phrases as "As we know from the reading of *Narcisse* and *Pygmalion*" ("Allegory," 210), "as we know from *Julie*" ("Excuses," 283), "As we know from the 'Préface dialoguée'" ("Excuses," 296). More compelling than these phrases, which one could write off as exercises in the stylistic conventions of critical rhetoric, the texts on Rousseau repeatedly suggest a movement within each essay of shifting from error to understanding. Thus, to take just one example, the essay "Self" first presents a reading of *Narcisse* as the straightforward, mimetic representation of Valère's vanity, in which his consciousness apparently moves from an initial bad faith to a triumphant good faith at the end of the play. De Man rejects this interpretation by reading a number of linguistic effects that such an interpretation fails to account for, effects that perform a suspension between self and other. He then counters this, his second interpretation, or suggests its containment, by pointing to the preface to *Narcisse*, which might be read as proof that Rousseau, as author, was definitely beyond the errors of his character. De Man comments on this interpretation by reading another text of Rousseau, *Pygmalion*, and, as one might expect, reverses his previous reading with the vacillation of a fourth interpretation.

More crucial than this sense of progress that can be traced within each essay[2] is the sense de Man gives his reader of a hierarchical schema of different critical levels of understanding. Thus, he distinguishes between tropological narratives such as the *Second Discourse* on the one hand and allegorical narratives such as *La Nouvelle Héloïse* that tell the story of the failure to read:

> The rhetorical mode of such structures can no longer be summarized by the single term of metaphor or any substitutive trope or figure in general, although the deconstruction of metaphorical figures remains a necessary moment in their production. They take into account the fact that the resulting narratives can be folded back upon themselves and become self-referential. By *refusing*, for reasons of epistemological rigor, to confirm the authority, though not the necessity, of this juxtaposition, Rousseau unsettles the metaphor of reading as deconstructive narrative and replaces it by a more complex structure. The paradigm for all texts consists of a figure (or a system of figures) and its deconstruction. But since this model cannot be closed off by a final reading, it engenders, in its turn, a supplementary figural superposition which narrates the unreadability of the prior narration. As distinguished from primary deconstructive narratives centered on figures and ultimately always on metaphor, we can call such narratives to the second (or the third) degree *allegories*. ("Allegory," 205)[3]

Side by side with these various modes of suggesting linear progress through time, one finds equally prevalent a disconcerting insistence on the text as "a series of repetitive reversals" ("Self," 162), "as a repetition of . . . [the tropological system's] aberration" ("Excuses," 301), as a repetition of a pattern that ruptures dialectical progress ("Self," 187). How can we account for this seeming contradiction?[4]

To put the question another way, how does time play its role in the performance of de Man's narrative? Already in the first essay, "Metaphor," we read that "the discovery of temporality coincides with the acts of transgressive freedom" ("Metaphor," 140) that necessarily take place when the boundaries of man's attempts at self-totalization or naming are seen to fail. Time is that which marks the realization of the impossibility of self-definition. In the essay "Promises," de Man speaks of time as "the phenomenal category produced by the discrepancy" between the "theoretical statement" of the law and its "phenomenal manifestation" that is necessarily delayed to a future moment ("Promises," 273). This is made clearer, if more unthinkable, in the essay "Self":

> And just as the indeterminacy of reference generates the illusion of a subject, a narrator, and a reader, it also generates the metaphor of temporality. A narrative endlessly tells the story of its own denominational aberration and it can only repeat this aberration on various levels of rhetorical complexity. Texts engender texts as a result of their necessarily aberrant semantic structure; hence the fact that they consist of a series of repetitive reversals that engenders the semblance of temporal sequence. ("Self," 162)

Temporality is a metaphor. It is generated out of a series of repetitions that give the illusion of sequence or linear temporal order. One begins to suspect that the distinction between linear dialectical progression and its disruption may not be all that clear, since, as we have just read, the semblance of sequence and therefore the semblance of time seems to coincide with the endless repetition of reversals.

If we return to the passage just cited, taken as it is from an essay in which the entire problematic is that of delineating the difference between self and other, one is struck by the juxtaposition of two sentences, the first of which begins, "A narrative endlessly tells the story of its *own* denominational aberration," and the second, "Texts engender [other] *texts* as a result of . . ." (emphasis mine). At stake here is not only the narrative line of an individual text but the relation between one text and another, a text and its other, the critical text that it necessarily engenders. For this reason, in reading de Man one is woven into the texture of the narrative to the point of making his text and ours into the dramatization of their own confusions.

Allegories of Reading moves like a dialectic that has no point of origin and no point of telos. Vacillation and progress cannot cancel each other out, since the text of these critical essays is, per definition, in a state of unpredictable change. Their mode of existence is necessarily temporal and historical, though in a strictly nonteleological sense. All critical progress takes place in the mode of asserting a series of irresolvable vacillations of nonpolar incompatibilities from which it implicitly exempts itself, locating these, as it does elsewhere, in the text of Rousseau: such vacillations as those between denomination and conceptualization, self and other, self and

God, mind and nature, personal and public happiness, promise
and fulfillment. And just as each of Rousseau's allegorical narratives invariably "resorts to the principles of authority that it under-
mines" ("Promises," 275), so de Man's allegorical performance necessarily "relapses into the figure it deconstructs" ("Promises," 275),
"reintroduc[ing] the metaphorical model whose deconstruction
had been the reason for its own elaboration" ("Promises," 257),
time. "It perform[s] what it has shown to be impossible to do"
("Promises," 275), to deconstruct. Like the author of the preface to
Narcisse in relation to the protagonist of that play, de Man might be
seen to claim for himself the authority he negates in the text at
hand, speaking in a "voice that, by the rigor of its negativity, finally
coincides with what it asserts" ("Self," 172). Like Galathea, Rousseau, and the reader in relation to Pygmalion, figures who merely
seem able to separate themselves from the errors of the artist, de
Man's text implicitly performs its blindness to the illusions of negative authority and is taken in by a vacillation it cannot coincidentally
assert and perform.[5]

Yet what is it that seems, if only momentarily, to allow the critical
text to escape the irresolution of the texts it deconstructs, if not its
belatedness, its coming after? If time is the phenomenal category
engendered out of the noncoincidence between a text's theoretical
statement and its phenomenal manifestation, then de Man's critical
text plays the role of that temporal passage, a temporal discrepancy
that could be equally located within the text read or between the
critical text and its object, for who after reading de Man could distinguish between that particular pair of self and other? *Allegories of
Reading* is an elaborate allegory of the impossibility of the fundamental condition of allegory, of the illusory nature of time and of
the misreading it engenders when it operates as critical progress.
Its time is, coincidentally, an act of transgressive freedom, a rupture, that marks the impossibility of textual definition and self-
definition. It performs this deception with respect to the texts it
reads and also with respect to the text it cannot and yet inevitably
does read: itself. It acts out, then, both the promise of progress and
its failure, making promises it cannot fulfill in the present, making
excuses rather than confessions for that which it might rather expose than hide, narrating endless fictions.

It is thus impossible to speak of this text as either knowledge or
ignorance, although as long as one assumes a rhetoric of linear
temporality, one seems bound to such distinctions. Perhaps it is
time to read a particular passage from *Allegories of Reading* rather

than simply citing it (openly and surreptitiously), an exemplary moment in which de Man's maddening irony is at play.

In the chapter entitled "Self" de Man follows the vacillating evolution of the relationship of Pygmalion as artist and author to his creation Galathea. At first, Pygmalion treats Galathea as an object of sexual aggression, desiring her "unmediated possession" ("Self," 182). But this moment of literality gives way to another gesture in which he reads the body of Galathea as symbolic of the beauty of her soul. When he rejects this interpretation, he regards her in turn as a *general* model for a particular being, and since Pygmalion has in fact created Galathea, she becomes a general Self who might well include the particular self of Pygmalion. In the play's central moment the temptation of a "totalizing identification" ("Self," 184) offers itself to Pygmalion, but, de Man maintains, no sooner does Pygmalion contemplate immolating himself so that artist and work might be one than he withdraws from any synthesis of self and other that would put the vacillations of the text to rest. When, de Man goes on to argue, shortly thereafter the statue comes to life and approaches Pygmalion, the final exchange between the two reiterates their antagonism, for no teleological closure of the general Self with the particular Self—in fact, no teleological closure of any kind—can take place.[6] "And there can be no doubt about their continued confrontation, in endless repetition, in the apparent conclusion of the text. The final exchange between Galathea and Pygmalion reiterates the situation that existed in the central passage when Pygmalion withdraws from ultimate identification with the most generalized form of selfhood" ("Self," 185).

But on what does he base his judgment, his justification for his positive assertion of the play's vacillation, the imbalance of final exchange between the two characters? "The play," he writes, "could, in principle, have come to a stop in the identifying echo of the two "moi's" uttered by the protagonists: *"Galathea* (touches herself and says): Moi. *Pygmalion* (transported): Moi!" (1:1230). The supplementary exclamation mark records the imbalance acted out in the final exchanges" ("Self," 185). What is it that de Man reads in these last lines but an exclamation point?

Things get worse, or, perhaps, de Man's play, his performance of critical assertion and vacillation, becomes better. For just after assuring us that Galathea's utterance on touching Pygmalion has all the ambiguity of the enigmatic "Ach!" that closes Kleist's play *Amphytrion,* de Man cites that statement and then insists on the absolutely univocal intention of Galathea.

"*Galathea* (with a sigh): Ah! encore moi" (1:1230–31). The tone is hardly one of ecstatic union, rather of resigned tolerance towards an overassiduous admirer. Since Galathea is the Self as such, she has to contain all particular selves including Pygmalion; as a statement of identity in which "encore moi" means "aussi moi" ("me as well"), it is a true enough affirmation. This is certainly how Pygmalion understands it. . . . But the line "Ah! encore moi" spoken with a sigh that suggests disappointment rather than satisfaction can also mean "de nouveau moi" ("me again"), a persisting, repeated distinction between the general Self and the self as other. Indeed, the separation between Galathea's coldness and Pygmalion's impetuousness could not be greater. ("Self," 185–86)

How does de Man "know" that the separation could not be greater? What can he possibly be interpreting in Galathea's "(with a sigh): Ah! encore moi"? He reads a series of singularly resistant signs, the "Ah," along with the exclamation point that follows it and a sigh, the difference between Ah! and Ah!, a tonality of voice that can nowhere be located in Rousseau's text, but only in the ironical gesture of de Man's commentary. He reads, moreover, "encore," the sign of the very critical doubling that one might claim de Man's writings to be about (in both senses of the word), "encore" which suggests both the temporal or spatial continuity of "still" and the rupturing discontinuity of "again." He reads that sign of doubling and fixes on one of its meanings, identifying it in a gesture of apparent critical certainty and progress as the sign of a rift between the artist (Pygmalion) and that which he has produced or, tellingly, between the author and that which he has written. Needless to say, the same is performed with respect to the last term of the phrase, with respect to that sign of the self ("moi") which has been the titular concern of the entire essay.[7]

But, perhaps, nowhere is de Man's irony more open to view than when he reads rhetorical figures of his own making. The question he raises in the lines cited below is the question raised earlier in relation to de Man's own text. How compatible are rhetorical resources with selfhood and to what extent does the deconstructor unlock the rhetoric of another self and expose the delusions of the concept of self, only to establish "the authority of a [deconstructive] self at the far end of its most radical negation" ("Self," 172)?

Rhetoric all too easily appears as the tool of the self, hence its pervading association, in the everyday use of the term, with persuasion, eloquence, the manipulation of the self and of others. Hence also the naïvely pejorative sense in which the term is commonly used, in opposition to a literal use of language that would not allow the subject to conceal its desires. The attitude is by no means confined to the popular use of "rhetoric" but is in fact a recurrent philosophical topos, a philosopheme that may well be constitutive of philosophical language itself. In all these instances, rhetoric functions as a key to the discovery of the self. ("Self," 173)

The passage is not yet lost in what de Man will soon speak of as "the epistemological labyrinth of figural structures" ("Self," 173). So far we see the way in. The door is not locked, since our sense of direction has not yet been frustrated. We read here of a first self that has used eloquence as a means to conceal. That same tool can, in the hand of the interpreter, serve as a key to open the passageway to the self.

> In all these instances, rhetoric functions as a key to the discovery of the self, and it functions with such ease that one may well begin to wonder whether the lock indeed shapes the key or whether it is not the other way round, that a lock (and a secret room or box behind it) had to be invented in order to give a function to the key. For what could be more distressing than a bunch of highly refined keys just lying around without any corresponding locks worthy of being opened? ("Self," 173)

As unsettling as this statement may be—and we will get to its content soon enough, but it is impossible to think what it is saying and how it is saying it all at once—as disorienting as this statement may be, its rhetorical mode is absolutely straightforward. It is not what de Man would call figural or metaphorical in Rousseau's sense, for its referential status is totally unproblematic.[8] The above assertion resides in the realm of mimetic language to which de Man has given us the key. One can read it by simply substituting "rhetoric" for "key" and "self" for "lock." While de Man's language remains unproblematically representational, what it speaks of is a rhetoric that may refuse access to a referent behind it. Yet it is not quite that rhetoric refuses access to a self behind it, for to bypass the distressing absence of corresponding locks (selves), is it not rhetoric itself that would have to invent them?

"Perhaps there are none," de Man continues, "and perhaps the most refined key of all, the key of keys, is the one that gives access to the Pandora's box in which this darkest secret is kept hidden" ("Self," 173).[9] The "key of keys" is not simply one key among others, but that which is the key to the functioning (or nonfunctioning) of all keys. And what it reveals is the secret that the keys with which we daily deal (rhetoric) have no corresponding locks. Yet to understand the passage in this way, as the straightforward assertion of an absence, is to fail to read the vacillation in the phrase "in which this darkest secret is kept hidden." Does the key of keys (rhetorical analysis of rhetoric) give us genuine access to the secret, or is it that we gain access only to a box in which the secret must, necessarily, be *kept* hidden, even at the very moment when we think we are revealing it? Surely this is the implication of the literary allusion to Pandora's box. In the myth of Pandora, last in the box was Delusive Hope, and it was this hope that kept Pandora from committing suicide—a hope, then, in the service of preserving the very self who revealed the self-threatening content of the box.

If the darkest secret of the absence of the self is *kept* hidden just at the moment that one speaks it aloud, this is because that rhetoric which is the key of keys surreptitiously reintroduces the authority of the self, however deconstructive. But if this is so, the structure of rhetorical control must come unhinged, and so it does. "This would imply the existence of at least one lock worthy of being raped, the Self as the relentless undoer of selfhood" ("Self," 173). The "key of keys," the key that implicitly turned all other keys to locks, has itself become a lock ("the Self as the relentless undoer of selfhood"), for all there is is rhetoric, which now assumes one role, now another. If before de Man spoke of a key that functions with remarkable ease, if afterwards of "locks worthy of being opened," the lock that closes this difficult passage must be approached with violent force (as one "worthy of being raped"). The movement is less one of opening locks than of their resistance, less one of entering into a space of selfhood or reference than a displacement away from that delusion that nevertheless repeats it.

To be sure, keys are no longer simply keys (rhetoric) and locks are no longer simply locks (selves), since each key serves as a lock for the next. We can no longer read by the controlled substitutions of coded terms that are the hallmark of mimetic language. De Man makes this all the clearer in the last line cited above, a line he, of course, lifted from Alexander Pope: "This would imply the existence of at least one lock worthy of being raped." Here the substantial hardware of the previous imagery, with all its implicit progress, ironized as it may be, gives way to the labyrinthine curl of the allusion to "The Rape of the Lock," [10] for when it is a question of metaphor, there is no telling where it may lead.

Where is all this insistence on de Man's irony bringing us if not to the endpoint of sorts that appears to close the volume *Allegories of Reading*?

> The anacoluthon is extended over all the points of the figural line or allegory; . . . it becomes the permanent parabasis of an allegory (of figure), that is to say, irony. Irony is no longer a trope but the undoing of the deconstructive allegory of all tropological cognitions, the systematic undoing, in other words, of understanding. As such, far from closing off the tropological system, irony enforces the repetition of its aberration. ("Excuses," 300–301)

If *Allegories of Reading* ends with the ironization of allegory, how could it be insignificant that another text of de Man's, "The Rhetoric of Temporality," closes with the allegorization of irony?

In that earlier essay to which the last lines of the book apparently refer, if only by reversal, the trajectory to its endpoint has hardly been simple. In the context of critical studies in German, English, and French letters, "The Rhetoric of Temporality" tells of an abandonment of the arbitrary and rational allegory of the eighteenth century in favor of the symbol. The symbol promises a union between itself (the representation of experience) and experience, between subject and object.[11] It displays the temptation of the self to "borrow . . . the temporal stability that it lacks from nature" (197). But de Man insists as well on the growth of another metaphorical style that arises just when the symbol is supplanting rococo allegory. This other style, a style that seems to constitute the blind spot of so many readings, de Man also chooses to call "allegory."

Tellingly enough, this other allegory, although outstripped by the symbol in the course of the nineteenth century, is able to account for the symbolic mode as a mere negative moment within its own structure. De Man arrives at this conclusion through a reading of Rousseau's *La Nouvelle Héloïse* in which he juxtaposes two landscapes in the text, that of the Meillerie episode with Julie's garden, Elysium. In the Meillerie episode the analogical continuity among the style of Saint Preux's impassioned writing, the scenery he describes, and the emotion he experiences is exemplary of the coincidence between "mind and nature" (193) or language and its referent. But the novel, we are told, presents this episode as a scene of temptation and error by contrasting it with Julie's garden, which is not only an emblem of virtue, but also, it would seem, an emblem of the allegorical. Thus, the passages concerning the garden operate as allegorical language in that they place the symbolic thrust of the text in the proper perspective of error. For, in contrast to the symbol that appropriates temporal stability where there is none, allegory always involves a temporal discontinuity in which a renunciation of a previous symbolic moment takes place. This de Man calls the "unveiling of an authentically temporal destiny" (206). If "time is the originary constitutive category" of allegory, it is time as a medium of rupture, "distance," "difference" (207).

The temporal relationships in the example of Julie's garden would seem to cut in all directions. For these allegorical descriptions not only assert a negative *self*-knowledge on the part of the novel (with respect to Saint Preux's language), but they also undercut any attempt to read this moment in Rousseau as confirmation of the other, to read it as a mirror of a world existing outside and prior to the text. It is not only that Rousseau refers to other texts rather than to a realm that we tend to call "reality"; in elaborating the literary sources of the Elysium, de Man demonstrates that it is less the content of those texts to which *La Nouvelle Héloïse* refers than their "allegorical diction" (203). The allegorical text, therefore, refers to an outside only as a "previous sign" of which it is the "essence . . . to be pure anteriority" (207), a temporally distant sign, in turn emptied of its referent—the very inverse, then, of the symbol.

If we have felt called upon to paraphrase the content of de Man's essay as he speaks of Rousseau, this is because it forms something of a commentary on de Man's own style. "The Rhetoric of Temporality" is divided into two sections concentrating, respectively, on the concepts of allegory and irony. Despite the apparent symmetry of the organization, the narrative modes of the inquiries prove to be critically dissimilar. The section entitled "Allegory and Symbol," as we have seen, tells a historical tale, that of a transition at the end of the eighteenth century from a concept of allegory as the key rhetorical term to that of symbol. The section on irony displays another narrative strategy, one that we will confront shortly.

Despite this disparity, allegory would seem to have a great deal in common with irony, for, as he nears the end of his essay, de Man has this to say:

> Our description seems to have reached a provisional conclusion. The act of irony, as we now understand it, reveals the existence of a temporality that is definitely not organic, in that it relates to its source only in terms of distance and difference and allows for no end, for no totality. . . . The temporal void that it reveals is the same

void we encountered when we found allegory always implying an unreachable anteriority. Allegory and irony are thus linked in their common discovery of a truly temporal predicament. They are also linked in their common de-mystification of an organic world postulated in a symbolic mode of analogical correspondences or in a mimetic mode of representation in which fiction and reality could coincide. (222)

But, no sooner does de Man reach this "provisional conclusion," an apparent state of definitional wisdom, than he ironizes it by putting it into a historical frame. Might it not be possible, he suggests, just as he traced the historical regression away from allegory, to also trace a parallel historical literary development that abandons the notion of irony?

> The regression in critical insight found in the transition from an allegorical to a symbolic theory of poetry would find its historical equivalent in the regression from the eighteenth-century ironic novel, based on what Friedrich Schlegel called "*Parekbase*," to nineteenth-century realism.
>
> This conclusion is dangerously satisfying and highly vulnerable to irony in that it rescues a coherent historical picture at the expense of stated human incoherence. (222)

The irony is directed at the attempt to historicize the question of literature, an irony therefore directed at the entire first part of de Man's own "Rhetoric of Temporality," where he had spoken of the "need for historical clarification as a preliminary to a more systematic treatment of an intentional rhetoric" (188).[12] But it would be naive to take irony as a force that simply questions the particular historical scheme of the essay at hand. For in a passage that is something of a turning point between the two sections of the essay, there is a certain laughter that reflects on and ironizes the text that precedes it in more ways than one:

> In the case of irony one cannot so easily take refuge in the need for a historical de-mystification of the term, as when we tried to show that the term "symbol" had in fact been substituted for that of "allegory" in an act of ontological bad faith. The tension between allegory and symbol justified this procedure: the mystification is a fact of history and must therefore be dealt with in a historical manner before actual theorization can start. But in the case of irony one has to start out from the structure of the trope itself, taking one's cue from texts that are de-mystified and, to a large extent, them-

selves ironical. For that matter, the target of their irony is very often the claim to speak about human matters as if they were facts of history. It is a historical fact that irony becomes increasingly conscious of itself in the course of demonstrating the impossibility of our being historical. (211)

If the "mystification [about symbolic language] is a fact of history," one might add that history is a mystification about facts and therefore a language that shares all the delusions of the symbol about an organic connection between itself and reality, the representation of experience and experience (188). History, like allegory, implies a past, but hardly a pure, unreachable anteriority. It is rather a past from which language borrows an unwarranted stability, a guarantee of its own significance.

But this is too obvious to be the crucial point at play here. What de Man also ironizes is what one might aptly call the allegorization of the question of allegory in part 1 of the essay—insofar as that spreading out in time was used to reach a satisfying historical conclusion. In question is not only the coherence of the historical picture but the implicit promise of moving away from the error of symbol to arrive at a coherence of a higher aletheic order. For while insisting on a regression in critical insight as conventional allegory gave way to symbol, de Man also speaks in that section of poetic figures such as Hölderlin, Wordsworth, and Rousseau, who were at the same time producing a different sort of allegorical text.

Nor is it simply a matter of a blindness in de Man's writing that a later moment of insight is able to set straight. His text performs in this what it is unable to avoid. If we look to his reading of Wordsworth's "A slumber did my spirit seal," the strange temporality of the allegorical text becomes more comprehensible.[13] As in Rousseau's Meillerie episode, there are "two stages of consciousness, one belonging to the past and mystified, the other to the *now* of the poem." "The stance of the speaker," de Man tells us, "who exists in the 'now,' is that of a subject whose insight is no longer in doubt and who is no longer vulnerable to irony. It could be called, if one so wished, a stance of wisdom" (224). But wishing does not make it so. For the temptation exists to misunderstand the nature of that wisdom, as though it might belong to an undivided self writing within the temporality of actual experience. Yet "the 'now' of the poem is not an actual now, but the ideal 'now,' the duration of an acquired wisdom."[14] It is never open to a unified subject to overcome the state of error, to put it behind him or her in a moment of transcendent understanding: "The fundamental structure of allegory reappears here in the tendency of the language toward narrative, the spreading out along the axis of an imaginary time in order to give duration to what is, in fact, simultaneous within the subject" (225).

If allegory can exist only within an ideal time and engenders a "duration as the illusion of a continuity that it knows to be illusionary" (226), if it is, therefore, never open to the individual to get beyond the moment of error, it is also never possible to avoid the attempt. Allegory is totally demystified as long as it remains within its language, but the writer is once again totally subject to renewed blindness as soon as he or she leaves that language for the empirical world, say, for the rhetoric of literary criticism. For the critical essay may recognize "inauthenticity but can never overcome it" (222). "To know inauthenticity is not the same as to be authentic [language]" (214).

Side by side with the satisfying history that culminates in such allegorical writers as Rousseau, there is, then, also that of de Man rewriting literary history to recognize and deconstruct a former state of error. The moment that "The Rhetoric of Temporality" turns its ironical or allegorical structures into a desire for stable knowledge, it performs its necessary "interplay with mystified forms of language . . . which it is not in . . . [its] power to eradicate" (226).[15]

Thus, in de Man's essay we can repeatedly trace a movement from the recognition of a former state of inauthenticity to the fundamentally symbolic gesture of turning this negative insight into positive knowledge of various sorts,[16] or, at least, a vacillation between the two. When de Man describes the relationship between allegorical and symbolic language in *La Nouvelle Héloïse*, for example, we read the following:

> The tension arises . . . between the allegorical language of a scene such as Julie's Elysium and the symbolic language of passages such as the Meillerie episode. The moral contrast between these two worlds epitomizes the dramatic conflict of the novel. This conflict is ultimately resolved in the triumph of a controlled and lucid renunciation of the values associated with a cult of the moment, and this renunciation establishes the priority of an allegorical over a symbolic diction. The novel could not exist without the simultaneous presence of both metaphorical modes, nor could it reach its conclusion without the implied choice in favor of allegory over symbol. (204)

De Man speaks in terms of "tension," "contrast," and "conflict." There is a "triumph," but it is the triumph of the emptying gesture of renunciation. There is a "priority of an allegorical over a symbolic diction," but this asserts itself as an "*implied* choice" (emphasis mine) in a novel that renounces, but never fails to insist on and employ, symbolic diction.

As de Man continues to describe the tension between symbol and allegory, he reminds his reader once again of a constitutive distance within allegory.

> Whereas the symbol postulates the possibility of an identity or identification, allegory designates primarily a distance in relation to its own origin, and, renouncing the nostalgia and the desire to coincide, it establishes its language in the void of this temporal difference. In so doing, it prevents the self from an illusory identification with the non-self, which is now fully, though painfully, recognized as a non-self. It is this painful knowledge that we perceive at the moments when early romantic literature finds its true voice. (207).

But if the knowledge gained in the language of allegory is painful, the tale about that knowledge often appears remarkably satisfying. Thus, in the context of his own critical progress, de Man can speak of changing the historical and philosophical pattern such that symbolic diction becomes a mere negative moment, a temptation to be overcome (204–5). Writing from the perspective of his own conclusion, he can speak in the temporal framework of a "now" in which symbolic language "no longer" plays a role. He employs a rhetoric in which truth and lucidity are clearly distinguishable from regressive self-mystification:

> We are led, in conclusion, to a historical scheme that differs entirely from the customary picture. The dialectical relationship between subject and object is no longer the central statement of romantic thought, but this dialectic is now located entirely in the temporal relationships that exist within a system of allegorical signs. It becomes a conflict between a conception of the self seen in its authentically temporal predicament and a defensive strategy that tries to hide from this negative self-knowledge. On the level of language the asserted superiority of the symbol over allegory, so frequent during the nineteenth century, is one of the forms taken by this tenacious self-mystification. Wide areas of European literature . . . appear as regressive with regard to the truths that come to light in the last quarter of the eighteenth century. (208).

This is the voice of a self that has escaped its temporal predicament, the void of temporal distance, caught, as it appears to be, in a defensive strategy that hides from negative self-knowledge. For it is in such a rhetoric that claims to dispense with the symbolic— where time as rupture has given way to the "now" of conclusions, where other texts are read for a gain in knowledge rather than for a genuine recognition of their allegoricity—that de Man's diction presents itself at its most "symbolic."

This is why, as de Man's irony becomes increasingly conscious of itself, it demonstrates the impossibility of being historical. It rejects its own temporal movement of correcting error to produce (illusory) wisdom and recognizes it or rather performs it as a problem that exists within the rhetoric of temporality. In speaking of other critics and other theories of language, de Man necessarily spreads out along the axis of imaginary time what is, in fact, simultaneous within his text. This is what the passage I called something of a turning point in the essay ironizes (211, cited on pp. 153–54 above), for that passage goes on to say:

> In speaking of irony we are dealing not with the history of an error but with a problem that exists within the self. . . . [A] great deal of assistance can be gained from existing texts on irony. Curiously enough, it seems to be only in describing a mode of language which does not mean what it says that one can actually say what one means. (211)

If de Man's text means what it does not and cannot say, this is partly because his ironization of allegory as we have seen it to take place is also, necessarily, an allegorization of sorts. For those vertiginous, ironical lines just cited might, ironically enough, be read as yet another attempt to move temporally from error to wisdom, this time from the error of the allegory[17] that makes up part 1 of the essay to the wisdom of irony. That is, we might read that ironization of allegory (ironized for its spreading out in time of what is actually simultaneous, for its conversion of allegorical duration into empirical knowledge, a conversion of time as distance into time as progress) we might read that ironization of allegory as itself an allegorization that privileges irony, one that must, in turn, be viewed ironically. Thus the movement of the literary text is restated and repeated on an increasingly conscious level by the critical reading that must, no less than irony, fail to overcome the inauthenticity of its own language. Things can never be left to rest at any point that one reaches, for the whole process takes place at an unsettling speed. One begins to experience a "dizziness to the point of madness" (215), a dizziness, it would seem, that is unavoidable. For the "dialectical play between the two modes, as well as their common interplay with mystified forms of language . . . make up," de Man tells us, "what is called literary history" (226).[18]

They make up what is called literary history: that is to say, they are not simply forces at a particular moment of our historical past. De Man may speak of allegory coming into its own "at *the very* [historical] *moment*" when symbolic modes were in full strength and go on to say, "*Around the same time* that the tension between symbol and allegory finds expression in the works and the theoretical speculations of the early romantics, the problem of irony also receives more and more self-conscious attention" (190, 208; emphasis mine). But whatever evidence its "content" may offer to the contrary, however much the subject in question seems to be a particular moment in time,[19] the play of allegory, symbol, and irony constitutes not only the historical story one tells about romantic literature, but also both literature in general and its theoretical (self-) commentary.

The kind of performance we have seen to take place in "The Rhetoric of Temporality" constitutes the movement of the Rousseau essays in *Allegories of Reading*. Time is an illusion created out of a series of repetitive reversals, for before the reversals can be recognized as such, they seem to mark the progress of a gain in knowledge, however negative. This is the allegorical thrust of the text, which is inevitably consumed by an irony that places the metaphor of time in perspective. That is to say, it collapses it, for de Man speaks of irony as "two irreconcilable . . . beings" "juxtaposed within the same moment" (226). Irony and allegory endlessly replace one another: this trajectory can be read as a text engendering other, critical texts or as a text reading itself, as a gain in critical knowledge or as an irresolvable split and endless vacillation.

After this long digression, which was, of necessity, both a definition and transgression of de Man's text, we might return to the original crises, that of saying not only what de Man means, but also what we mean when we say de Man. No doubt this essay, I confess, in de Man's own words, produces "a darkness more redoubtable than . . . [any] error . . . [it might] dispel" ("Allegory," 217). To be sure this is no excuse.[20] But whatever I may have done in reading his text, if the reader will forgive the rhetorical question,[21] would it not still be possible to assert that it is "Ah! encore de Man"?

7

The Unimaginable Touch of Time: Wordsworth's "Tintern Abbey," Crossing the Alps, and "Intimations of Immortality"

How to return again to "Tintern Abbey," a text we seem to know so well, or at least come back to so often that it has a place like almost no other text of Wordsworth in our literary memory: How does one go back to that spot, of place and time, so often revisited since its writing in 1798 by every major commentator on Wordsworth? What can one possibly expect to hear and see there that hasn't been remarked before? Moreover, when one visits the banks of the Wye as critic, isn't one all too likely to do so much in the manner of the young Wordsworth and his friend Robert Jones as they traipsed through the Alps in the summer of 1790 like "keen hunters in a chase . . . / Eager as birds of prey" (1850 *Prelude* VI, 497–98)?[1] Isn't the entire enterprise of criticism all too often, perhaps ineluctably, a seeking for the trophies and spoils that we fancy are to be found in the progress through another's verse? Even when we cull what may be flowers of dejection, it is, after all, with the promise of the abundant recompense of our own and universal reason.

159

Let me ask you, then, to accompany me first on a variegated journey through the images and forms of "Lines Composed a Few Miles above Tintern Abbey," and on the way to tread the terrain of the Immortality Ode and the crossing of the Alps in book VI of *The Prelude*. It will be a march of great speed, I admit, but one in which we can trace trajectories that mark a distancing from former modes of understanding. One could argue for similar trajectories elsewhere in Wordsworth's poetry, in "Lucy Gray," for example, "To a Highland Girl," "A Slumber Did My Spirit Seal," or "The Boy of Winander."

"Tintern Abbey" tells not only of our, but first and foremost, of course, of Wordsworth's return to the banks of the Wye in 1798. The first paragraph is a description of place and would seem to speak of the poet's experience as one of rather immediate sense perception since verbs of hearing and seeing govern and overwhelm most of the lines.

> Five years have past; five summers, with the length
> Of five long winters! and again I hear
> These waters, rolling from their mountain-springs
> With a soft inland murmur.—Once again
> Do I behold these steep and lofty cliffs,
> That on a wild secluded scene impress
> Thoughts of more deep seclusion; and connect
> The landscape with the quiet of the sky.
> The day is come when I again repose
> Here, under this dark sycamore, and view
> These plots of cottage-ground, these orchard-tufts,
> Which at this season, with their unripe fruits,
> Are clad in one green hue, and lose themselves
> 'Mid groves and copses. Once again I see
> These hedge-rows, hardly hedge-rows, little lines
> Of sportive wood run wild: these pastoral farms,
> Green to the very door. . . .
> (TA 1–17)[2]

Yet this perspective of immediate description is made considerably more complicated in that the place of which Wordsworth speaks is itself a space in which the world of human order and the wildness of nature meet, and one in which the border between the two has lost its clarity. On this "wild secluded scene" the cliffs "impress / Thoughts of more deep seclusion," paradoxically either anthropomorphizing the scene by endowing it with the capability of thought or introducing the human observer at the very moment of insisting on his or her exclusion. The hedgerows, would-be outlines of demarcation between nature and cultivated land, that which civilization establishes to separate the two, have become "sportive wood run wild":[3] the plots of cottage ground and the orchards lose themselves in groves and copses. Wordsworth tells of his own, his human encounter with the landscape, and the scene before him, it would seem, repeats the same tale; for this is a landscape in which man's dwelling and nature meet. What Wordsworth speaks of, despite the claims of so many readers to his pantheism,[4] then, is no simple encounter with nature,[5] but rather, an encounter with a landscape that in turn thematizes the uncertainty of both the human and the natural and of what it means when they meet.

Our predicament in knowing just how to read these lines is redoubled when one reconsiders the phrases in which that experience of nature, ostensibly through the senses, is related: "and again I hear" (2), "Once again / Do I behold" (4–5), "I again repose . . . and view" (9–10), "Once again I see" (14). As one readily senses, the hearing and seeing is repeatedly coupled with the reminder that it is taking place "*again.*" This is no static repose in nature (despite lines 9–10) but a re-pose, the gesture of positing the once again.[6] What Wordsworth tells of is less any sensory experience of the natural landscape than a mediation through the memory of a former experience with woods, cliffs, and pastoral landscape that are themselves already the complex locus of such uncertain encounters.[7] Perhaps this explains the indistinctness verging on extinguishment of the voice Wordsworth hears, the murmur of the mountain springs (4), the quiet of the sky (8).

And perhaps it is only mildly surprising, then, that Wordsworth closes the paragraph with a double reading of an ambiguous sign.

> and wreaths of smoke
> Sent up, in silence, from among the trees!
> With some uncertain notice, as might seem
> Of vagrant dwellers in the houseless woods,
> Or of some Hermit's cave, where by his fire
> The Hermit sits alone.
>
> (TA 17–22)

It is, after all, a reflection on how to understand the scenes we have just read, both a reflection on the dilemma of understanding per se and on the uncertain figure of man's position with respect to nature. It is an interpretive moment to which the close of the poem will return us.

Yet to be precise, the poem does not quite begin with the description of which I have spoken, for it is prefaced by the plaintive lines "Five years have past; five summers, with the length / Of five long winters!"—lines that suggest, perhaps, a nostalgia for a return to that past, certainly a sense of loss. It opens, then, with the temporal lapse between Wordsworth's two visits, with the pastness of the first with respect to the second, and this tells us both much about the passage that follows and much about the poem's final lines, where another temporal rupture, a very different one, is proposed.

The second paragraph speaks of the intervening years between his two visits. The beauteous forms of the Wye did not desert the poet but, rather, lifted him from the weariness of the world.[8] Wordsworth describes this as a threefold debt.

> These beauteous forms,
> Through a long absence, have not been to me
> As is a landscape to a blind man's eye:
> But oft, in lonely rooms, and 'mid the din
> Of towns and cities, I have owed to them
> In hours of weariness, sensations sweet,
> Felt in the blood, and felt along the heart;
> And passing even into my purer mind,
> With tranquil restoration:—feelings too
> Of unremembered pleasure: such, perhaps,
> As have no slight or trivial influence
> On that best portion of a good man's life,
> His little, nameless, unremembered, acts
> Of kindness and of love. Nor less, I trust,
> To them I may have owed another gift,
> Of aspect more sublime . . .
>   (TA 22–37)

One can trace a progressive etherealization both within each description and as Wordsworth moves from each to the next. He first speaks of "*sensations* sweet" that move from the blood to the heart to the "purer mind" and bring "tranquil restoration" from the din of the cities; then of "*feelings*" associated with categories of moral rectitude (30–35),[9] and finally of that "serene and blessed mood" (TA, 41) that doubles the first movement (from blood to heart to purer mind) in its pattern of intensification through and beyond the corporeal and on to the "living soul."[10]

> that blessed mood,
> In which the burthen of the mystery,
> In which the heavy and the weary weight
> Of all this unintelligible world,
> Is lightened:—that serene and blessed mood,
> In which the affections gently lead us on,—
> Until, the breath of this corporeal frame
> And even the motion of our human blood
> Almost suspended, we are laid asleep
> In body, and become a living soul:
> While with an eye made quiet by the power
> Of harmony, and the deep power of joy,
> We see into the life of things.
>
> (TA 37–49)

Yet the passage that follows tells us that we, like Wordsworth, may have been led on (TA 42), however gently, that the promise of extraordinary insight, an eye, given the power of harmony, that can "see into the life of things," is "but a vain belief."

> If this
> Be but a vain belief, yet, oh! how oft—
> In darkness and amid the many shapes
> Of joyless daylight; when the fretful stir
> Unprofitable, and the fever of the world,
> Have hung upon the beatings of my heart—
> How oft, in spirit, have I turned to thee,
> O sylvan Wye! thou wanderer thro' the woods,
> How often has my spirit turned to thee!
>
> (TA 49–57)

Wordsworth may well have turned to the Wye to escape "the fretful stir" and "fever of the world," but even that most sublime and blessed mood only "lightened" (TA 41) the burden of the world's unintelligibility, "the burthen of the mystery" (TA 38), and never truly lifted its "weary weight" (TA 39).

Here in "Tintern Abbey"—with a sense of blessed progress, through repetition and intensification—we shift, however naively it may prove, from a world of sensation to one of ethereal serenity. "Ode: Intimations of Immortality," which in its epigraph is also a

celebration of continuity, tells in its middle paragraphs (V–VIII) of
the reverse, of a morally tainted descent into sensation from the
ethereal past of childhood.[11] But while apparently caught up in
that much misread myth of childhood, it raises once again the question of "weight" in relation to philosophical insight.

Although the stanza before is heavily laden with unmistakable
ironies, although it portrays the child's bliss as endless theatrical
scenes of rehearsed imitation,[12] the eighth stanza of the Immortality Ode abruptly seems to return to the vision of the child close to
heaven's glory:[13]

> Thou, whose exterior semblance doth belie
>   Thy Soul's immensity;
> Thou best Philosopher, who yet dost keep
> Thy heritage, thou Eye among the blind,
> That, deaf and silent, read'st the eternal deep,
> Haunted for ever by the eternal mind,—
>   Mighty Prophet! Seer blest!
>   On whom those truths do rest,
> Which we are toiling all our lives to find,
> In darkness lost, the darkness of the grave.
>   (IO 109–18)

In the second paragraph of "Tintern Abbey," just as Wordsworth
is about to vaunt the sight that lets him see into the life of things,
he speaks of "beauteous forms" that have not been to him "As is a
landscape to a blind man's eye." The child of the Immortality Ode
is also celebrated as a "Seer blest," an "Eye among the blind" in a
passage that resonates remarkably with echoes of the similar moment in "Tintern Abbey"—blindness, seeing, eye, soul, blessedness.

Yet, in one as in the other, the figure of weight fails to carry with
it the promised supernatural vision. In "Tintern Abbey" the weight
of unintelligibility, despite an overall exuberance that almost belies
the fact, is merely "lightened" rather than lifted and therefore stays
as reminder of the vanity of such beliefs in blessed insight. In the
Immortality Ode there are other impediments that also cannot be
put by:

> Thou, over whom thy Immortality
> Broods like the Day, a Master o'er a Slave,
> A Presence which is not to be put by;

Thou little Child, yet glorious in the might
Of heaven-born freedom on thy being's height,
Why with such earnest pains dost thou provoke
The years to bring the inevitable yoke,
Thus blindly with thy blessedness at strife?
Full soon thy Soul shall have her earthly freight,
And custom lie upon thee with a weight,
Heavy as frost, and deep almost as life!
                                    (IO 119–29)

The paragraph closes with the threat of earthly freight and custom, and yet Immortality looms over the boy in a figure that menaces with at least as oppressive a weight.[14] The "glory" that since stanza V has ostensibly marked the distinction between childhood and manhood, Immortality, is a "Presence" that cannot be lifted, brooding over the boy like a master over a slave. "Heaven-born freedom," despite the exterior semblance of the phrase, is, paradoxically, "*on* [his] being's height." And the openly announced threat of human custom finally appears with a lightness strikingly in contrast with these ominous blessings, for custom lies upon the child with the astonishing insubstantiality of frost.

As in "Tintern Abbey," the voice of moral glory, with all its rhetorical gravity, obscures the disorientations brought about by the figure of weight. In both texts the passages take place in the name of profound sight and understanding, "see[ing] into the life of things," an "Eye" (TA 49; IO 111) granted astonishing "power" (TA 47), a "Seer blest"(IO 115). Yet in both texts it is precisely in those moments that the pathos is so at odds with the disturbing logic of the actual phrasing that the text threatens to blind the reader to the significance of what actually takes place.

Perhaps what follows, then—the casting off of the "heaven-born freedom" (IO 123) and of the "Delight and liberty" (IO 137) that prove so burdensome—goes without saying.

O joy! that in our embers
Is something that doth live,
That nature yet remembers
What was so fugitive!
The thought of our past years in me doth breed
Perpetual benediction: not indeed
For that which is most worthy to be blest;
Delight and liberty, the simple creed

Of Childhood, whether busy or at rest,
With new-fledged hope still fluttering in his breast: —
Not for these I raise
The song of thanks and praise.

(IO 130–41)

In this difficult section Wordsworth relinquishes his allegiance to a simple creed of childhood and rethinks remembrance or recollection in its relation to immortality, thus questioning the three critical terms of the poem's cumbersome title: "Ode: Intimations of *Immortality* from *Recollection* of Early *Childhood*." The vision of the child "trailing clouds of glory" (IO 64) whether busy, as in stanza VII, or at rest, as in VIII, is no longer the object of the poet's celebration.

Still, nature is said to "remember,"[15] and it is the thought of past years that breeds benediction. Yet what nature recollects is less the former presences of an earlier time that one might fix as "childhood" than the past as that which "was so fugitive," somewhat like Yeats, who will later write, "Man is in love and loves what vanishes" ("Nineteen-hundred-nineteen").

Not for these I raise
The song of thanks and praise;
But for those obstinate questionings
Of sense and outward things,
Fallings from us, vanishings.

(IO 140–44)

Wordsworth sings in praise of questioning sense and the outward experience of the world. This is a singing, then, that distances itself from the close of stanza III and the opening of IV (IO 25–50), where an overflowing and almost raucous joy of hearing, seeing, and feeling is bound to the over-full sensual bliss of nature's spring and that simple creed of childhood ("Child," "boy," "Babe"). Wordsworth writes a poetry now which is, rather, a language of doubt— that doubt with which stanza IV, in any case, inevitably it seems, already culminates: "Whither is fled the visionary gleam? / Where is it now, the glory and the dream?" (IO 56–57). The song lauds a mode of language that questions and thereby performs "Fallings from us, vanishings" (IO 144). This was almost what the opening lines of the ode were about:

There was a time when meadow, grove, and stream,
The earth, and every common sight,

> To me did seem
> Apparelled in celestial light,
> The glory and the freshness of a dream.
> It is not now as it hath been of yore; —
> Turn wheresoe'er I may,
> By night or day,
> The things which I have seen I now can see no more.
>
> .   .   .   .
>
> But yet I know, where'er I go,
> That there hath past away a glory from the earth.
> (IO 1–9, 17–18)

The first stanzas announce fallings and vanishings, yet they do so with a sense of loss. This is mitigated only by a progression to knowledge—"But yet I know"—in passing from the first to the second stanzas, a knowledge which the later lines choose to unsay.

> But for those obstinate questionings
> Of sense and outward things,
> Fallings from us, vanishings;
> Blank misgivings of a Creature
> Moving about in worlds not realised,
> High instincts before which our mortal Nature
> *Did* tremble like a guilty Thing surprised.
> (IO 142–48; emphasis mine)

The opening lines of the ode may speak of that which has disappeared but only as full misgivings for a past, as a former experience of guilt and of the Fall.

Yet the mood in stanza IX is one of joy (IO 130), for those fallings and vanishings before which the poet once mistakenly "Did tremble like a guilty Thing surprised" are now "High instincts." It is for these obstinate questionings that Wordsworth raises his song and for what he also calls both "first affections" and "shadowy recollections."

> But for those obstinate questionings
> Of sense and outward things,
> Fallings from us, vanishings;
>
> .   .   .   .
>
> But for those first affections,
> Those shadowy recollections,

> Which, be they what they may,
> Are yet the fountain light of all our day,
> Are yet a master light of all our seeing;
> Uphold us, cherish, and have the power to make
> Our noisy years seem moments in the being
> Of the eternal Silence; truths that wake,
> To perish never.
>
> (IO 142–57)

Although they are unlikely enough terms to be in apposition, "those first affections" and "shadowy recollections" are another way of speaking of "those obstinate questionings." Affection and recollection, then, are less a gathering back of the past here than a questioning of outward things, a making vanish. Thus, in an earlier version those first affections and recollection "Throw off from us, or mitigate, the spell / Of that strong frame of sense in which we dwell."[16] We see in stanzas I–VIII that they are not the desire for being given or regiven nature, heaven, childhood, but rather a blank mis-giving, a moving about in such worlds recognized as never having been realized and never realizable.[17] They are the strange master light of our seeing, for, paradoxically, we see by means of the shadowy, which has the power to make things seem other than they are ("shadowy recollections / Which . . . have the power to make / Our noisy years seem . . ."). The noisy years of conventional childhood, in which the "little Actor cons" one part after another, holding forth in dialogues that imitate the adult world, (stanza VII) can be made to appear in the aura of a "mighty Prophet" and "best Philosopher" as moments in the "being / Of the eternal Silence" (IO 155–56)—the eternal and immortal that prove so questionable in stanza IX.

> Hence in a season of calm weather
> Though inland far we be,
> Our souls have sight of that immortal sea
> Which brought us hither,
> Can in a moment travel thither,
> And see the Children sport upon the shore,
> And hear the mighty waters rolling evermore.
>
> (IO 162–68)

Recollection as the power, not to regain, but to make vanish, can transform and turn the noisy years into an emblem of immortal truths. Thus, "in a season of calm weather," in those "years that bring the philosophic mind" (187), however far removed we may be from the locus of any "immortal sea," "*in thought*" (IO 172; emphasis mine)[18] we can "have sight" (164) of that "vision splendid" (74). This is not as in stanza VIII, where the pathos of sight and immortality blurs syntax and diction: but it is here rather an act of creating the eternal as illusory, making both the noisy years and the eternal silence fall away from us, as the obstinate questioning which imagination is.

It would not then be that the child is father of the man, as the famous epigraph suggests:

> The child is Father of the Man;
> And I could wish my days to be
> Bound each to each by natural piety.

We might venture to say, rather, that the father is father of the child, a banal and commonsensical proposition if father and child are two different individuals but intriguingly disquieting in the master light of the epigraph. The epigraph compels one to reread the usually distinct nouns, father and child, as uniting the figures in a continuity of subject as well as temporal development. They are understandable, the apparent paradox dissolves, only insofar as the child and father are bound each to each, insofar as the child grows into the (selfsame) man. Yet what stanza IX speaks of is no simple creed of childhood innocence as the origin (that "which brought us hither") of a mature, philosophic "eye / That hath kept watch o'er man's [im]mortality" (IO 198–99). In light of these lines, father and child remain, apparently, the same, but the one creates other, not in a gesture of a growth, but in a leap of the father's imagination to a shore of childhood that is made to vanish, declared never to have existed ("shadowy recollections, / Which . . . have power to make / Our noisy years seem moments in the being / Of the eternal Silence. . . . Hence . . . / Our Souls have sight of that immortal sea"). In a sense the philosophic mind is what book VI of *The Prelude* will call a "fatherless vapour," a fatherless father who demystifies his own origins. "The philosophic mind" (IO 187) performs a radically redefined act of recollection as obstinate questionings of outward reality, as the causing to fall away from us rather than bringing back of a fictional point of departure. This is a recollection that transforms the past into that which it never was, so that we can mark the vast distance of our inland locus to an immortal sea of childhood as ostensible origin.

In the "Intimations Ode" Wordsworth shifts from an illusory triumph over blindness in the semblance of the child's prophetic and philosophical sight, to the obstinate questionings that redefine recollection. In "Tintern Abbey," where we last left it, there is a similar shift. Rather than pure intelligibility, rather than seeing "into the life of things" (TA 49), Wordsworth (in the fourth paragraph) comes to accept "perplexity" (TA 60), "recognitions" that are both "dim and faint" (TA 59), the "gleams of half-extinguished thought" (TA 58).

> And now, with gleams of half-extinguished thought,
> With many recognitions dim and faint,
> And somewhat of a sad perplexity,
> The picture of the mind revives again.
>
> (TA 58–61)

Indeed the key terms are "thought" and "thinking," terms that appear eight times in the fourth paragraph though not at all in the second and third, for "thought" is anything but the sublime intelligibility of the second paragraph.

What Wordsworth leaves behind, then, in this progress through his verse is a series of vain beliefs. He marks these in an autobiographical tale of the different stages of his life, boyhood, 1793, 1798.[19] Tellingly enough, he does not present his story chronologically, but the fourth paragraph gives half-extinguished glimpses of his former state of mind.

> And so I dare to hope,
> Though changed, no doubt, from what I was when first
> I came among these hills; when like a roe
> I bounded o'er the mountains, by the sides
> Of the deep rivers, and the lonely streams,
> Wherever nature led: more like a man
> Flying from something that he dreads than one
> Who sought the thing he loved. For nature then
> (The coarser pleasures of my boyish days,
> And their glad animal movements all gone by)
> To me was all in all.—I cannot paint
> What then I was. The sounding cataract
> Haunted me like a passion: the tall rock,
> The mountain, and the deep and gloomy wood,

Their colours and their forms, were then to me
An appetite; a feeling and a love,
That had no need of a remoter charm,
By thought supplied, nor any interest
Unborrowed from the eye.

                                        (TA 65–83)

In his "boyish days" Wordsworth lived the "coarser pleasures" of "animal movements," but by 1793, although he still compares himself to a roe (TA 67), the distance between himself and nature was already marked.[20] The natural scene came to him as "appetite," as "feeling," and as a "love" which had no "interest / Unborrowed from the eye," no interest unborrowed from the senses. He followed wherever nature led (TA 70), and yet, even though nature "was all in all" to him, this was more like flying from something dreaded than seeking something loved. And now, in 1798, Wordsworth's interest is no longer that of "thoughtless youth." Consequently, his present enterprise cannot be to "paint / What then I was," for in giving up those interests borrowed from the eye, as in the Immortality Ode, he also gives up an aesthetics that might claim to relive, represent, or recuperate a past. Moreover, thought replaces, as we have seen, not only the correlative aesthetics of his 1793 state of mind, but also those of the intervening years, which insisted on a vain belief in aberrant forms of recollection, in memory that offered feelings of pleasure as solace for world weariness, and a delusive sense of pure intelligibility.

What Wordsworth chooses, or what seems to choose him, is another kind of picture, one that brings with it the burden of mystery, of perplexity, and which he calls "the picture of the mind" (TA 61). The opening paragraph, as we saw, was about this if about nothing else,[21] less about the banks of the Wye than about the again-ness of his return, a picture of Wordsworth contemplating himself contemplate the scene, a landscape which is itself already a reflection on the relation between the human and the natural. The time of "dizzy raptures" (TA 85) is past (83), replaced by a "presence that disturbs" (94), one that is no longer sensation, feeling, or the intelligibility of sublime insight (in paragraph III):

                    —That time is past,
And all its aching joys are now no more,
And all its dizzy raptures. Not for this
Faint I, nor mourn nor murmur; other gifts

Have followed; for such loss, I would believe,
Abundant recompense. For I have learned
To look on nature, not as in the hour
Of thoughtless youth; but hearing oftentimes
The still, sad music of humanity,
Nor harsh nor grating, though of ample power
To chasten and subdue. And I have felt
A presence that disturbs me with the joy
Of elevated thoughts; a sense sublime
Of something far more deeply interfused,
Whose dwelling is the light of setting suns,
And the round ocean and the living air,
And the blue sky, and in the mind of man:
A motion and a spirit, that impels
All thinking things, all objects of all thought,
And rolls through all things.
                              (TA 83–102)

What Wordsworth has the sense (TA 95) of, however perplexing, is
"A motion and a spirit, that impels / All thinking things, all objects
of all thought," the sense of the driving force that links thinker and
the object of thought. This is not an abandoning of the "world / Of
eye, and ear" (TA 106) so much as its inevitable redefinition, a redefinition that takes place, in another form, also in the last stanza
of the Immortality Ode. Wordsworth tells us that he has had to un-
learn (TA 88–92) his earlier conceptions of the relationship between language and that of which it speaks. For the natural world
is no longer the object of appetite and passion. Perhaps it never
was—never the object, then, of simple perception: Wordsworth
recognizes nature as bound to what he calls "the language of the
sense" (TA 108), a sense which is language to begin with and which
creates its object no less than perceives it.[22]

Let us remember why Wordsworth now turns to Dorothy. The
fourth paragraph might well have ended "Tintern Abbey," and
have ended it with a sense of utter stability.

              well pleased to recognise
In nature and the language of the sense
The anchor of my purest thoughts, the nurse,
The guide, the guardian of my heart, and soul
Of all my moral being.
                              (TA 107–11)

The earlier lines that in thinking the relation of mind and object spoke of a presence that disturbs (TA 94), of interfusion (TA 96), of motion (TA 100), have given way to the fixity of anchor, guide,[23] and guardian, to the certainty and purity of soul and of morality. The implicit movement of differential progression from boyhood days to 1793 to 1798 that has defined the poet's story dissolves before the teleological superlative: purest thoughts.[24]

And yet the fifth paragraph does not repose there but introduces, however covertly, the imbalance of "Nor perchance," a perchance that casts the poet back to the beginning just when he had apparently achieved his end. It ponders an alternate path to what Wordsworth has called thought, a path that will lead elsewhere.

> Nor perchance,
> If I were not thus taught, should I the more
> Suffer my genial spirits to decay.
> (TA 111–13)

If Wordsworth had not come to the contemplation of thought through a hermetic turning inward, a reflection on his own past in relation to nature and on the nature of such reflection, he could turn instead to his sister Dorothy, his fellow dweller in the houseless wood. There, it would seem, by regarding Dorothy as an image of a former self, he might return to the shores of childhood and avoid the spiritual decay that suddenly seems to threaten. He might stay time in its course or even reverse it, recapture a former self in what, after all, is a roundabout way of painting "what then [he] was," of recuperative autobiography, another version of the anchor and stability of the previous lines. All of this takes place under the aegis of loving exhortation, lending a certain power to Wordsworth's voice in which he serves as guide to Dorothy's moral being.

Wordsworth turns to his sister Dorothy with lines that one cannot but feel to be an act of kindness and love in which he teaches her to see into her future life. One is nevertheless puzzled by the discrepancy between a touching insistence on the friendship between them—"thou my dearest Friend, / My dear, dear Friend" (TA 114–15), "My dear, dear Sister!" (TA 121)—and the progressive turn to the inward life of solitude that Wordsworth's exhortation calls for.

How to think this shift? We might return to that other vacillation, at the end of the first stanza, that should haunt us at this juncture. Wordsworth spoke of the uncertain interpretation of wreaths of smoke sent up from among the trees (17–22). He reads them, on the one hand, as the sign of "vagrant dwellers in the houseless woods," of the natural setting as a space where, paradoxically, its dwellers have a community in numbers and yet experience a deprivation, the dislocation of man from home.[25] But he also sees wreaths of smoke as sign, perhaps, of "some Hermit's cave, where by his fire / The Hermit sits alone," the trace of the abode of a figure who in choosing the deeper seclusion of the solitary life has willingly cast aside both the concept of a social dwelling-place and of a oneness with organic nature.

At the juncture between the fourth and fifth paragraphs, this ambiguity is doubly relevant. It reflects on our understanding of the new way in which the poet has "learned / To look on nature," and it also reflects on the way in which we are to understand the beautiful passage to come where the love between Dorothy and William in this address is at odds with its contents.

Moreover, what reader can fail to catch the added strangeness of juxtaposing those phrases of personal endearment with a metaphorical diction that transforms Dorothy into a text?

> thou my dearest Friend,
> My dear, dear Friend; and in thy voice I *catch*
> The *language* of my former heart, and *read*
> My former pleasures in the shooting lights
> Of thy wild eyes. Oh! yet a little while
> May I behold in thee what I was once,
> My dear, dear Sister!
> (TA 114–19; emphasis mine)

Wordsworth makes the prayer that he might behold in his sister "what [he] was once," but what he sees in her eyes is the text of his "former pleasures," what he beholds is "the language of [his] former heart," a recuperative autobiography that while dissolving the subjectivity of Dorothy also recuperates no-thing and no one.

Wordsworth does read, in a sense, what he was once, in that the lines that follow systematically echo the vocabulary earlier used in "Tintern Abbey," a self-citation rather than a return to a lost past. They speak of his state in 1793 (TA 123–25 echoing 67–70); they echo as well the years between his two visits to the Wye, both the promise of healing from "the dreary intercourse of daily life" (TA 126–34 echoing 25–35) and the sublime "sweet sounds and harmonies" that bring a "healing" from the burden of the mystery (TA 134–45 echoing 35–49).[26]

One can behold the figure of Dorothy here as a participant in the intersubjective relation marked by the passion of Wordsworth's voice: there to recapitulate in a predictably chronological manner the autobiographical tale that we had to piece together earlier in this very poem. She reiterates so well that William apparently forgets his figures of reading in a rhetoric of exhortation and prediction that seems destined to fulfillment.

The closing fourteen lines in no way forfeit the tone of passion; nevertheless, something unforeseen takes place. It is no longer a question of tension between regarding Dorothy as the object of his reading and the object of William's love or between a rhetoric of text and one of realization. In the same unsettling "Nor perchance" that opened the last paragraph, with almost the same lack of logical continuity registered by that repetition, Wordsworth goes on:

> Nor, perchance—
> If I should be where I no more can hear
> Thy voice, nor catch from thy wild eyes these gleams
> Of past existence—wilt thou then forget
> That on the banks of this delightful stream
> We stood together; and that I, so long
> A worshipper of Nature, hither came
> Unwearied in that service: rather say
> With warmer love—oh! with far deeper zeal
> Of holier love. Nor wilt thou then forget,
> That after many wanderings, many years
> Of absence, these steep woods and lofty cliffs,
> And this green pastoral landscape, were to me
> More dear, both for themselves and for thy sake!
> (TA 146–59)

Are these lines simply a hedge against decay and mortality: does Wordsworth call on Dorothy because "his salvation, as man and poet, is dependent upon the renovation he celebrates," as one critic has put it?[27] Is the "utilization of memory" a "lie against time"?[28]

Wordsworth posits his own death. The poem opens with the lapse of five years and closes with the lapse of a whole lifetime.[29] The citation of Milton's *Samson Agonistes* in the opening lines of the paragraph already foreshadowed this. Wordsworth seemed determined at that junction not to "suffer [his] genial spirits to decay." The vaunted sight of the second paragraph ("Those beauteous forms, / Through a long absence, have not been to me / As is a

landscape to a blind man's eye") had been cast off, along with all
interest borrowed from the eye (paragraph 4). Yet no sooner does
Wordsworth turn to Dorothy than sight returns with a renewed
promise of power (114–19). But those lines of Wordsworth run
wild in their echoing of Milton, for Samson's dejection in feeling
his "genial spirits droop" is accompanied by no assertion of renewal
through the faculty of sight—rather, by the certainty not only of
his blindness but also of his coming death.

> All otherwise to me my thoughts portend, —
> That these dark orbs no more shall treat with light,
> Nor th' other light of life continue long,
> But yield to double darkness night at hand;
> So much I feel my genial spirits droop,
> My hopes all flat: Nature within me seems
> In all her functions weary of herself;
> My race of glory run, and race of shame,
> And I shall shortly be with them that rest.
> (*Samson Agonistes* 590–98)[30]

If the echo of Samson's voice implicitly posits Wordsworth's death
early in the paragraph, here in the last lines of the poem Wordsworth does so openly. These lines mark Wordsworth's radical displacement from that spot a few miles above Tintern Abbey where
the title implies (perhaps fictionally) that he composed the poem,[31]
a displacement from Dorothy in which there can now truly no
longer be an interest borrowed from the eye (TA 83) or ear ("If I
should be where I no more can hear / Thy voice, nor catch from
thy wild eyes these gleams / Of past existence" [TA 147–49]). It is a
displacement from his sister almost at the very moment when
Wordsworth's progressive narrative of Dorothy's future would have
had her coinciding with his present state, what might have been the
culmination in identity promised by "My dear, dear Friend," "My
dear, dear Sister."

It is a separation as well from the moment in time so carefully
specified in the extended title of the poem and from the possibility
of return also suggested by the title ("Lines Composed a Few Miles
above Tintern Abbey, on Revisiting the Banks of the Wye during a
Tour, July 13, 1798"). Wordsworth will no longer be able to perceive or reperceive the landscape, which will now indeed be to him
as to a blind man's eye (TA 24); nor will he be able to hear the language of his former heart nor read his pleasures even in his sister's

eyes (146–49, although a case for a certain kind of reading no longer based on perception could be made). He is no longer able to hear his own voice and behold his own past, much less see into the life of things as in the simulation of death at the end of paragraph 2.

Dorothy, only one year younger than William, is less the figure of his descendant and spiritual heir, as the earlier lines might suggest, than of his double:[32] where he remembered himself, it is now she who must remember, not, reflexively, herself, but him. Perhaps even "remember" is too active a term here, for whereas line 145 openly asks that Dorothy "remember me," the last lines are in the less forceful form of "Nor . . . wilt thou then forget" (146–49, 155). The Hermit of the cave (certainly not of the mansion for all lovely forms) will sit, after all, alone, not even present to himself, for in positing this rupture into the future, Wordsworth makes the present moment past: he makes it vanish and with it himself.[33] Dorothy is left simply as the possible agent of recollecting the past, but no longer with nostalgia or the will to recuperation (as in TA 119–20). Nor will there be promise of the continuity that a relation either to another or to one's own earlier self might seem to offer. Paradoxically, she is called upon not to forget ("Nor wilt thou then forget"), but in order to do so, in order to imagine her future, she must forget the same present she is to remember—in an act of obstinate questionings, of imagination that thinks William's death and her own aging by leaping over them.

In a sudden shift to the future, with a blank misgiving or loss of the present, we cannot choose but read a prefiguration of the imagination in book VI of *The Prelude*. There, the imagination arises in the course of a narrative that speaks of a gap in time and space in relation to a negative enlightenment. As in "Tintern Abbey," that lapse is preceded by a lengthy tale of error in which an economy of gain and of false sublimity operates. Wordsworth describes his journey crossing the Alps in Switzerland with Robert Jones in the summer of 1790. He prefaces the famous moment by mocking the young men's desire for spoils (comparing them to "keen hunters" and "eager . . . birds of prey" [VI, 496–97]), mocking as well the way they misread the book of Nature:

> Whate'er in this wide circuit we beheld,
> Or heard, was fitted to our unripe state
> Of intellect and heart. With such a book
> Before our eyes, we could not choose but read

> Lessons of genuine brotherhood, the plain
> And universal reason of mankind,
> The truths of young and old.
>
> *(Prelude* VI, 541–47)

Wordsworth openly derides reading nature reductively as an ideological text about "genuine brotherhood" or "the universal reason of mankind." He rejects the false aesthetics that misuses nature in a poetry of conventional, formal allegory, rejects their composed fictions of sorrow to yield pleasure. For Wordsworth is going to tell of or rather be overwhelmed by, if not another mode of sorrow, then by another mode of poetry.

As the passage continues, it is still a question of how to read the landscape.[34] Wordsworth and Jones, left by their guide, search the terrain for the Simplon Pass as the proper path to fulfill their expectations. What they seek and what they find is a track readily available to a reading, signs congruent with, and that willingly yield the available spoils of meaning. They also yearn for a trajectory that will flatter their "unripe state / Of intellect and heart," one that offers "Conspicuous invitation to ascend [the] lofty" (572–73) heights of the sublime setting:

> Along the Simplon's steep and rugged road,
> Following a band of muleteers, we reached
> A halting-place, where all together took
> Their noon-tide meal. Hastily rose our guide,
> Leaving us at the board; awhile we lingered
> Then paced the beaten downward way that led
> Right to a rough stream's edge, and there broke off;
> The only track now visible was one
> That from the torrent's further brink held forth
> Conspicuous invitation to ascend
> A lofty mountain. After brief delay
> Crossing the unbridged stream, that road we took,
> And clomb with eagerness, till anxious fears
> Intruded, for we failed to overtake
> Our comrades gone before. By fortunate chance,
> While every moment added doubt to doubt,
> A peasant met us, from whose mouth we learned
> That to the spot that had perplexed us first
> We must descend, and there should find the road,
> Which in the stony channel of the stream

Lay a few steps, and then along its banks;
And, that our future course, all plain to sight,
Was downwards, with the current of that stream.
Loth to believe what we so grieved to hear,
For still we had hopes that pointed to the clouds,
We questioned him again, and yet again;
But every word that from the peasant's lips
Came in reply, translated by our feelings,
Ended in this, — *that we had crossed the Alps.*
                              (*Prelude* VI, 563–591)

The pass itself is not marked by a visible guide, transparent signs whose readability is guaranteed; nor is it that which "point[s] to the clouds" (a loftiness and etherealization that Wordsworth ironizes), for the obvious way had been "broke[n] off," and was, rather, "downwards." It is a movement, then, marked with the perplexities ("to the spot which had perplexed us first / We must descend"), doubt, and sadness which Wordsworth, in "Tintern Abbey," associates with *thought*. And as in that earlier poem, the ultimate form taken by this crucial understanding has to be proposed across a gap in time. If Dorothy must in the future speak of the poem's present as having vanished, if she must, moreover, mark the difference between what will then be the past of 1798 and the visit of 1793 that preceded it, if it is only in this manner that a critical understanding can take place, so the crossing can only be understood at the double remove of a past tense, in a statement that needs to be translated, questioned again and again.[35]

But, having understood one has crossed the Alps, a crossing that takes place in a mountainous blank of consciousness and whose dim recognitions barely come across as translation,[36] one is all the more lost. Not only Wordsworth but also we, as readers, are destined to double the experience of Jones and Wordsworth, halted insofar as we may wish to follow the continuity of Wordsworth's story, the tale of a progressive path through the Alps. Here, and for very obvious reasons, since Wordsworth suddenly ceases to paint past events, in a formal break that recapitulates that of the two pilgrims, there is a rupture in the continuity of the text.[37] In order to close the gap in the chronological narrative of the outward path, one would have to skip the next twenty-five lines to where "the melancholy slackening that ensued / Upon those tidings by the peasant given / Was soon dislodged" (617–19). Twice told, then, are both the questionability of generating the present seamlessly out of the past, and that of painting in the present what came before. What rises up to thwart such enterprises are those famous and perplexing lines in which Wordsworth speaks of the imagination.

> Imagination—here the Power so called
> Through sad incompetence of human speech,
> That awful Power rose from the mind's abyss
> Like an unfathered vapour that enwraps,
> At once, some lonely traveller. I was lost;
> Halted without an effort to break through;
> But to my conscious soul I now can say—
> 'I recognize thy glory:' in such strength
> Of usurpation, when the light of sense
> Goes out, but with a flash that has revealed
> The invisible world, doth greatness make abode.
>   (VI, 592–602)

To be sure, earlier versions of these lines might have told of what rose before the poet's "mental eye," of his immediate reaction on having spoken with the peasant:

> Imagination at that moment rose
> Imagination, here that awful Power, in
> The awful Power, before my mental eye
> Before the retrospective song rose up
> Then suddenly depressed before me rose.[38]

In a passage which explicitly and with harsh self-irony rejects conspicuous reading (1850 *Prelude* VI, 541–47, 570–73), this return to an earlier version would reveal, retrospectively, the reader's wish to find and insert the missing biographical indication to close the rupture in the poem's readability. One turns to the palimpsests of manuscripts that haunt this moment in the *Prelude,* as well one might, as though a turn to the past might mend the break.

If the manuscript (cited above) seems to continue the narration of the encounter with the peasant, the 1805 version insists on something else.

> Imagination!—lifting up itself
> Before the eye and progress of my song
> Like an unfathered vapour, here that power,
> In all the might of its endowments, came

Athwart me. I was lost as in a cloud,
Halted without a struggle to break through.
(1805 *Prelude* VI, 525–30)

Robert A. Brinkley has lucidly marked this version as indicating an interruption in the writing taking place in 1804.[39] If nothing more were said, this would once again read the scene as a biographical chain of events. Imagination, even in the 1850 version, might well be that which comes athwart the song-as-progress and the song as fashioned by a controlling, retrospective eye.[40] Indeed, the suggestions both of progress and of a song necessarily endowed with eye seem to vanish in the 1850 version.

Yet why should Imagination be regarded either as an interruption in the course of a particular moment of writing or in a certain concept of writing, and why might it be described both as a general gap in consciousness (1850 *Prelude* VI, 592–98) and also as the particular gap in consciousness on crossing the Alps?

Crossing the Alps is a figure for the Imagination, a power which marks "the incompetence of human speech" in any simple gesture of naming. The failure of "conspicuous invitation" to mark the path and the difficulties in understanding the peasant suggest this even before (VI, 588–89). In "Tintern Abbey" the poet's desire to behold himself in Dorothy, to read and thereby recuperate himself in the lights of her eyes and to use language as exhortation directed towards a self-satisfying goal give way to "retrospective" song of another order, one that displaces both the present and future of the narrative subject. In *The Prelude* Wordsworth tells of giving up various modes of illusion that made him like a bird of prey and that made the landscape readable for personal spoils (readability through sense perception, delusory sublimity, control). What replaces these is the non-place of the Imagination taking its place only when the light of sense perception goes out.[41]

In the 1850 *Prelude* the power of the self with all its ideological ramifications, figured by the climbing of the "lofty mountain," gives way to the power of the abyss, an abyss understood, retrospectively, as the mind's abyss. The rising up of Imagination is that which brings about the fall, a fall from the heights of the Alps all the more precipitous because not literal. It is that which both marks the "incompetence of human speech" and renders the mind unnameable—or nameable only as the unnameable, as abyss, as the unfather. Imagination is like that which enwraps the lonely travellers as they cross the Alps, which halts them. It is that which ruptures conventional concepts of language and poetry while redefining them as a usurpation upon a living thought, soulless image, unfathered vapor, which were, before the crossing, regarded as disaster.

> That very day,
> From a bare ridge we also first beheld
> Unveiled the summit of Mont Blanc, and grieved
> To have a soulless image on the eye
> That had usurped upon a living thought
> That never more could be.
>
> (VI, 523–28)

Whatever can now be uttered, whatever recognition, whatever song of praise comes forth, it must speak once again of usurpation and the going out of the light of sense,[42] of making the present past or deferred to the future.[43] As in "Tintern Abbey," Imagination rises in the aura either of a lost past (that of crossing the Alps, that in which "that awful Power rose from the mind's abyss") or of a future in which what Rilke calls an "endlich noch Erreichtes" (what is finally attained), what Wordsworth calls prey, spoils, or trophies, is joyfully discounted.

> Our destiny, our being's heart and home,
> Is with infinitude, and only there;
> With hope it is, hope that can never die,
> Effort, and expectation, and desire,
> And something evermore about to be.
> Under such banners militant, the soul
> Seeks for no trophies, struggles for no spoils
> That may attest her prowess, blest in thoughts
> That are their own perfection and reward,
> Strong in herself and in beatitude
> That hides her, like the mighty flood of Nile
> Poured from his fount of Abyssinian clouds
> To fertilise the whole Egyptian plain.
>
> (VI, 604–16)

Something that one might call Imagination is also at stake in "Tintern Abbey." If, in reflecting on earlier phases of Wordsworth's life, paragraph 4, written in 1798, announces with some self-satisfaction "that time is past" (TA 83), the closing lines raise the stakes and make the present of 1798 past. The fifth paragraph recapitulates Wordsworth's life for the first time chronologically, and this gives a sense of continuity with a former self, with the object of Wordsworth's love, Dorothy, and also a sense of progress. It is not, however, with the soul, a guardian, an anchor, that this paragraph culminates (as did paragraph 4), but in a gesture of an imagined, radical recollection in the future that ironizes both concepts of teleological progress and of a naive recuperative eye that feign to connect one's childhood with the quiet of the future.

Dorothy's thoughts are transformed into what the Immortality Ode calls "obstinate questionings / Of sense and outward things / Fallings from us, vanishings." For "Intimations of Immortality" also gives up a mythological version of immediacy and connection,[44] the connection of "So was it, . . . so is it . . . so be it" (lines tellingly omitted from the ode's epigraph, where Wordsworth cites his own "My Heart Leaps Up" partially), to move toward "the philosophic mind." Dorothy's (unheard) voice will apparently repeat[45] the same tale that "Lines Composed a Few Miles above Tintern Abbey" now chooses to tell. What is to be not forgotten—if not precisely remembered—is the difference in the ways of regarding the landscape: that Wordsworth returned to the Wye no longer a simple worshipper of nature but rather with a *different,* a warmer love and deeper zeal, in which woods and cliffs are dear but not because they heal or lighten the burden of William and certainly not because they promise him the power to see into the life of things. They are more dear, not for *his* sake but "both for themselves and for [Dorothy's] sake." Dorothy has become a figure of the poetical voice in its complex relation to the landscape, a relation that conspicuously leaves William out of the present and future picture: it is for the sake of this leaving out that the landscape has become more dear. The self-satisfaction of "abundant recompense" (TA 88) that marked the passage of time before 1798 ("That time is past" [TA 83]) vanishes in the proposed lapse into the future. The teleological quicksand towards which it reaches leaves behind the superlatives of "purest thought" and "dearest Friend" to mark the difference of an absence with comparatives ("warmer," "deeper," "holier," "more dear").[46]

Wordsworth calls for Dorothy to become a voice he will not be able to hear; he will no longer behold in her what he was once. Dorothy becomes a text but one that is different from and must therefore be read altogether differently from William reading his former pleasures in her wild eyes. The text she will become ruptures the connection to William as a continuity with self or other: it speaks not at all of sense perception but only of the difference that William's double absence (the intervening years, death) has made to these banks, of transformations to a new mode of thought and a new mode of reading, one in which the poet can no longer hear the voice that speaks of him, nor see through eyes that connect to a "past existence." Perhaps that connection to past existence was uncertain even in its most direct description. The first paragraph closes, after all, less with the certainty of experiencing the landscape than with questionable notice:

> and wreaths of smoke
> Sent up, in silence, from among the trees!
> With some uncertain notice, as might seem
> Of vagrant dwellers in the houseless woods,
> Or of some Hermit's cave, where by his fire
> The Hermit sits alone.
>   (*TA* 17–22)

The wreaths of smoke sent up "in silence" are a first extinguishing of sound that portends the last. Already, then, a precariousness of knowledge and of the powers of interpretation that prefigure the poem's end. Smoke arises "from among the trees," and trees have been repeated figures in the previous lines—the sycamore, the orchard tufts, the groves and copses, the hedgerows. The smoke signals, perhaps, along with much else as well, a barely suggested conflagration of the substantiality of what came before.[47] For here Wordsworth looks upon the scene, not as in the lines before, where interest borrowed from the eye and ear might seem at least to be his preoccupation. From the uncertain sign Wordsworth reads back to imagine. "The wreaths of smoke / Sent up in silence" are akin to the "unfathered vapour" of the Imagination in *The Prelude*, originless, save in what the poet half-creates as a merely possible source.[48] And what Wordsworth reads or invents hardly undoes the incertitude but, rather, marks a pivotal point between two modes of understanding suggested elsewhere in "Tintern Abbey" in different ways. The choice seems that between companionship and solitude on the one hand, an implicit paradox, as we saw, in the address to Dorothy that shifts from the one to the other. The former, however, leaves the dwellers houseless and vagrant, no cottage ground, no pastoral farm to root them in the greenness of nature. And the other alternative fails to do this as well, for the Hermit's cave is a space not simply of seclusion from, but also of exclusion of, the world of both man and nature, somewhat like that of Wordsworth's final stance. It seems significant, therefore, that the choice is not between vagrant dwellers and the Hermit, but rather between the wanderers and the *cave* of the Hermit, the hollowed-out dwelling itself where by his fire the Hermit happens to sit. It is between these two, in a sense, that much of the poem resonates, however unnoticeably, however uncertainly.

Thus, the distancing of the human figure from the natural landscape is signaled in lines 17–22 by the necessity and difficulty of interpreting the wreaths of smoke sent up in silence. But from the beginning and before this overt call to read the scene as unfathered sign, "Lines Composed a Few Miles Above Tintern Abbey" was about William's distance from, rather than presence at, the banks of the Wye: not only because, as we have seen, the poem opens with the "picture of the mind," which is to say the againness of his visit, or a landscape that already reflects on the human encounter with nature. In 1797, one year before the date of "Tintern Abbey," Wordsworth wrote:

> Yet once again do I behold the forms
> Of these huge mountains, and yet once again
> Standing beneath these elms, I hear thy voice
> Beloved Derwent, that peculiar voice
> Heard in the stillness of the evening air
> Half-heard and half created.[49]

These lines about the Derwent, it would seem, might just as well do for what Wordsworth has to say about the Wye. What is repeated of them, with inevitable ironic resonance, in "Tintern Abbey" is a text that in its earlier as well as later versions insists on the particularity of scene ("*these* huge mountains," "*these* elms") and peculiarity of voice ("*thy* voice," "*that* peculiar voice"—emphasis mine).

This is rather disconcerting for any reading that emphasizes Wordsworth's pantheism or his passion for the specificity of that spot, or that takes literally the claim to moral restoration through a direct (re)experience of nature. For what Wordsworth remains faithful to is far less any actuality than the theater of distancing himself from what seems a commitment to a former immediacy, a distancing marked in both tales by a half-creating (above, line 6, and TA 106). The very gesture of half-citing the lines about the Derwent in lines ostensibly *about* the valley of the Wye already says as much.

The Immortality Ode, too, with a very different gesture, displaces what seems the specificity of the particular in nature for a nature that echoes the poet's voice—and does so precisely at the moment that the poet most completely and delusively enters into blissful unity with the natural scene (stanza IV). Just when he is convinced that he can hear its voice perfectly, nature—somewhat unnaturally for the heart of May—repeats the same message of dejection about his separation from it that opened the poem:

> I hear, I hear, with joy I hear!
> —But there's a Tree, of many, one,
> A single Field which I have looked upon,
> Both of them speak of something that is gone:
>   The Pansy at my feet
>   Doth the same tale repeat:
> Whither is fled the visionary gleam?
> Where is it now, the glory and the dream?
>   (IO 50–57)

Nature loses its particularity before our eyes (or is it our ears?) as the line slides from many to one to a single, generalized field; it is as though we are called upon to witness an object lesson in the impossibility of naming the individual (and this has much to do, as we have seen, with the whole point of the Immortality Ode). Nature tells the same tale that Wordsworth told us earlier: "The things which I have seen I now can see no more" (IO 9), echoed in line 56, and "But yet I know, where'er I go, / That there hath past away a glory from the earth" (17–18), echoed in line 57. Nature cannot be a figure of present delight. It cannot even speak in the affirmative but, rather, in the open-ended form of unanswered questions. Nature, misunderstood in the opening lines of stanza IV as the sensual fullness of May, turns out to be a linguistic repetition and intensification of the poet's initial distance from it. It remembers what was so fugitive. It makes us remember what we would rather forget, that neither recollection nor any other form of singing nature will solve the dilemmas of the opening four stanzas.

In "Tintern Abbey," too, there is no anchor—not in a moment in the past, nor in the transcendence of a mistaken sublime (TA 37—48), nor in that which the self-satisfaction of learning and thought appears to be able to bring (85–88, 105–11), nor in the passion for another and the illusion it gives of access to oneself (112–46), and certainly not in the apparent particularity of the landscape (157–58).[50] If "these steep woods and lofty cliffs, / And this green pastoral landscape" became more dear to Wordsworth "for themselves," this has nothing to do with the uniqueness or self-identity of natural place.

"Tintern Abbey" culminates with yet another uncertain reading, the positing of distances, and readings between. (The critical no less than the narrative eye is dispossessed of the illusion of progression.) It culminates, or pretends to, with a gesture that Wordsworth calls upon us to interpret and that, necessarily and understandably, has been taken as a will to immortality. But with some uncertain notice, it must also be read differently—as the lurch to a future in which Wordsworth no longer hears and no longer sees (TA 147–48) his surroundings, his past, his present, his sister—not even as catching or reading the *language* of their sense—in which the "dear, dear Friend" and "dear, dear Sister" has become "More dear" as she no longer promises connection to the self, the past, the other, in which the landscape of ironized particularity, or pictures of the mind, or uncertain notice also becomes more dear from the lofty and steep perspective of an eye that, in not forgetting, keeps unimaginable watch over man's mortality.

8

Time Mirrors: Rilke's Sonnets to Orpheus (II-3)

Sonnet II-3 from Rilke's Sonnets to Orpheus

1	Spiegel: noch nie hat man wissend beschrieben,	Mirrors: never yet has one knowingly described,
2	was ihr in euerem Wesen seid.	what you in your essence are.
3	Ihr, wie mit lauter Löchern von Sieben	You, as though filled purely with sieve holes
4	erfüllten Zwischenräume der Zeit.	Interstices of time.
5	Ihr, noch des leeren Saales Verschwender—,	You, still squanderers of the empty hall—,
6	wenn es dämmert, wie Wälder weit . . .	When it dusks, like woods far . . .
7	Und der Lüster geht wie ein Sechzehn-Ender	And the chandelier goes like a sixteen-pointer
8	durch eure Unbetretbarkeit.	Through your impenetrability.
9	Manchmal seid ihr voll Malerei.	Sometimes you are full of painting.
10	Einige scheinen *in* euch gegangen—,	A few seem to have gone *into* you—,
11	andere schicktet ihr scheu vorbei.	Others you sent shyly by.
12	Aber die Schönste wird bleiben—, bis	But the most beautiful one will remain—, until
13	drüben in ihre enthaltenen Wangen	over there in her withheld cheeks
14	eindrang der klare gelöste Narziß.	penetrated the clear released Narcissus.

Rilke's "Turning" (1914)

1	Lange errang ers im Anschaun.	For a long time he achieved it by looking.
2	Sterne brachen ins Knie	Stars sank to their knees
3	unter dem ringenden Aufblick.	beneath the wrestling upward glance.

. . . .

14	Tiere traten getrost	Animals passed over consoled
15	in den offenen Blick, weidende,	in the open glance, grazing,
16	und die gefangenen Löwen	and the captured lions
17	starrten hinein wie in unbegreifliche Freiheit;	stared into it as into incomprehensible freedom;

. . . .

22	Und das Gerücht, daß ein Schauender sei,	And the rumor that there was a gazer
23	rührte die minder,	touched the lesser,
24	fraglicher Sichtbaren,	more questionably visible ones,
25	rührte die Frauen.	touched the women.
26	Schauend wie lang?	Looking how long?
27	Seit wie lange schon innig entbehrend,	For how long already ardently doing without,
28	flehend im Grunde des Blicks?	fleeing in the ground of the glance?
29	Wenn er, ein Wartender, saß in der Fremde; des Gasthofs	When he, waiting, sat in the foreignness: of the inn's
30	zerstreutes, abgewendetes Zimmer	dispersed, turned-aside room
31	mürrisch um sich, und im vermiedenen Spiegel	sullen about himself, and in the avoided mirror
32	wieder das Zimmer	again the room
33	und später vom quälenden Bett aus	and later from the torturing bed
34	wieder:	again:
35	da beriets in der Luft,	there it was counseled in the air,

36	unfaßbar beriet es	ungraspably it was counseled
37	über sein fühlbares Herz,	over his feelable heart,
38	über sein durch den schmerzhaft verschütteten Körper	over his through the painfully shaken body
39	dennoch fühlbares Herz	still feelable heart
40	beriet es und richtete:	it was counseled and ruled:
41	daß es der Liebe nicht habe.	that love was lacking.
	. . . . .	. . . . . .
43	Denn des Anschauns, siehe, ist eine Grenze.	For to looking, see, there is a limit.
44	Und die geschautere Welt	And the more looked-at world
45	will in der Liebe gedeihn.	wishes to flourish in love.
46	Werk des Gesichts ist getan,	Work of sight is done,
47	tue nun Herz-Werk	Do heart-work now
48	an den Bildern in dir, jenen gefangenen; denn du	on the images in you, those captured ones, for you
49	überwältigtest sie: aber nun kennst du sie nicht.	conquered them, but now you do not know them.
50	Siehe, innerer mann, dein inneres Mädchen,	See, inner man, your inner maiden,
51	dieses errungene aus	she who was won from
52	tausend Naturen, dieses	a thousand natures, this
53	erst nur errungene, nie	only yet gained, never
54	noch geliebte Geschöpf.	yet loved creature.

In 1923, Rainer Maria Rilke, late in life and therefore with an inevitable retrospective glance, writes the *Sonnets to Orpheus*. Given their title, how could these works not ponder the nature of poetry, death, and time? There is one among them that, like "Tintern Abbey," ultimately situates its reflection on these in an abrupt shift between past and future.

And yet it does not come to such a pass by ostensibly tracing a belabored autobiographical progression in the mind's relation to nature and its own history. Already in its first lines the sonnet openly ponders the issues with which "Tintern Abbey" culminates; or, rather, it inverts those implicit questions into a negative assertion. Rilke, like Wordsworth, broods over the definition of poetic reflection and links that meditation to time. Never yet, Rilke writes, has one knowingly described what mirrors are in their essence—an enigma in which it takes very little to see that mirrors are metaphorical for his own enterprise. The definition he immediately offers is that mirrors are like "interstices of time." What has time to do with the essence of such reflection?

1   Spiegel: noch nie hat man wissend beschrieben,
2   was ihr in euerem Wesen seid.
3   Ihr, wie mit lauter Löchern von Sieben
4   erfüllten Zwischenräume der Zeit.
                    (*SO* II-3)[1]

1   (Mirrors, never yet has one knowingly described,
2   what you in your essence are.
3   You, as though filled purely with sieve holes
4   Interstices of time).

Why should the medium of poetic reflection also be called "time," or rather "*interstices* of time"? And are they quite precisely called that? For it is uncertain in the German just how far the simile extends. Are mirrors merely *like* interstices of time, or are mirrors quite certainly to be understood as interstices of time whose seeming is limited to their being filled with sieve holes? Where do we locate the power of the "like"? And does the floating of the marker for figuration have any significance in a poem that announces a past failure to define the instrument of figuration—"never yet has one knowingly described" what mirrors are?

Zwischenräume ("interstices") are quite literally *spaces* between, so that the time in terms of which mirrors are described takes on a strangely spatial dimension.[2] These interstices of time are (as though) filled with sieve holes. It is not, then, that mirrors are like sieves, instruments with the purpose of catching essential substance while letting the inessential pass through. Rilke compels us to come to terms as best we can, rather, with that which is nothing but sieve holes—arrived at, one can only imagine, by the operation of a sieve upon itself, a sieve sifting a sieve. Where does this leave us, though, if not holding an object that contains all *but* that we wished to reflect on? What inevitably escapes the grasp in such a strange version of self-reflection are the holes, which both refuse to contain and to be contained, which are experienced only as elusion: and this, Rilke tells us, is what constitutes mirrors, appearances to the contrary. One begins to suspect that the concepts of essence (*Wesen*) and description (*Beschreibung*) in the opening lines ("Mirrors, never yet has one knowingly described, / what you in your essence are") may be out of place.

But what of the interstices of time? It is not only that mirrors are (like) interstices of time: in a sense the entire sonnet is poised around the abyss of such a temporal interstice between the "still" ("noch") of the present moment in stanza 2 and the moment negatively posited in line 1, "never yet" ("noch nie"): this is a future in which mirrors might someday be defined—perhaps, we are led to anticipate, in this very text.[3]

If the two stanzas that follow make no substantial progress toward definition, they tell us nevertheless what it might mean to come face to face with mirrors, for they describe various confrontations between mirrors and their objects—the empty hall, the chandelier, and painting. One cannot be lulled, as with Wordsworth, even temporarily, into believing in an immediate relation of mind or poetry to what one might be tempted to call either nature or reality. All of Rilke's late work is a denial of such possibilities. And, we are told, mirrors neither produce nor reproduce their objects: they squander them.

> 5   Ihr, noch des leeren Saales Verschwender—,
> 6   wenn es dämmert, wie Wälder weit . . .
> 7   Und der Lüster geht wie ein Sechzehn-Ender
> 8   durch eure Unbetretbarkeit.
>
> 9   Manchmal seid ihr voll Malerei.
> 10   Einige scheinen *in* euch gegangen—,
> 11   andere schicktet ihr scheu vorbei.

> 5   (You, still squanderers of the empty hall—,
> 6   When / if it dawns / dusks, like woods far . . .
> 7   And the chandelier goes like a sixteen-pointer
> 8   Through your impenetrability
>
> 9   Sometimes you are full of painting.
> 10   A few seem to have gone *into* you—,
> 11   others you sent shyly by.)

Mirrors send their objects forth into an untreadable (*unbetretbar*) space, although this is an inaccessibility we have yet to understand. If they are "Verschwender" of the empty hall, they are not only squanderers of it, but, in the earlier sense of the verb (*verschwinden machen*), mirrors make their objects disappear, perhaps through transformation, a critical term of Rilke's concept of poetry, for nothing passes into mirrors as itself.

However radical this variation on traditional mimesis may be, the sonnet gives us any number of indications that such a solution to the original enigma of defining mirrors is at best stopgap. Stanzas 2 and 3 are riddled with qualifications: the reflection of the hall takes place in the "still" preceding the deferred but proposed moment of essential definition, the "never yet" of line 1. The reflection of the chandelier is at a particular time of the day (dawn or dusk), paintings are reflected there only part of the time ("manchmal"), and the "scheinen" of line 10 is a term often indicating a mere seeming in Rilke's late work.

The question of mere appearance has a good deal to do with perspective. Lines 5–11 observe mirrors from the outside: reflecting on mirrors as external objects that, in turn, reflect objects outside themselves—a point of view that cannot possibly penetrate to "what [mirrors] in [their] essence are." If we turn to an earlier text, "Turning," we see a remarkable and remarkably literal commentary on this kind of observation, what Rilke calls "Anschaun" ("looking at") and "Werk des Gesichts" ("work of sight").

1   Lange errang ers im Anschaun.
2   Sterne brachen ins Knie
3   unter dem ringenden Aufblick.

      .   .   .   .

14   Tiere traten getrost
15   in den offenen Blick, weidende,
16   und die gefangenen Löwen
17   starrten hinein wie in unbegreifliche Freiheit;

      .   .   .   .

22   Und das Gerücht, daß ein Schauender sei,
23   rührte die minder,
24   fraglicher Sichtbaren,
25   rührte die Frauen.

26   Schauend wie lang?
27   Seit wie lange schon innig entbehrend,
28   flehend im Grunde des Blicks?

29 Wenn er, ein Wartender, saß in der Fremde; des Gasthofs
30 zerstreutes, abgewendetes Zimmer
31 mürrisch um sich, und im vermiedenen Spiegel
32 wieder das Zimmer
33 und später vom quälenden Bett aus
34 wieder:
35 da beriets in der Luft,
36 unfaßbar beriet es
37 über sein fühlbares Herz,
38 über sein durch den schmerzhaft verschütteten Körper
39 dennoch fühlbares Herz
40 beriet es und richtete:
41 daß es der Liebe nicht habe.

(*SW* 2:82–83)[4]

1 For a long time he achieved it by looking [*Anschaun*].
2 Stars sank to their knees
3 beneath the wrestling upward glance [*Aufblick*].
. . . .
14 Animals passed over consoled
15 in the open glance [*Blick*], grazing,
16 and the captured lions
17 stared into it [*starrten hinein*] as into incomprehensible
freedom;
. . . .
22 And the rumor that there was a gazer [*Schauender*]
23 touched the lesser,
24 more questionably visible ones,
25 touched the women.
26 Looking [*Schauend*] how long?
27 For how long already ardently doing without,
28 fleeing in the ground of the glance [*Blicks*]?
29 When he, waiting [*ein Wartender*], sat in the foreignness; of the
inn's
30 dispersed, turned-aside room
31 sullen about himself, and in the avoided mirror
32 again the room
33 and later from the torturing bed
34 again:
35 there it was counseled in the air,
36 ungraspably it was counseled

37   over his feelable heart,
38   over his through the painfully shaken body
39   still feelable heart
40   it was counseled and ruled:
41   that love was lacking.)

As in the sonnet, we find here figures of animals, women, the room, and finally of mirrored images with which the poet has not yet come to terms, on which he has not properly reflected. The 1914 "Turning" tells of a poet of considerable if questionable Orphic powers over his surrounding world. What it specifically criticizes is an earlier form of consciousness that attempts to capture that world through external perception, what Wordsworth called "interest [borrowed] from the eye" ("Tintern Abbey," 82–83). Rilke insists on turning from a vocabulary of power associated with the figure of the writer—winning, achieving, capturing[5]—and calls instead for "heart-work . . . / on the images in you," for a reflection on the images within:

43   Denn des Anschauns, siehe, ist eine Grenze.
44   Und die geschautere Welt
45   will in der Liebe gedeihn.

46   Werk des Gesichts ist getan,
47   tue nun Herz-Werk
48   an den Bildern in dir, jenen gefangenen; denn du
49   überwältigtest sie: aber nun kennst du sie nicht.
50   Siehe, innerer mann, dein inneres Mädchen,
51   dieses errungene aus
52   tausend Naturen, dieses
53   erst nur errungene, nie
54   noch geliebte Geschöpf.
                                 (*SW* 2:83–84)

43   (For to looking [*des Anschauns*], see, there is a limit.
44   And the more looked-at world
45   wishes to flourish in love.

46   Work of sight is done,
47   Do heart-work now
48   on the images in you, those captured ones, for you
49   conquered them, but now you do not know them.
50   See, inner man, your inner maiden,
51   she who was won from

52   a thousand natures, this
53   only yet gained, never
54   yet loved creature.)

The poem was originally sent in a letter of 1914 with the com-
ment that it "present[ed] the turning that must indeed take place if
I am to live" (*Briefe*, no. 217).[6] As though the sonnet were a pro-
grammatic fulfillment of the aesthetic imperatives in "Turning," it
shifts its gaze from the stag, the room, and the images of painting
(*SO* II-3, 5–11) outside it. In the closing stanza of the sonnet, something apparently privileged is about to take place. The "But" announces a confrontation with mirrors that will no longer be quali-
fied and marred by the limitations of happening only at particular
moments or to particular objects—all that replaced by a temporality first of duration ("will remain") and then of future fulfillment
("until"). The figures of this confrontation are no longer, even apparently, borrowed from nature (the woods, the stag) nor from an
everyday reality, however aesthetic (painting)—not the work of art
as object but the stuff of which works of the imagination are made,
the abstract and mythological:

12   Aber die Schönste wird bleiben—, bis
13   drüben in ihre enthaltenen Wangen
14   eindrang der klare gelöste Narziß.

12   (But the most beautiful one will remain—, until
13   over there in her withheld cheeks
14   penetrated the clear released Narcissus.)

This is a remaining that might well be seen to promise, perhaps,
the spatial and temporal stability of definitions, the "never yet" finally come to pass—"never yet has one knowingly described" (*SO*
II-3, 1). The sonnet speaks, just as "Turning" demanded of an "inner Man" who sees his "inner maiden," each won long ago and long
since internalized. For in the images of the most beautiful one and
of Narcissus we can recognize those of whom Rilke said years earlier in his letters that it was only through such internalized figures
that he maintained a connection with mankind:

Und dann: ich habe kein Fenster auf die Menschen, endgültiger-
weise. Sie geben sich mir nur so weit, als sie in mir selbst zu Worte
kommen, und da teilen sie sich mir während dieser letzten Jahre
fast nur aus zwei Gestalten mit, von denen aus ich im großen auf die
Menschen zurückschließe. Was zu mir vom Menschlichen redet, im-

mens, mit einer Ruhe der Autorität, die mir das Gehör geräumig macht, das ist die Erscheinung der Jungverstorbenen und unbedingter noch, reiner, unerschöpflicher: *die Liebende.* In diesen beiden Figuren wird mir Menschliches ins Herz gemischt, ob ich will oder nicht. (*Briefe,* no. 149, January 23, 1912)

(And then, I have no window on humans definitively. They give themselves to me only in so far as they come to words in myself, and there they communicate with me in the last years almost exclusively in two shapes [*Gestalten*], from whom I reason back in general about humans. What speaks to me of the human, immensely, with a calm of authority, which makes my hearing spacious, that is the appearance of those who died young and more absolutely still, purer, more inexhaustibly, *the lover.* In these two figures the human is mixed into my heart whether I wish it or not.)

It is these two figures who, here too, will create a strange spaciousness in this final interstice of our hearing. "The most beautiful one" appears as the lover who patiently waits for Narcissus to penetrate.[7] She is also the figure of one who died young, for Rilke wrote the sonnets as a monument for Vera Oukama Knoop and writes of their coming without his willing it, in association with a girl who died young (*Briefe,* no. 363, May 19, 1922). Narcissus, too, is of course both one who loves and one of those who died young, a male version in his double role, then, of the most beautiful one, for he too comes before the mirror.

The most beautiful one and Narcissus each fuse within themselves the figure of lover and dead youth. If they are, in the last lines of the sonnet, then, joined together, this is not only due to the event of penetration described there. Through an endless mirroring of the constellations of Rilke's work these images become one another, interchangeably. The relationship between them marks the vibrations not only of images within the literary text, but between the poet and his creation as well. For the beautiful girl is, in the words of "Turning," the "inner maiden" of the poet and also his "Geschöpf," not only his creature, but his creation. She is both the self of the poet as Narcissus who seeks his own reflection, and his unattainable other, perhaps Eurydice to his Orpheus.[8]

But what do the last lines of the sonnet tell us of this attempt to merge once again with Eurydice, of the attempt of the Orphic voice to transform its past, perhaps recuperate its losses, of Narcissus to regain his self? If the last lines are the successful solution to the enigma of the opening lines, if they, however enigmatically, are the ultimate definition of mirrors and poetry, can this be ascribed, as

"Turning" would have it, to the fact that, for the first time, the poetical text now incessantly mirrors its own images—those who died young, the lover, Narcissus, Orpheus, Eurydice? And are we to understand these images as once "won from a thousand natures" that might be located in an earlier "work of sight"?

It is easy to be drawn in by the myth that "Turning" narrates, of an external nature, first caught and won, yet to be internalized, whose lack is that it is yet to be known and loved.[9] It is as though the questionable and mildly violent rhetoric of imprisonment and struggle ("ringenden" [3], "gefangenen" [16, 48], "unbegreifliche Freiheit" [17], "überwältigtest" [49], "errungene" [51, 53]) might be sanctified and transformed once the internalization is coupled with knowledge and love ("Turning," 49, 54). It is the myth of the happy relationship of poet to his creation with all the ecstasy of a Narcissus able to love and possess what is within himself as other, of an Orpheus finally united with Eurydice.

In the sonnet, however, what separates the final stanza from that which comes before is not a simple distinction between the mirror that captures external objects and the poetic self-allusion seeming to indicate, perhaps, self-knowledge in the last lines. There is much in the poem to suggest that, but the third stanza already concerns the mirroring of works of art rather than external images. And stanza 2 may systematically note images that "Turning" denigrates as work of sight (the figures of animal and room), but the relationship of the hall and the sixteen-pointer to the mirrors is not that of observation from the outside ("Anschaun").

Although it is difficult to catch at first glance, the empty hall is less an external object than a precise definition of the two essential elements of mirroring, the looking-glass walls and a source of light (the chandelier). When the mirrors make the empty hall disappear, there is no "capturing" or "conquering" as "Turning" pretends to have it. Everything takes place through the semblance of simile that is precisely the inverse of what we have come to expect of conventional poetry. Rather than converting nature into artifice, rather than internalizing a sense-experienced nature, "work of sight," through reflection, knowledge, or heart-work (Herz-Werk), the emblems of conventional reflection (the mirrored walls and light source) become *like* woods through which the chandelier passes *like* a stag. The apparently natural wood and sixteen-pointer are, therefore, an illusion, figures marked by simile, "like." They result from a nonreflection that squanders the evidence of its mirroring elements by transforming glass and chandelier into woods and stag.

This may well be an ironical commentary on what Rilke describes elsewhere as the"continual transformation [*Umsetzungen*] of the beloved visible and tangible into the invisible vibration and animation of our own nature" (*Breife*, no. 410). It reverses as well what might seem the simple schema of the first sonnet in the series, where in the presence of Orpheus's singing "Animals of stillness pressed out of the clear / released wood from den and nest" ("Tiere aus Stille drangen aus dem klaren / gelösten Wald von Lager und Genist"). The Orphic voice here dissolves the natural wood (in a phrase identical to that in line 14 of II-3) and offers the animals "temples in hearing." Yet in the other sonnet the natural wood and stag are figures created by mirroring. What is clear and released is Narcissus.

There is not only a difference to be marked between the two sonnets but also within II-3 in moving from the middle stanzas to the last: in the closing lines of the poem there is no longer even a descriptive illusion of the natural, nor does the poetic diction continue to voice its power of analogy ("wie") or appearance ("scheinen"), nor are the visual elements of conventional reflection (mirror and light) overtly named. If the third stanza could abandon the natural to speak both of what stands in front of mirrors and what is in them as artifice (Malerei), the last stanza takes this one step further. In these lines poetry speaks (of) poetry, but this is not simply because, as we saw earlier, Narcissus and the most beautiful one awaken a din in the echo chamber of Rilke's earlier images. The critical moment is one of silence.

That same first sonnet of the Orpheus poems (however different its enterprise in other respects) tells also of a transformation that takes place in silence.[10]

> Und alles schwieg. Doch selbst in der Verschweigung
> ging neuer Anfang, Wink und Wandlung vor.
>
> (*SO* I-1, 3–4)

> (And all was silent. Yet even in the silencing
> new beginning, sign, and transformation went forth.)

In one of Rilke's French poems this silence takes place in the movement of a fountain:

1   Je ne veux qu'une seule leçon, c'est la tienne,
2   fontaine, qui en toi-même retombes,—
    .   .   .   .
13   Mais ce qui plus que ton chant vers toi me décide
14   c'est cet instant d'un silence en délire
15   lorsqu'à la nuit, à travers ton élan liquide
16   passe ton propre retour qu'un souffle retire.

                                            (*SW* 2:530)

1   I want but one single lesson, it is yours,
2   fountain, who fall back into yourself,—
    .   .   .   .
13   But that which more than your song towards you decides me
14   it is this instant of a silence in delirium
15   when to the night, across your liquid expanse
16   passes your own return that a breath pulls back.

If the earlier lines of the mirror sonnet already constitute themselves through a meditation on the elements of reflection, if the
object of their mirror has, from the beginning, been mirrors themselves, in what sense are we to understand the implied, singular
success of the closing lines? The silence of their performance, like
that of the fountain, falls back within itself. That which is silenced
in the final tercet has something to do not merely with the voice of
the poem or with a change in mirrored object, but with our own
stance. The moment of definition takes place as a transformation
in the way in which we regard both ourselves and mirrors.

12   Aber die Schönste wird bleiben—, bis
13   drüben in ihre enthaltenen Wangen
14   eindrang der klare gelöste Narziß.

12   (But the most beautiful one will remain—, until
13   over there in her withheld cheeks
14   penetrated the clear released Narcissus.)

Although we can locate the crucial problems here, we are hard
pressed to say just where we stand. In a text that calls for a conscious fixing of definitions, there is a disconcerting rupture in its
spatial and temporal orientation. Where is this "over there" ("drüben"), and why, when we are syntactically tensed towards a present
or future form, does the verb "penetrate" appear in the imperfect?[11]

The merging of Narcissus with the most beautiful one, the ultimate performance of what might seem to be reflection and self-
consciousness, marks a break with the preceding stanzas because,
for the first time, mirrors are no longer addressed. They are no
longer spoken to as an interlocutor with whom the poet stands face
to face. They no longer maintain the potential to utter an answer.
Nor, for that matter, are mirrors spoken of referentially, the object
of what "Turning" calls observation. We have apparently stood outside mirrors to observe their confrontation with an empty hall, its
chandelier, and painting (stanzas 2 and 3). But the most beautiful
one will come before the mirror until . . . over there, Narcissus penetrated. Where? Over there, where she stands, in front of the mirror. If the space before the mirror is suddenly "over there," this can
only be because we, along with the poet, are, suddenly, over here—
within the mirror. In the silent interstice between lines 12 and 13,
the perspective of the poem has flipped.[12] The reader falls to the
other side, squandered. To attempt reflection on mirror-texts is
sooner or later to be deflected by them, to be taken in by them, to
become an unimaginable image in their impossible space. *When* did
all this take place? In the same non-moment, in the same interstice
of time announced by the "until" at the close of line 12, in which
Narcissus penetrated to the cheeks of the most beautiful one,
reader and narrative voice pass through the mirror of sieve holes.
The sonnet silences this moment: all this takes place in a delirious
and unreadable silence ("silence en dé-lire"[*SW* 2:530, hyphen
mine]), in one of silence's excesses between the words ("excès de
silence, / de ce silence entre les mots" [*SW* 2:568]). It is marked by
the imperfect tense, "penetrated" ("eindrang"), where one expects
the present. The moment comes only as a promise of stability ("will
remain") that dissolves into the movement of penetration—a rupture into a future experienced as loss.

"Spiegel: noch nie hat man wissend beschrieben / was ihr in eu-
rem Wesen seid." ("Mirrors: never yet has one knowingly described / what you in your essence are.") The attempt to define the
essence of mirrors from the outside (lines 3–11) proves impossible,
for conscious description can only mark a disparity between the
describer and the object. If the final stanza no longer describes mirrors, it nevertheless "beschreibt" in another sense of the word: just
as "describing a circle" means marking out its path, the final stanza
carries through or performs what mirrors are. And if this execution cannot take place knowingly or consciously, we might still be

"wissend" in the sense of "initiated."[13] The task then becomes one of "carrying through in an initiated state what mirrors in their essence are."[14] We solve the poem's enigma (and its call to language as definition) only at the price of dissolving it, squandering it, and transforming it, and only in being utterly transformed by it. The lyric itself cannot escape its own deflection.

What this definition of mirrors / poems brings about both for the text and for ourselves is anything but a consciousness that makes the self present to itself. As in Wordsworth, giving up the power to paint the external world goes hand in hand with giving up the power to paint oneself. The appearance of "images in [the poet]" ("Turning"), the "dead youth" and the "lover," marks a withdrawal from that on which the 1912 letter seemed to insist, what might have been understood as authority in all its calmness, becomes rather a "Ruhe der Autorität" as authority's sleep and silence. The standpoint of narrative and critical perception, of poet and reader, is one of noncoincidence with their narcissistic doubles. Just as the narrator and reader move to join what might be the image of themselves, Narcissus, who becomes enfigured only at this critical moment, passes to the side of the mirror on which they had previously stood: the most beautiful one, the narrator, and the reader outside the mirror in line 12, the narrator and reader within and the girl and Narcissus outside in line 14. Never are the two sides what we would call mirror reflections; their relation takes place, rather, as passing one another by. Neither poet nor reader finds his or her self in the mythological figure. Nor is Narcissus's penetration to the cheeks of the most beautiful one a sign of unambiguous union, for he enters her "*enthaltenen* Wangen," cheeks that are at once contained and withheld.[15] What is staged as a scene of reflection in the concluding lines deflects the possibility of self-possession for poet and reader alike, for whom authority is, by definition, out of the question.

Rilke rewrites the myths of Narcissus, not only Ovid's but also that of his own two poems entitled "Narcissus," (both written in 1913), that balance two opposing versions of his death. The first speaks in the third person, of a youth to whom it was given to see himself. Such insight, however ecstatic, closes the circle of forms that constitutes both Narcissus's self and his vision of himself.

> Er liebte, was ihm ausging, wieder ein
> Und war nicht mehr im offnen Wind enthalten

und schloß entzückt den Umkreis der Gestalten
Und hob sich auf und konnte nicht mehr sein.
(*SW* 2:56)

(He loved what went out of him again in
And was no longer contained / withheld in the open wind
and closed in ecstasy the circumference of the figures
And cancelled / preserved himself and could no longer be.)

Narcissus turns from being contained ("enthalten") by the open wind and chooses instead the ecstasy of self-closure.

The second of the poems tells not of closure but of the unceasing dissolution of a self that can find no containing boundaries ("alle meine Grenze haben Eile, / stürzen hinaus" ["all my boundaries are in a hurry, / dash out"]), of a "yielding middle," a "kernel full of softness" in the self. The sonnet pointedly echoes the rejected "enthalten" of the first poem and insists on a movement into the other that both of the earlier texts relinquish.

Moreover, the sonnet's Narcissus sidesteps Ovid's act of self-reflection altogether (even though narrator and reader do not) and is neither defined nor lost in the attempt to know himself. The non-moment when mirrors carry through what they are is the force that seems to first produce him. He is indeed thereby "gelöst," not dissolved as Ovid's text suggests, but liberated.[16] "Gelöst" also, perhaps, in the sense that a riddle is solved or deciphered, for Narcissus's paradoxical encounter with himself is replaced by a different scene. Narcissus is no longer a tragic figure: he neither comes to know nor loses himself.

The sonnet implicitly asks the question of its own status, asks what poetry is by asking what mirrors are. If stanza 2, as we have seen, already ponders the elements of reflection by radically producing the illusion of nature from the force of simile, nevertheless the tercet reflects on mirrors mirroring in an altogether different manner. It places the narrative poetic voice in front of the mirror: it requires the reader to stand there too. Poetry, reflection, and time-as-lapse are, if not exactly equivalent, at least implicitly announced as interchangeable in the opening lines. If poetic (non) reflection as interstice of time does not enable a reproduction or grasping of the object, of the self,[17] of the lover, if it does not allow a conscious, iterable definition of mirrors-poetry-time,[18] nevertheless something has taken place—or, one is tempted to say, something has taken time. There is a movement in the text from the "never yet," its promise for the future, to the pastness of the closing verb. One cannot say what transpires in the present tense. It is at once a dissolution of and also a solution to the initially announced enigma, but this solution is not a knowledge. It allows one to assert, albeit in the past, what mirrors are / were about. Yet, like the poet, we do not so much win our reflection as become it or, rather, assume its place. Such an achievement gives all the delusions of progress, of moving from a never yet at the beginning of the poem to its fulfillment in the closing lines. But that which might pose as knowledge can only be experienced retrospectively, as a fall into the mirror and as a blank in consciousness: nowhere does the text tell us explicitly what has happened to our perspective, spatially and temporally: we have to *figure it out* afterwards. If indeed the critical perspective is abruptly jolted to the other side of the mirror, this is never spoken *about:* the sudden production and shift of Narcissus is all that takes place, which is really beside the point. It in no way *represents,* literally or figuratively, what happens to us, even if we must read our displacement in its wake. The trajectory described by the poem is less progress than liberation, a liberation from a temporality of presence and progress, and from much else as well.

The sonnet to Orpheus is an answer of sorts, after all, to the question of what mirrors are, but its pseudo-progression refuses to describe what mirrors in their essence are. We have seen their enigma to demand a thoroughgoing rewriting of the conceptual givens of definition: knowledge, description, essence. The sonnet begins, ostensibly, as a reflection on mirrors—which is to say, on texts such as the sonnet itself and therefore as a self-reflection— but one that performs radical transfigurations rather than representation in which the terms of representation cannot maintain a fixed meaning. It is a performance in which the classical figure seeking self-identity, and failing, turns to his radical other instead. Perhaps this explains the "like" of stanza 1 whose terms of comparison cannot be fixed. It is the staging of a mirroring in which figures on the two sides of the mirror have no similarity to that which they figure. All this takes place over a gap in time that we can only consciously recognize later, as a blank in our own understanding. All this takes place, doubly then, in an interstice of time and as an interstice of time, that gets us nowhere fast—in which the questioning voice is deflected into and transformed by the mirror and with it the enterprises of definition and reflection. Poetry is a mirror in which we seek to know ourselves critically, in the course of time:

time is a loss of the present to a future that is—before we know it—always past.

More or less this lurch to the future is what takes place in crossing the Alps or what is called for in positing the poet's death in "Tintern Abbey"—Wordsworth's call to his sister not to forget. It is what inevitably happens in that semblance of temporal sequence in which, as de Man puts it, time is a metaphor—marking the space we call criticism or that Benjamin calls translation. Lévi-Strauss will speak of the double distances between the anthropologist and the primitives of South America, and then again between the writer and those crumbling figures of his earlier years, and finally of a future apocalypse that mirrors the whole show; Ford will ironize the pretense to truth of literary historians, memoirists, and impressionist narrators delighted and doomed to mistell the past. Lessing will fetishize the concept of temporal priority in an extended joke about the nature of origin and representation, the laughter of which reverberates in his allegorical reading of Homer. When we reflect on it, in each instance time forces us to rethink telling and even casts us to the other side of the mirror.

Notes

· · · · · · · · · · · · · ·

Prologue: Telling, Time

The epigraph is from Jorge Luis Borges, *Ficciones* (New York: Grove Press, 1962), 99–100.

1. All references to the "Theses on the Philosophy of History" are marked by the thesis number. They appear in the German edition under the title "Uber den Begriff der Geschichte" ("On the Concept of History"): see Walter Benjamin, *Gesammelte Schriften* I.2 (Frankfurt: Suhrkamp, 1974), 693–704. The English version is in *Illuminations* (New York: Schocken, 1969), 253–64.

2. Walter Benjamin, *Gesammelte Schriften* II.1 (Frankfurt: Suhrkamp, 1974), 204–10.

Chapter 1: Architectures of Oblivion

1. All citations from *Tristes Tropiques* refer to Claude Lévi-Strauss, *Tristes Tropiques* (Paris: Plon, 1955), in the French original, and to *Tristes Tropiques*, trans. John and Doreen Weightman (New York: Atheneum, 1974), in English. These are referred to in the text by page numbers followed by *F* and *E*, respectively. All citations from *Structural Anthropology* refer to Claude Lévi-Strauss, *Structural Anthropology*, trans. Claire Jacobson and Brooke Grundfest Schoepf (New York: Basic Books, 1963), in English and to *Anthropologie Structurale* (Paris: Plon, 1958) in the French original. These are referred to in the text by *SA* followed by page numbers, which in turn are marked with *F* and *E* for the French and English editions, respectively. The translations have been, more often than not, greatly modified.

2. See also 38F, 37–38E; 100–101F, 90–91E; 173F, 153E; 364–65F, 316E; 380–81F, 330E, 383–84F, 333E. See Jeffrey Mehlman, *A Structural Study of Autobiography* (Ithaca: Cornell University Press, 1971), 188–90, where he also discusses the scene at Sainte Anne's Hospital.

3. Also with respect to his teachers—Dumas, for example (16–18F, 19–21E).

4. There are further ironies in that the closing pages of *Tristes Tropiques* praise the neolithic way of life, first in the name of Rousseau and then in the name of Lévi-Strauss (451–52F, 391E); and also in that Lévi-Strauss

uses something of the same image to describe the way in which European civilization denudes the tropics: "Like a bush fire fleeing in front of the consumption of its substance, in one hundred years the agricultural blaze had crossed the State of Sao Paulo" (104F, 93E).

5. See James A. Boon, "An Endogamy of Poets, and Vice Versa: Exotic Ideals in Romanticism/Structuralism," *Studies in Romanticism* 18, no. 3 (1979): 339–41.

6. In the passage just preceding the above lines, although it slips through the fingers of the translators, Lévi-Strauss, suddenly, and with enormous pathos, speaks directly to the primitives who have been cannibalized by the Western appetite for self-mystification. He marks his identification with the savage tribes, then, grammatically, by a striking shift to the second person, even before he metaphorically announces himself "like the Indian of the myth" (43F, 41E).

On the question of the relationship to the South American Indians as to the Other, see the superb essay of Eugenio Donato, "*Tristes Tropiques:* The Endless Journey," *Modern Language Notes* 81 (1966): 270–87.

7. Debris also plays a crucial role when Lévi-Strauss speaks of mythical thought in "The Science of the Concrete": "The specificity of mythic thought, as of bricolage, on the practical plane, is to elaborate structured sets, not directly with other structured sets, but by using the remains and debris of events" (Claude Lévi-Strauss, *La pensée sauvage* [Paris: Plon, 1962], 32; *The Savage Mind* [Chicago: University of Chicago Press, 1966], 21–22).

8. This contamination never ceases to be a preoccupation. See, for example, 173F, 153E; 245F, 215E; 375F, 326E.

On the impossibility of the ethnographer's finding the pure primitive, see Maurice Blanchot, "L'homme au point zéro," *La Nouvelle Revue Française,* 4e année, no. 40 (1956): 686–88.

9. See Donato, "The Endless Journey," 273–74.

10. Thus, later in *Tristes Tropiques* Lévi-Strauss finds the Munde Indians, in some senses the answer to his wish of having lived in the days of real journeys. Here he sees the splendor of a spectacle that has not yet been blighted and polluted, as originary as that encountered by the earlier explorers. It is a moment, as earlier, at once of perfect proximity—the savage almost the mirror image of the ethnographer—and also of noncomprehension.

> They were there, all ready to teach me their customs and beliefs, and I did not know their language. As close to me as a reflection in the mirror, I could touch them but would not understand them. I received at once my recompense and my punishment. . . . Were I to guess what they were like, they would shed their strangeness: I could have just as well stayed in my own village. Or if, as was here the case, they kept it, then it serves no purpose for me because I am

then not even capable of grasping what makes their strangeness theirs. (384F, 333E)

On this passage, see Mehlman, *Structural Study*, 193–94 and 197.

11. Donato speaks of this as a switch on the part of Lévi-Strauss from seeking others to finding himself—a privileged position of "temps retrouvé" and self-discovery ("The Endless Journey," 274–75). Yet with this shift both that self and its past crumble.

12. It no doubt makes sense in the strange logic of the other that Richard Macksey in writing of Proust should speak far more perceptively of Lévi-Strauss than so many others who write of *Tristes Tropiques:* "There is for Proust a similar reflective character in his *prise de conscience,* which suggests the final dimension of his edifice: Time: This destroyer of all external objects of desire becomes, in turn, a creative force: it allows recollection" (Richard Macksey, "The Architecture of Time: Dialectics and Structure," in *Proust: A Collection of Critical Essays,* ed. René Girard [Englewood Cliffs: Prentice Hall, 1962] p. 119). This will explain how "The Architecture of Time" becomes "Architecture of Oblivion."

13. See Georges Bataille, "Un livre humain, un grand livre," *Critique* 12, no. 105 (February 1956): 100: "Ethnography is not only simply one domain of knowledge among others; it is a placing in question of the *civilization of knowledge,* which is the civilization of the ethnographers." See also Boon, "An Endogamy of Poets," 341.

14. In the essay that appears as the Afterword to *The End of the Line* (New York: Columbia, 1985), 217–39, Neil Hertz outlines a structure of the relation among author, reader, the author's surrogate, and what poses as a possible axis for representation, reflection, doubling, or difference. Hertz elaborates this structure in remarkable readings of Courbet, Wordsworth, Flaubert, Eliot, and himself. What takes place in *Tristes Tropiques's* first geological metaphor, where Lévi-Strauss has his narrator speak of a former self in relationship to the past, could very productively be assimilated to Hertz's line of meditation.

15. Donato also places the two geological metaphors side by side but reads them for their similarity rather than contrast. He sees their significance in the fact that geological differences are rooted in nature rather than in culture. See Eugenio Donato, "Lévi-Strauss and the Protocols of Distance," *Diacritics* 5, no. 3 (Fall 1975): 4.

16. See Georges Balandier, "Grandeur et servitude de l'ethnologue," *Cahiers du Sud* 43, no. 337 (1956): 450–51.

In a fascinating essay Carl Rubino relates literature and science and the question of time, particularly with respect to general relativity. He brings together Lévi-Strauss's *Tristes Tropiques* and Wordsworth's poetry, which is, of course, my enterprise as well. Where I find it difficult to follow him is in his placing side by side Lévi-Strauss's geological metaphor just cited and the enterprise of "Ode: Intimations of Immortality." See Carl Rubino,

"Winged Chariots and Black Holes: Some Reflections on Science and Literature," *Genre* 16 (1983): 347–49.

17. Towards the end of *Tristes Tropiques*, Lévi-Strauss will recapitulate several of his encounters precisely in terms of travel back to various layers of time: "After the Nambikwara in the Stone Age, it was no longer the 16th century to which the Tupi-Kawahib had brought me back, but rather yet the 18th century such as one could imagine it in the little ports of the Antilles or on the coast. I had crossed a continent. But the end—quite close— of my voyage was first made palpable [*sensible*] to me by this reascent from the depths of time" (430F, 372E). See Mehlman, *Structural Study,* 207.

18. Susan Sontag emphasizes only Lévi-Strauss's relation to doubt as his "*philosophical* stance" ("The Anthropologist as Hero," *Claude Lévi-Strauss: The Anthropologist as Hero,* ed. E. Nelson Hayes and Tanya Hayes [Cambridge: MIT Press, 1970], esp. 188–89).

19. Thus, Lévi-Strauss begins by distinguishing himself from the scientist "for whom dawn and twilight are one and the same phenomenon" (68F, 62E).

20. Twenty-five years after publishing *Tristes Tropiques,* Lévi-Strauss, in an interview, claimed this passage to be in fact the only remaining fragment of a novel begun and abandoned in 1939 ("Ce que je suis," *Le Nouvel Observateur,* no. 816 [1980]: 50).

21. The sunset reappears in the last volume of *Mythologiques:*

> Having arrived at the evening of my career, the final image that myths leave me, and through them this supreme myth that the history of humanity tells, also the history of the universe in the midst of which the other unfolds, joins again then the intuition which at my beginnings, as I told it in *Tristes Tropiques,* made me seek in the phases of a sunset, watched from the setting in place of a celestial decor which became progressively complicated to the point of undoing itself and abolishing itself in the nocturnal passage into nothingness, the model of the facts that I was to study later . . . vast and complex edifice, it also was radiant with a thousand colors which unfold under the eye of the analyst and closes itself again to sink slowly far away as though it had never existed. (*L'Homme nu, Mythologiques IV* [Paris: Plon, 1971], 620).

See Donato, "Lévi-Strauss and the Protocols of Distance," 3.

For another take on the pivotal role the sunset plays in Lévi-Strauss, see Tom Conley, "The Sunset of Myth: Lévi-Strauss in the Americas," in *Twentieth-Century French Fiction: Essays for Germaine Brée* (New Brunswick: Rutgers University Press, 1975), esp. 226–29.

22. Elsewhere, nevertheless, Lévi-Strauss is insistent on the discontinuity between "the lived" and "the real":

> Phenomenology shocked me in so far as it postulated a continuity between the lived and the real. I was in agreement in recognizing

that the latter enveloped and explained the former—I had learned from my three mistresses [geology, psychology, and Marxism] that the passage between the two orders is discontinuous, that to reach the real, one must first repudiate the lived, even if only to reintegrate it afterwards, in an objective synthesis stripped of all sentimentality. (62–63F, 58E)

For another reading of "Sunset" see Boon, "An Endogamy of Poets," 342–43. Boon and others note Lévi-Strauss's return to the image of the sunset in *L'Homme nu*, 619–21.

23. A few pages later the sunset will paradoxically be called always "identical" and yet "unforeseeable," and in the same breath compared to a geological upheaval in which each color mysteriously is transformed into its complement:

> Nothing is more mysterious than the ensemble of always identical but unforeseeable processes by which night follows day. Its mark appears suddenly in the sky accompanied by incertitude and anguish. No one would know how to sense in advance the form—this time unique among all the others—that the nocturnal geological upheaval will adopt. By the impenetrable alchemy each color comes to metamorphose itself into its complement. . . . For the night the mixing [of colors] has no limit because it inaugurates a false spectacle. . . . Thus night enters by way of a piece of trickery [*supercherie*]. (73–74F, 67E)

24. There are moments in *Tristes Tropiques* where this interplay of demarcation lines haunts the "real" landscape as well: "Europe offers forms that are precise in a diffuse light. Here the role, which for us is traditional, of the sky and the earth are inverted. Above the milky trail of the *campo* the clouds build the most extravagant constructions. The sky is the region of forms and of volumes; the earth keeps the softness of primeval ages" (237F, 209E). See also 380F, 330E.

25. See Donato, "Lévi-Strauss and the Protocols of Distance," 3.

26. One has assurances, at least, that the drawings culled both fifteen years later and forty years previous are identical to those brought back by Lévi-Strauss.

> How surprised I was to receive . . . an illustrated publication of a collection made fifteen years later. . . . Not only did the documents seem to be of an execution as sure as mine, often the motifs were identical. During all this time, the style, the technique, and the inspiration had remained unchanged just as had been the case in the forty years that had passed [*ecoulés*] between Boggiani's visit and mine. (211–12F, 185–87E)

> Let it suffice then to remember that these paintings have been known since the first contacts with the Guaicuru in the seventeenth

century and that they do not seem to have evolved since that time. (*SA* 276F, 251E)

The tone is one of self-certainty although elsewhere Lévi-Strauss confesses to having believed that he had arrived at the last possible moment (211F, 185E).

27. Or does he? For, given what he tells us, how are we to assess the value of his other photographs of the Caduveo?

28. Similar imaginings of comprehensive reduction appear elsewhere in Lévi-Strauss's work—as, for example, in *La Pensée Sauvage*, where he speaks of transferring all available data on Australian tribes to computer punch cards (*La Pensée Sauvage*, 117; *The Savage Mind*, 89).

29. This image of the deal of the cards returns in *La Pensée Sauvage*. The passage begins: "First, man is like a player taking in hand, when he takes his place at the table, cards which he has not invented, because the game of cards is a given of history and of civilization. Secondly each deal of the cards among the players results from a contingent distribution and takes place unknown to them" (*La Pensée Sauvage*, 126; *The Savage Mind*, 95).

30. It is relevant for much of the discussion of Caduveo body art that it is repeatedly women's art that radically questions the gestures of the anthropologist. Therefore it is too simple a response to charge Lévi-Strauss with rendering women objects or with making human beings invisible. The questions of representation are far more involved both on the side of Lévi-Strauss and on the part of the artists and art works he discusses. See in relation to this Page DuBois, "*Tristes Tropiques:* Framing the Woman Question," *Massachusetts Review* 21, no. 2 (1980): 340–41.

31. There is an interesting moment when Lévi-Strauss later talks about the Mundé Indians in which the language of the systematic returns but with an understanding that his hypotheses "may relate only to the distinctive features of the particular society" (383F, 332E).

32. There is a passage in *Structural Anthropology* that suggests quite the opposite, however:

> It is clear that the artist did not plan to draw a face [*visage*] but a facial painting. . . . Even the eyes that are indicated summarily are there only as points of reference for the two large inverted spirals into whose architecture they merge. The artist drew the facial design in a realistic fashion, which is to say in respecting the true proportions as though she had painted on a face and not on a flat surface. (*SA* 284F, 258E)

33. "How far did this intimacy go? It was very difficult to suppose [*admettre*] that the bachelors, on learning to know them, could resist the attraction of the young Indian girls half nude on holidays with the body patiently decorated with delicate black or blue scrolls [*volutes*] which seemed to merge a sheath of precious lace with their skin" (191F, 168E). See also 214F, 188E; *SA* 279F, 255E; and *SA* 282F, 257E.

34. Although the opening lines of *Tristes Tropiques* insist that "adventure has no place in the ethnographic profession" (13F, 17E), it manages to reappear elsewhere: 369F, 321E; 383F, 332E; 435F, 376E.

35. Here Lévi-Strauss distinguishes the Caduveo with respect to their neighbors on either side of the geographic mark. In other passages it is a refrain that insists on the power of Caduveo eroticism to draw others from the far reaches of those banks (214F, 188E; *SA* 280F, 155E).

36. And yet in a seven-line paragraph, almost forgotten in the grandiose finale of chapter 20, the question of priority does arise.

> Must one consider this complex structure of three hierarchical classes and two balanced moieties as one interdependent system? It is possible. It is also tempting to distinguish the two aspects and to treat the one as older than the other. In this case there would be no lack of arguments in favor of the priority either of classes or of moieties. (222F, 196E)

That the two oppositional forces might equally be regarded as more fundamental is somewhat dissimulated in the closing passage.

See Mehlman, *Structural Study*, 203.

37. Jacques Derrida, *Of Grammatology*, trans. Gayatri Chakravorty Spivak (Baltimore and London: Johns Hopkins University Press, 1974), 101–40.

Chapter 2: Poor Timing

1. Ford Madox Hueffer, *Memories and Impressions* (New York and London: Harper, 1911), xviii. All subsequent citations from Ford's works are indicated by the following abbreviations and page numbers in the text:

EN	*The English Novel: From the Earliest Days to the Death of Joseph Conrad* (Philadelphia: J. B. Lippincott, 1929)
GS	*The Good Soldier* (New York: Vintage, 1951)
HJ	*Henry James* (New York: Octagon Books, 1972)
IWN	*It Was the Nightingale* (New York: Octagon Books, 1975)
JC	*Joseph Conrad: A Personal Remembrance* (New York: Octagon Books, 1971)
MaI	*Memories and Impressions* (New York and London: Harper, 1911)
MoL	*The March of Literature from Confucius' Day to Our Own* (New York: The Dial Press, 1938)
NC	Joseph Conrad and Ford Madox Hueffer, *The Nature of a Crime* (London: Duckworth and Co., 1924)
OI	"On Impressionism," *Poetry and Drama* 2 (June and December 1914)
PfL	*Portraits from Life* (Boston: Houghton Mifflin, 1937)
Te	"Techniques," in *Southern Review* 1 (July 1935): 20–35
TtR	*Thus to Revisit* (New York: E. P. Dutton, 1921)

2. Vincent J. Cheng, "A Chronology of *The Good Soldier*," *English Language Notes* 24, no. 1 (1986): 91–97; Arthur Mizener, "Chronological Se-

quence of Events in *Parade's End*," in Sondra J. Stang, *Ford Madox Ford* (New York: Ungar, 1977), 132–37.

3. William Gass, "Ford's Impressionism," *Antaeus* 56 (1986): 24, 27 (hereafter referred to as Gass).

4. Samuel Hynes, "The Epistemology of *The Good Soldier*," *Sewanee Review* 69, no. 2 (1961): 226–27.

5. See Max Saunders, who aptly speaks of "Ford's reminiscences" as "works of the imagination," in "A Life in Writing: Ford Madox Ford's Dispersed Autobiographies," *Antaeus* 56 (Spring 1986): 47, 66. Also see Grover Smith, *Ford Madox Ford* (New York: Columbia University Press, 1972), 3, and Stang, *Ford*, 130.

6. On these passages as well as other issues related to this essay see the chapter that follows, "*The* (too) *Good Soldier*, 'a real story.'"

7. It is in *Joseph Conrad*, where Conrad's experience has been replaced by observation, observation by a recording of his impressions in writing, his writing read by Ford, who also knew the man well, Ford's impressions rendered in a writing that admittedly may not be true to fact.

8. Could it be a question of hypocrisy on the part of Ford, claiming sincerity and "pious scrupulosity" there, reveling in the conscious control of his effects here? "The objector will here interpolate that all that is a very old story. Hypocrites have always existed and been unveiled by writers" (*MoL* 806), even when the hypocrites are the writers themselves. In the passage just cited Ford goes on to place the blame for hypocrisy at least equally on the eyes of the observer who misinterprets the pseudonobility of the hypocrite—allegorically, then, a blame placed on the reader.

9. One has only to glance at other pages of the dedication to *Memories and Impressions*, where it is a "forgetting [of] childhood" (x), "the end of an epoch, the closing of a door" (xii), that mark the point of departure for writing.

10. Robert Lowell, Introduction to Ford Madox Ford, *Buckshee* (Cambridge: Pym-Randall Press, 1966), xii; Georges Jean-Aubry, *The Sea Dreamer: A Definitive Biography of Joseph Conrad* (Hamden, Conn.: Archon Books, 1967), 232; H. G. Wells, *Experiment in Autobiography* (New York: Macmillan, 1934), 526.

11. See Smith, *Ford Madox Ford*, 7.

12. That phrase which speaks of equation through the "is" is reminiscent of Ford's elaboration on the juxtaposition of situations:

> The juxtaposition of the composed renderings of two or more unexaggerated actions and situations may be used to establish, like the juxtaposition of vital word to vital word, a sort of frictional current of electric life that will extraordinarily galvanize the work of art in which the device is employed. That has the appearance of being a rather hard aesthetic nut to crack. Let us put it more concretely by citing the algebraic truth that $(a = b)^2$ equals not merely $a^2 + b^2$, but

a^2 plus an apparently unearned increment called $2ab$ plus the expected b^2. (*MoL* 804)

There is a small slip of the algebraic pen here, for to be entirely accurate, Ford would have had to write $(a + b)^2 = a^2 + b^2 +$ "the apparently unearned increment called $2ab$." But isn't it precisely when trying to claim equality, say of lies and figurative truths, that things go awry and the unexpected and slightly unfathomable inserts itself?

13. Such distintegration is very different from the "multiplicity of meanings," "gap," "dialectic," etc. described by Paul B. Armstrong. These take place solely in the framework of retrospective "acts of reflection" that seek to clarify and in a fundamentally ordered temporal structure either of recuperation or of loss, a reflection and temporality which is certainly there, but not the whole story. See "The Hermeneutics of Literary Impressionism: Interpretation and Reality in James, Conrad, and Ford," *Centennial Review* 27, no. 4 (1983): 244–69, and "The Epistemology of 'The Good Soldier': A Phenomenological Reconsideration," *Criticism* 22 (1980): 230–51.

Chapter 3: *The* (too) *Good Soldier*

The epigraph is taken from Joseph Conrad and Ford Madox Hueffer, *The Nature of a Crime* (London: Duckworth, 1924), 66.

1. All citations are from Ford Madox Ford, *The Good Soldier* (New York: Vintage, 1951). Page numbers are given in the text.

2. Ford wrote of this theory of Impressionism: "We accepted without much protest the stigma 'Impressionists' that was thrown at us. . . . [W]e saw that Life did not narrate, but made impressions on our brains. We in turn, if we wished to produce on you an effect of life, must not narrate but render impressions" (Ford Madox Ford, *Joseph Conrad* [Boston: Little, Brown, 1924], 194–95). "It seems to me that one is an Impressionist because one tries to produce an illusion of reality—or rather the business of Impressionism is to produce that illusion" (Ford Madox Hueffer, "On Impressionism," *Poetry and Drama* 2 [June and December 1914]). On these passages see the preceding chapter.

3. See Hugh Kenner: "If one seeks for a centre, one is driven through ironic mirror-lined corridors of viewpoint reflecting viewpoint and this is the book's essence, an optical illusion of infinite recession. . . . The gap between presentation and 'values' is never bridged" ("Conrad and Ford: The Artistic Conscience," *Shenandoah* 3 [1952]: 54).

4. An obvious pun, noted repeatedly in readings of *The Good Soldier*. See, for example, Mark Schorer, preface to *The Good Soldier* (New York: Vintage, 1961), p. xv; T. J. Henigan, "*The Desirable Alien:* A Source for Ford Madox Ford's *The Good Soldier,*" *Twentieth-Century Literature* 11 (1965–66): 27; and T. A. Hanzo, "Downward to Darkness," *Sewanee Review* 74 (1966): 838.

5. The argument about the reliability of the narrator in *The Good Soldier* has become a given proposition, not to say a commonplace, in Ford Madox Ford criticism. See, among many others, Samuel Hynes, "The Epistemology of *The Good Soldier*," *Sewanee Review* 69 (1961): 225–35; James Hafley, "The Moral Structure of *The Good Soldier*," *Modern Fiction Studies* 5 (1959–60): 121–28; Mark Schorer's preface (in many respects the most subtle of these essays); and Grover Smith, *Ford Madox Ford* (New York: Columbia University Press, 1972). A simple questioning of narrative "truth" is not the point of this essay, for even an apparently complete renunciation of epistemological certainty such as one finds in the essay of Joseph Weisenfarth ("Criticism and the Semiosis of *The Good Soldier*," *Modern Fiction Studies* 9 [1963–64]: 39–49) does not begin to take up the ultimate critical problematic. Here it is not a matter of once again reforming the same question, but of per-forming the method of its textual madness.

6. I use the term according to the text's own double definition of "intimacy," or at least according to that of Nancy's mind—which ultimately may be the best figure we have for the text. "Intimacy" is at the same time the telling of secrets and the act of adultery: "So these matters presented themselves to Nancy's mind. But later on in the case she found that Mr. Brand had to confess to a 'guilty intimacy' with someone or other. Nancy imagined that he must have been telling someone his wife's secrets" (218).

7. This is certainly the movement of the opening paragraph of the novel.

8. Just as Dowell misreads Leonora's words in order to repress the violence they camouflage, so Leonora, Edward, and Nancy will render the cruelty of their daily scenes as illegible as Dowell could wish in his first weeks at Branshaw Telegraph. "Still there it is. And there it is also that all those three presented to the world the spectacle of being the best of good people. I assure you that during my stay for that fortnight in that fine old house, I never so much as noticed a single thing that could have affected that good opinion" (246).

9. "His face hitherto had, in the wonderful English fashion, expressed nothing whatever. Nothing. There was in it neither joy nor despair; neither hope nor fear; neither boredom nor satisfaction. . . . I never came across such a perfect expression before and I never shall again" (25).

10. This interpretation is less scandalous than it seems. Elsewhere in the novel the "black and white" specifically refers to a written text. As Nancy reads of the Brand divorce case, we read: "That was incredible. Yet there it was—in black and white" (219).

11. "I suppose that I should really like to be a polygamist; with Nancy, and with Leonora, and with Maisie Maidan, and possibly even with Florence" (237).

12. It is the comprehension of this relationship between the sacramental text of the marriage service and its meaning that defines reason: "I should marry Nancy if her reason were ever sufficiently restored to let her appreciate the meaning of the Anglican marriage service. But it is probable that

her reason will never be sufficiently restored to let her appreciate the meaning of the Anglican marriage service. Therefore I cannot marry her, according to the law of the land" (236).

13. Thus Florence's mode of discourse in interpreting the significance of the "Protest" renders literal and figural language mutually exclusive. She uses a figural language of inversion whereby she claims Edward to be clean-lived in order to say she wishes he weren't. Yet the literal truth of the matter (the fact that Edward is not clean-lived) renders Florence's attempt at figural inversion senseless. The historical facts behind the scene will explain the significance of this mutual exclusion.

14. This scene of the cows has often been mentioned as a hint of the action to come, but the brief readings always remain at the level of limited allegory. See for example Jo-Ann Baernstein, "Image, Identity, and Insight in *The Good Soldier*," in *Ford Madox Ford: Modern Judgements,* ed. Richard A. Cassell (London: Macmillan, 1972), 119; John A. Meixner, *Ford Madox Ford's Novels,* (Minneapolis: University of Minnesota Press, 1962), 168; Richard A. Cassell, *Ford Madox Ford: A Study of His Novels* (Baltimore: Johns Hopkins Press, 1962), 187; and R. W. Lid, *Ford Madox Ford: The Essence of His Art* (Berkeley and Los Angeles: University of California Press, 1964), 57.

15. The good literary historian might well protest at this point. As Violet Hunt relates the *real source* of this passage, it was none other than Ford himself who called the piece of paper "the Protest." As Hunt, Ford, and Ford's mother toured the castle at Marburg, it was Ford who played the role of Florence, saying: " 'There, that is what I have brought you to see. The Protest of Zwingli, Luther and Bucer. That bit of paper *is* Protestantism. It all began with the signing of that bit of paper.' And turning to me: 'That is what you mean when you say you are a Protestant!' " (Violet Hunt, *The Desirable Alien at Home in Germany* [London: Chatto and Windus, 1913], as cited in Henigan, *The Desirable Alien,* 159–60). Who at this point could have confidence in the word of Ford filtered through that of Violet Hunt, through that of Florence, and through that of the novel's narrator once again? Still, if I have rejected this bit of literary history in favor of actual history, it is partly because of the decade Ford spent preparing a biography of Henry VIII. He knew his Protestant history, then, better than he here lets on.

The complex reverberations of that history in the tale of *The Good Soldier* exceed the scope of this study. Henry VIII, for example, is on the one hand openly associated in the novel with the possibility of divorce (220–21) and therefore with having had six wives one after another. But he is also a figure whose history raises the spectre of incest as inextricable from marriage. This says much about the aura of incest that threatens the relationship between Edward and Nancy.

Marc Shell elaborates the accusations of incest aimed at Henry VIII in *The End of Kinship* (Stanford: Stanford University Press, 1988), 109–13.

Shell's discussion is no simple historical reportage. He explores the way in which incest operates in the quasi-factual arena of event as inextricable from a reading of Elizabeth's translations, essays, and carefully crafted political speeches, and from Shakespeare's *Henry VIII.* Moreover, the kinds of figural exchanges and disguises that Shell shows to be critical in *Measure for Measure* have much resonance with the relation of the literal and the figural in Ford. What Shell demonstrates is that such issues have no narrow religious and linguistic limits. The irresolvable distinction between literal and figural kinship in general and its relation to incest (Shell, 4) has vast political implications.

16. Ford Madox Hueffer, *Memories and Impressions from Confucius' Day to Our Own* (New York and London: Harper and Brothers, 1911), xviii.

17. This took place, incidentally, "under the protection of" Philip of Hesse (not Ludwig the Courageous) who (much later) wished to have two (not three) wives at once.

18. Martin Luther, *Luther's Works* (Philadelphia: Fortress Press, 1971), 37. This work is hereafter cited in the text with the abbreviation *LW* followed by the page number.

19. This is not to say that the status of the words "This is my body" is not repeatedly questioned (*LW* 19, 22, 24, 27, 41, 56). But the question is always immediately shifted beyond the confines of the colloquy: their role as language in the text of the argument is all but forgotten. Nevertheless, the discussion of the phrase puts the defender of a literal reading into something of a predicament. Once Luther insists on the bodily presence of Christ in the bread, he is forced to depend on a series of backup mechanisms to guarantee that presence. The words "This is my body" must be added to bring the body into the bread, and the words are in turn meaningless unless guaranteed by the authority of God. The problematic of literal versus figurative language thus becomes far more complex than I am able to indicate clearly in the text.

20. This is the same logical double-bind as Florence's discourse on the Protest, in which a figural language that operates by inversion and a literal language of truth are mutually exclusive. See note 13, above.

Chapter 4: Fictional Histories

1. Citations from Virgil, *The Aeneid of Virgil*, trans. Rolfe Humphries (New York: Charles Scribner's , 1951).

2. For a brief commentary on the context for this polemic, see Gotthold Ephraim Lessing, *Werke* (Munich: Winkler Verlag, 1969), 2:1164–65).

3. Gotthold Ephraim Lessing, *Sämtliche Schriften,* ed. Karl Lachmann and Franz Muncker (Stuttgart: Göschen, 1886–1924), 11:3. Most references to Lessing's works other than the *Laocoön* refer to this edition. They are indicated in the text by Lachmann and volume and page.

4. Polemics for Lessing, then, is hardly reducible to the reproduction of

the traditional form of juxtaposing citation with refutation, as suggested by Norbert W. Feinäugle, "Lessings Streitschriften: "Überlegungen zu Wesen und Methode der literarischen Polemik," *Lessing Yearbook* 1 (Munich: Max Hueber Verlag, 1969), 126- 49.

5. References to the German edition of the *Laocoön* are to volume 9 of the Lachmann edition, marked in the text by the page number and *G*. The subsequent number followed by an *E* refers to the page of the English translation—Gotthold Ephraim Lessing, *Laocoön*, trans. Edward Allen McCormick (Baltimore: Johns Hopkins University Press, 1984)—which also supplies, in an appendix, translations of the Latin quotations from Pliny. With few exceptions the English translations as they appear in the text have been modified, sometimes radically.

6. We should not be misled by the apparently haphazard appearance of the image of the critical path. It is one of the guiding metaphors of the *Laocoön*. We come across it in the preface, in chapter 20, and elsewhere in the text.

At the same time that Lessing was writing the *Laocoön*, he was planning another critical work entitled *Hermäa*. In the preface to that text we find the following passage:

> Hermäa were what the Greeks called all that was found by chance on the road. For Hermes was for them, among other things, also the god of the road and of chance.
>
> Consider a man of unlimited curiosity, without a penchant for a particular field of study. Incapable of giving a fixed direction to his mind, he will wander through all fields of learning in order to satisfy his curiosity. . . . If he is not entirely without genius, he will note a great deal but probe little. . . .
>
> And these his comments, his traces, his discoveries, his views, his caprices . . . how could he better name them than Hermäa. They are riches that a fortunate accident [*Zufall*] allows him to find on the path, more often on secret paths than on the highway. (Lachmann 14:290–91)

What chapter 26 and other moments in the *Laocoön* pose as potential error (following one's caprices, wandering from the main path) is announced, therefore, as the conscious nonmethodology of another work. The irony this lends to the self-corrective moments in the *Laocoön* is obvious.

7. For the "true" historical genesis of the *Laocoön*, see *Laokoon—Lessing, Herder, Goethe: Selections*, ed. William Guild Howard (New York: Henry Holt, 1910), cxli–cxliv, and Henry Hatfield, *Winckelmann and His German Critics* (New York: King's Crown Press, 1943), 49–55.

8. Cf. Howard, *Laokoon*, cxlii.

9. Ibid., 316.

10. What many have read clearly, however, is that Lessing copied Winckelmann, and implicit in such accusations or explanations is a concept of the

text's essence as coincident with its content. Hatfield writes that "Lessing did not abandon his plan of attacking Winckelmann's earlier interpretation of the statue, although he well knew that his predecessor had revised his views" and that "he was by no means candid in his treatment of his predecessor" (*Winckelmann and His German Critics*, 53–54). See, for example, F. Andrew Brown, *Gotthold Ephraim Lessing* (New York: Twayne, 1971), 88–89; N. G. Tschernyschewski, "Fortschrittliche Ideen in der Aesthetik Lessings," *Neue Welt*, Maiheft 1952; Howard, *Laokoon*, cxliv; Hugo Blümner, *Lessings Laokoon* (Berlin, 1880), 97; and Erich Schmidt, *Lessing: Geschichte seines Lebens und seiner Schriften* (Berlin, 1884–92), 12, as cited by Elida Maria Szarota, who gives an excellent and detailed synopsis of critical reaction to this problem in *Lessings "Laokoon"* (Weimar: Arion Verlag, 1959), 9–10. (Szarota herself sees Lessing's fictional history as evidence of his tact and respect for Winckelmann.)

Similar accusations have been leveled with regard to Lessing's borrowings from Spence and Caylus. See, for example, Brown, *Lessing*, 82–83 and 85; and Donald T. Siebert, Jr., "*Laocoön* and *Polymetis*: Lessing's Treatment of Joseph Spence," *Lessing Yearbook* 3 (1971): 71–83. Howard's long introduction to Lessing's text is a masterful description of its debt to many other texts as well: see esp. lxix–lxxi. Ernst Cassirer, on the other hand, is at once able to write of Lessing, "He did not create this content but found it almost entirely ready at hand," claiming that "there is scarcely a single aesthetic concept and scarcely a single principle in Lessing which did not have its exact parallel in contemporary literature." Lessing's originality, he maintained, lay elsewhere than in the content of his concepts. See Ernst Cassirer, *The Philosophy of the Enlightenment* (Boston: Beacon Press, 1955), 357ff.

11. As Lessing himself says about the relation between original and imitation, "If the imitator is a man who has confidence in himself, then he seldom imitates without wishing to embellish; and if, in his opinion, the embellishment is successful, then he is fox enough to brush over with his tail the footprints that would betray the path by which he came" (37–38G, 172E).

12. Thus Lessing praises Voltaire (by citing his translator) precisely because his history does not obey the traditional laws of ordering (Lachmann 4:364–65).

13. This latter position had been the contention or at least hypothesis of Lessing in chapters 5 and 6 (38G, 35E).

14. All this also allows Lessing to enjoy the elaborate extended joke of chapter 27. There, it is once again a question of evidence that the statue was made in the later period. To this end, Lessing cites a passage from Pliny:

> Yet lest I should seem to be altogether attacking the Greeks, I
> should like to be thought to belong to those first masters of painting
> and modeling, whom you will find in these books writing on their

completed works (works which we are never tired of admiring) an inscription denoting incompleteness, as "Apelles was making," or "Polycletus," as if the work was ever inchoate and imperfect; so that from the varieties of criticism the artist might have a way of escape towards pardon, as being ready to correct whatever was desired, if he had not been cut off. How modest it was of them to inscribe all their works, as if they were their last, and as if in each case they had been meanwhile cut off by fate. Three works and no more, I believe, which I shall describe in their turn, are said to have been inscribed, as if finished, "he made," by which it appeared that the artist had the greatest confidence in his work, and for this reason all these were regarded with great dislike. (169G, 148E [Latin] and 235E [English trans.])

Might we not also think of Lessing as a "first master," one who preceded Winckelmann, one whose writing of the *Laocoön* was cut off by fate at the end of chapter 25 by the publication of the *History*, one whose extreme modesty admits his own work as "inchoate and imperfect" and prevents him from venturing another step until he has read Winckelmann? Yet Pliny himself describes such modesty as a way of escape towards pardon for whatever errors the work may contain. And Lessing, in the closing paragraph of the chapter, admits that the use of the more modest phrasing does not definitively place one in the early period nor ensure that such modesty is necessarily to be taken at its word: "If all artists who used ἐποίησε [made] belong with the late ones, still not all those who made use of ἐποίει [was making] belong therefore with the more ancient. Even among the later artists there might have been some who really possessed this modesty so becoming to a great man and others who feigned to possess it" (168G, 149E).

15. Lessing insists several times in the course of the *Laocoön* that similarities between works do not necessarily indicate that the one has imitated the other: see 33–34G (33E), 51G (45E), 58G (47E).

16. For those who read Lessing's problematic literally, Blümner gives an impressively detailed gloss of the various responses to the question of how to read the *similiter* (*Lessings Laokoon*, 300–301).

17. Despite my designation of one of these readings as proper and the other as a misreading, one could make equally powerful claims for a reversal of labels; See Blümner, *Lessings Laokoon*, 300. Lessing does both, in fact. On the one hand, he claims critical precision for reading the similiter as a *temporal* analogy, yet he immediately afterwards recognizes that his reader will insist on another interpretation. What is significant here is not which reading is "correct" but that Lessing pretends to distinguish at all between correct readings and misreadings.

18. In light of such a passage, it is remarkable, although perhaps inevitable, that Lessing's critics arrive at his theory of language through a literal reading of his statements on language; and these, in turn, have often been taken as coincident with stylistic strategies. See, for example, Eric A. Black-

all, *The Emergence of German as a Literary Language, 1700–1775* (Cambridge: Cambridge University Press, 1959), 361ff., and Detlev Droese, *Lessing und die Sprache* (Zurich: Juris Druck und Verlag Zürich, 1968), 110–12.

19. The title page of the essay reads "Laocoön; or, On the Limits of Painting and Poesy," followed by the epigraph from Plutarch: "They distinguish themselves from one another in their objects and mode of imitation."

20. Cf. 5G, 5E; 52G, 46E; 60G, 190E; 60G, 48E.

21. In light of the implications of Lessing's discussion of the disgusting, it makes perfect sense that Socrates' mouth should be filled with excrement.

22. The similarity between this discussion of the disgusting in Lessing and its ultimate relationship to the question of vomiting is an obvious recall of Jacques Derrida's discussion of the disgusting and vomit in Kant ("Economimesis," in *Mimesis des articulations*, ed. Sylviane Agacinski et al. [Paris: Flammarion, 1975], 55–93). That I have copied Derrida seems to go without saying, the dates of publication alone proving whose text has precedence. It is not a case, however, of simple ventriloquism, just as the relation of Lessing to Mendelssohn and of Kant, in turn, to both Lessing and Mendelssohn is not one of perfect assimilative repetition but of a certain kind of incorporation. In the case of Lessing, although the disgusting is strategically situated to mark an endpoint of disruption in the progress of his text, such disruptions of conventional schemes of representation are at work even when Lessing most cogently insists on describing the role of the beautiful. The disgusting, or at least its implications, do not operate (as for Kant) as an exception to the rules of mimesis.

23. In the case of what Lessing calls "the poetic painting," the ideal poetic experience is one in which the reader loses consciousness of the means of representation (words) such that "we . . . believe we feel the true palpable impression of their objects" (101G, 85E). The matter, however, is not quite so simple, as a reading of chapter 16 will show.

24. See Paul de Man, "Self," in *Allegories of Reading* (New Haven: Yale University Press, 1979), 160–87.

25. Lessing offers the following definition of allegorical language in his "Essay on the Fable": "*Allegory* does not say that which, according to the words, it seems to say, but rather something similar. The new teachers of rhetoric remember, that this *something other* is to be restricted to *something similar*, because otherwise every *irony* would be an *allegory*" (Lachmann 7:421). This saying other than what it seems to say becomes critical in Lessing's allegorical reading of a passage from Homer in chapter 16. There, irony and allegory do not exclude one another, however.

26. Howard's gloss on this passage would therefore miss the point: "In poetry . . . personified abstractions are not allegorical; they are what they represent" (*Laokoon*, 380).

27. Clearly, much more is at stake in the question of portraying the invisible than yet another distinction between painting and poetry. It is perhaps

not entirely beside the point that in chapter 12, in relation to poesy, as in chapter 10, in relation to painting, the power of figural and allegorical representation is linked to raising "a mere figure to a higher being" (73G, 60E). ("Through the painterly destruction of the difference between visible and invisible beings, at the same time all the characteristic features are lost through which this higher race raises itself above the lesser one" [82G, 66E].) Nor is it simply a matter, here in the later passage, of distinguishing between the literal categories of mortals and gods. The godly—which is to say, not only the realm of the invisible but also the power of making invisible (or, as we have seen, the power of figuration)—is, according to Lessing, bound in Homer with a whole series of readerly gestures, the free play of the imagination (82G, 66E), a violation of reasonable proportions (82G, 67E), and an escape from the logical constraints of cause and effect (83G, 67E).

28. Can it be insignificant that Howard, one of the pillars of *Laocoön* scholarship, suppressed the last sentence of the passage just cited as well as the entire paragraph that follows? In his commentary on the term *Ausschweifungen* in the preface (*Laokoon*, 342), he explains that it ordinarily means "excesses" but should here be read as "digressions, excursuses." He adds: "Many of these digressions are omitted from the present edition"— in the name of what implicit law against excess, we might conjecture.

In a similar gesture of repression E. M. Butler writes: "As an aesthetic treatise *Laocoön* was unfinished and remained so; dramatically it was complete at the end of Chapter XXII; for the lengthy considerations about the representation of the ugly and the disgusting are in the nature of a digression, and could willingly be spared" (*The Tyranny of Greece over Germany* [New York: Macmillan, 1935], 68).

29. Szarota reads the passage as just such a mimetic chain. Lessing, she maintains, naively assumed the *artist* had to be beautiful in order to create beauty (*Lessings "Laokoon,"* 33).

30. Each of the Laocoön passages in Virgil is followed by a scene that revolves around the questions of truth, lies, and misinterpretation. Sinon appears after the first passage to convince the Trojans, with a long fabrication, that the horse is an innocent image. Cassandra appears after the last: like Laocoön, she speaks the truth in warning the Trojans, only to have her word doubted.

31. Thus it would seem quite futile to label Lessing, as Szarota does, in her book *Lessings Laokoon*, as an "enemy of allegory" struggling for a realistic art form (pp. 59–60, for example, and throughout her text). The performance of Lessing's text is an endless refutation of such assertions. It has understandably become a commonplace even among the *Laocoön*'s most sophisticated readers to point out that Lessing speaks here and there of metaphor as that which brings the arbitrary signs of language back towards the natural. See, for example, Tzvetan Todorov, "Asthetik und Semiotik im 18. Jahrhundert. G. E. Lessing: Laokoon," in *Das Laokoon-Projekt*, ed.

Gunter Gebauer (Stuttgart: J. B. Metzler, 1984), 18; Karlheiz Stierle, "Das bequeme Verhältnis: Lessings *Laokoon* und die Entdeckung des ästhetischen Mediums," in the same volume; and David Wellbery, *Lessing's Laocoön* (Cambridge: Cambridge University Press), 194–95.

In addition, Lessing's famous letter to Nicolai of May 26, 1769, which has received much-deserved attention, again speaks of figures and similes bringing arbitrary signs closer to natural signs. (See Wellbery, *Lessing's Laocoön*, 226, as well as the volume by Victor Anthony Rudowski, *Lessing's Aesthetica in Nuce* [Chapel Hill: University of North Carolina Press, 1971].) That same letter has also been used to clarify and reduce the seeming contradictions in the *Laocoön* on the relationship among natural and arbitrary signs, painting and poetry.

It can hardly be a question of denying the existence of such assertions in Lessing's work. But figural language in Lessing—say in the complex operation of *similiter* or in the representation of hunger by a strange kind of potential satiety—never performs quite according to the ideal rules the scholars tend to seek and cite, those scholars who always look to the authoritative source, as though it could speak in natural language, always reading it as saying the thing itself.

32. As one example among many, see Brown, *Lessing*, 87.

33. I quote from the Richard Lattimore translation of the *Iliad* (Chicago: University of Chicago Press, 1951).

34. Eric Blackall says of Lessing's critical writing: "Someone is being addressed nearly all the time. It is a vivid style punctuated by accents of arraignment or appeal. An orator pleading a case . . ." (*German as a Literary Language*, 366). If this is so, Lessing ironically locates such implications of his style within the history of a decadent desire for polemical power.

Chapter 5: The Monstrosity of Translation

1. Translated by Harry Zohn as "The Task of the Translator," in Walter Benjamin, *Illuminations* (New York: Schocken, 1969). Zohn's lucid translations have made a decidedly meaningful contribution to the understanding of Benjamin by an English-speaking audience. The criticism that appears here and there in my text should be recognized more as a play between possible versions than as a claim to establish a more "correct" translation. References to Zohn are marked as *Z* followed by the page number.

Unless otherwise noted, however, all citations to Benjamin are from Walter Benjamin, *Gesammelte Schriften* (Frankfurt a.M.: Suhrkamp Verlag, 1972). The translations, such as they are, are my own.

2. All references to "Die Aufgabe des Übersetzers" are to vol. 4, pt. 1, of *Gesammelte Schriften* and are hereafter cited by page number in the text.

3. For a general discussion of the concept of symbolic language which the Baudelaire piece poses, see Paul de Man, "The Rhetoric of Temporality," in *Blindness and Insight* (Minneapolis: University of Minnesota Press,

1971), as well as Walter Benjamin, *Ursprung des deutschen Trauerspiels,* 1, pt. 1:336–37 and 342.

4. The connection between original and translation "may be called a natural one," Benjamin writes, "more precisely a connection of life," ("ein Zusammenhang des Lebens," 10). To make his meaning clear, he repeats the syllables *Leben* sixteen times in the course of the paragraph, and midway through clears it of its traditional meaning. The "life" to which translations are bound is itself woven into textual history: "The sphere of life must ultimately be fixed in history, not in nature. . . . Thus, the task arises for the philosopher to understand all natural life through the more encompassing life of history" (11).

5. Zohn translates "Entfaltung" as "flowering"—and understandably so, for this extension of the metaphorical web is a natural one. It is not, however, Benjamin's.

6. "Translation is then ultimately expedient for the expression of the innermost relation of languages to one another. It cannot possibly reveal [*offenbaren*] this hidden relationship itself, cannot possibly establish it [*herstellen*], but can perform it [*darstellen*] by a germinating or intensive realization" (12).

7. "Here as in every other essential regard, Hölderlin's translations, especially those of the two Sophoclean tragedies, present themselves as a confirmation. The harmony of the languages is so deep in them, that the meaning [*Sinn*] is touched by the language only as an aeolian harp is touched by the wind. Hölderlin's translations are originary images [*Urbilder*] of their form: they relate themselves even to the most perfect translations of their texts as the originary-image to the example." (20–21). ("Hierfür wie in jeder andern wesentlichen Hinsicht stellen sich Hölderlins Übertragungen, besonders die der beiden Sophokleischen Tragödien, bestätigend dar. In ihnen ist die Harmonie der Sprachen so tief, daß der Sinn nur noch wie eine Äolsharfe vom Winde von der Sprache berührt wird. Hölderlins Übersetzungen sind Urbilder ihrer Form; sie verhalten sich auch zu den vollkommensten Übertragungen ihrer Texte als das Urbild zum Vorbild.")

8. Zohn's translation is perhaps more logical, certainly more optimistic, but doesn't quite form itself in detail according to the strange mode of Benjamin's meaning: "In the same way a translation, instead of resembling the meaning of the original, must lovingly and in detail incorporate the original's mode of signification, thus making both the original and the translation recognizable as fragments of a greater language, just as fragments are part of a vessel" (Z 78).

9. Gershom Scholem, in writing about this text, relates the figure of the angel of history to the *Tikkun* of the Lurianic Kabbalah. Yet at the same time, Benjamin has in mind the kabbalistic concept of the *Tikkun,* the messianic restoration and mending which patches together and restores the original Being of things, shattered and corrupted in the "Breaking of Ves-

sels," and also (the original Being of) history ("Walter Benjamin und sein Engel," in *Zur Aktualität Walter Benjamins* [Frankfurt: Suhrkamp, 1972], 132–33). If Scholem recognizes the failure of the angel of history to carry out this task, he nevertheless sees evidence of this redemption elsewhere in Benjamin (ibid., 133–34).

Scholem might have turned to "Die Aufgabe des Übersetzers," where the image of the broken vessel plays a more direct role. Harry Zohn's (mis)translation of this passage (cited in n. 8 above) along with Benjamin's carefully articulated messianic rhetoric seem to speak here of the successful realization of the *Tikkun*. Yet whereas Zohn suggests that a totality of fragments are brought together, Benjamin insists that the final outcome of translation is still "a broken part." In the Lurianic doctrine, then, translation would never progress beyond the stage of the *Shevirath Ha-Kelim*. (For a description of this "Breaking of Vessels" as Benjamin knew it, see Gershom Scholem, *Major Trends in Jewish Mysticism* [New York: Schocken, 1973].) In the closing passage of "Die Aufgabe des Übersetzers," the messianic valorization of the Holy Scriptures ironically serves to usher in the fundamental fragmentation which interlinear translation performs.

10. Benjamin speaks at length of the concept of *Kritik* in the early romantics in *Der Begriff der Kunstkritik in der deutschen Romantik* (1, pt. 1:11–22).

Chapter 6: The Metaphor of Temporality

This chapter was originally written in 1984, the year following de Man's death, and it bears the marks of that event. Other events followed: the discovery and publication of Paul de Man's wartime writings and the proliferation of subsequent responses. The former made painfully clear how necessary it is to read a text in relation both to the question of history and to the implications of its concept of the historical, and made clear that what a text says and performs with respect to these issues has everything to do with the political. Some of the responses analyzed these questions with great intelligence in readings both of the early and the late works. What appears here in relating questions of temporality, authority, and rhetoric hardly begins to place "The Rhetoric of Temporality" and *Allegories of Reading* in political perspective, but its insights and blindsights are perhaps, nevertheless, some of what such meditations have to take into account.

The epigraph is from what later became a chapter of *The Rhetoric of Romanticism* and was first published in Paul de Man, "Shelley Disfigured," in Harold Bloom et al., *Deconstruction and Criticism* (New York: Seabury Press, 1979), 68.

1. Paul de Man, *Allegories of Reading* (New Haven: Yale University Press, 1979). All references to *Allegories of Reading* are noted in the text by the title of the chapter followed by the page number.

2. De Man creates the sense of progress in this essay, ironically enough, by a movement that vacillates between vacillation and progress.

3. See de Man's essay on the *Social Contract:* "We call *text* any entity that can be considered from such a double perspective: as a generative, open-ended, non-referential grammatical system and as a figural system closed off by a transcendental signification that subverts the grammatical code to which the text owes its existence. The 'definition' of the text also states the impossibility of its existence and prefigures the allegorical narratives of this impossibility" ("Promises," 270).

4. The problem of teleological progression is raised in the essay "Self" with regard to Rousseau's play *Pygmalion:* "The provisional syntheses that are achieved along the way in the course of the action do not necessarily mark a progression and it is the burden of the reading to decide whether the text is the teleology of a selfhood that culminates in the climactic exclamation 'Moi!' or a repetitive vacillation" ("Self," 176).

But the question is, can "reading" ever be in a position to divest itself of this burden by making a definitive decision?

5. One can trace this general movement of revelation and recoil in other of de Man's texts. See, for example, "Literature and Language: A Commentary," in *Blindness and Insight* (Minneapolis: University of Minnesota Press, 1983), 281, 289.

6. In ways that are too involved to outline here and for reasons that are all too easy to imagine, this evolutionary tale is almost a parodic recapitulation of the arguments of the first two chapters on Rousseau, "Metaphor" and "Self."

7. The "moi" functions both as a general Self that can bridge the gap and include the particular self of Pygmalion and as a self that marks the rupture between Galathea and Pygmalion as other.

8. In the opening essay of *Allegories of Reading* de Man writes: "The grammatical model of the question becomes rhetorical not when we have, on the one hand, a literal meaning and on the other hand a figural meaning, but when it is impossible to decide by grammatical or other linguistic devices which of the two meanings (that can be entirely incompatible) prevails. Rhetoric radically suspends logic and opens up vertiginous possibilities of referential aberration. And although it would perhaps be somewhat more remote from common usage, I would not hesitate to equate the rhetorical, figural potentiality of language with literature itself" ("Semiology and Rhetoric," 10). See also "Self," 166f.

9. Elsewhere, de Man uses a simplified version of this metaphor to speak of false models of reading: "The attraction of reconciliation is the elective breeding-ground of false models and metaphors; it accounts for the metaphorical model of literature as a kind of box that separates an inside from an outside, and the reader or critic as the person who opens the lid in order to release in the open what was secreted but inaccessible inside" ("Semiology and Rhetoric," 5).

10. No sooner does de Man refer to "one lock worthy of being raped" than he goes on to speak of "the epistemological labyrinth of figural struc-

tures." The wit of the allusion to Pope can be found in Canto II of "The Rape of the Lock," where a similar slide between lock and lock in the name of a labyrinth takes place. Here, Belinda's ringlets become labyrinths that chain her admirers:

> This nymph, to the destruction of mankind,
> Nourish'd two locks, which graceful hung behind
> In equal curls, and well conspired to deck
> With shining ringlets the smooth ivory neck.
> Love in these labyrinths his slaves detains,
> And mighty hearts are held in slender chains.
> (lines 19–24)

11. "The Rhetoric of Temporality" in Paul de Man, *Blindness and Insight*, 188. Subsequent references to this essay are noted in the text by page number.

12. In a 1980 interview de Man had this to say: "But irony is for me something much more fundamental than [reading the text against the overt claim of control]. One gets beyond problems of self-reflection, self-consciousness. For me, irony is not something that one can historically locate, because what's involved in irony is precisely the impossibility of a system of linear and coherent narrative. There is an inherent conflict or tension between irony on the one hand and history on the other, between irony on the one hand and self-consciousness on the other" ("Interview with Paul de Man," *Yale Review* 73 [Summer 1984]: 580).

13. Ironically enough, this passage follows closely upon de Man's ironization of his own historicizing of the question of allegory.

14. Paul de Man, "The Rhetoric of Temporality" in *Interpretation: Theory and Practice*, ed. Charles S. Singleton (Baltimore: Johns Hopkins Press, 1969), 206. (The phrase is inadvertently omitted in the reprinting of the essay.)

15. Walter Benjamin's *Ursprung des Deutschen Trauerspiels*, a text de Man invokes at the outset of his essay, distinguishes between what Benjamin calls the truth of the philosopher from mere knowledge, which tries to stabilize and capture its object: "Truth, realized in the round dance of performed [*dargestellten*] ideas, escapes being projected by whatever means into the realm of knowledge. Knowledge is a possessing. Its object itself defines itself as that which must become possessed by consciousness—even if it is transcendental" (Walter Benjamin, *Gesammelte Schriften* [Frankfurt a. M.: Suhrkamp Verlag, 72], 1, pt. 1: 209, my translation).

16. The parallel insight in *Allegories of Reading* surfaces at any number of moments, say, for example, when de Man speaks of the subject, denied in the literary text by the author or reader, being "reborn in the guise of the interpreter," ("Self," 174). "Is this not the best way to reintroduce the authority of a self at the far end of its most radical negation, in the highly

abstracted and generalized form of a deconstructive process of self-denial?" "Self," 172).

17. See de Man's commentary on Shelley in a similar predicament: "Shelley Disfigured," in *Deconstruction and Criticism,* 68.

18. Something similar takes place in the essay "Semiology and Rhetoric" in *Allegories of Reading,* where the grammatization of rhetoric as an assertion of negative knowledge, of a deconstruction of metaphor, alternates with the rhetorization of grammar that brings us to a "suspended uncertainty" ("Semiology and Rhetoric," 16).

19. See the pseudomelancholic preface to de Man's *Rhetoric of Romanticism,* where history, each time it is introduced, ironically gives way to phrases such as "a rhetorical analysis of figural language" or "theoretical inquiries into the problems of figural language" (de Man, *The Rhetoric of Romanticism* [New York: Columbia University Press, 184], viii).

20. On the question of confessions and excuses, see the final chapter of *Allegories of Reading,* entitled "Excuses."

21. On the question of rhetorical questions see the opening chapter of *Allegories of Reading,* "Semiology and Rhetoric."

Chapter 7: The Unimaginable Touch of Time

1. Unless otherwise indicated, *The Prelude* is cited from William Wordsworth, *The Prelude, 1799, 1805, 1850,* ed. Jonathan Wordsworth, M. H. Abrams, and Stephen Gill (New York: W. W. Norton, 1979). Passages in the text are from the 1850 *Prelude* unless otherwise noted and are indicated by book and line number.

2. All poetry of Wordsworth (with the exception of passages from *The Prelude*) is cited from William Wordsworth, *The Poetical Works of William Wordsworth,* ed. E. de Selincourt and Helen Darbishire, 5 vols. (Oxford: Clarendon Press, 1947). "Lines Composed a Few Miles above Tintern Abbey" is marked as TA in the text; "Ode: Intimations of Immortality from Recollections of Early Childhood" is marked as IO.

3. See Albert S. Gérard, *English Romantic Poetry* (Berkeley and Los Angeles: University of California Press, 1968), who sees this ambiguity as an "element of pervasive unity" (99).

More precisely "little *lines* / of sportive wood run wild," a phrase which in the same gesture transforms the humanly cultivated into that which is wild and also, in the echoing of "Lines" from Wordsworth's title (and from so many other Wordsworth titles as well), suggests that poetry itself has something to do with this transformation. (The pun on "lines" is noted in an unpublished paper of Jonathan Baldo.)

4. See, for example, Melvin Rader, *Wordsworth: A Philosophical Approach* (Oxford: Clarendon Press, 1967), 59–60; John Beer, *Wordsworth in Time* (London: Faber and Faber, 1979), 53; Eugene L. Stelzig, *All Shades of Con-*

sciousness (Paris: Mouton, 1975), 86; and Gérard, *English Romantic Poetry*, 109–10.

5. For a partial gloss on various critical views of this question see Gérard, *English Romantic Poetry*, 91–99.

6. See Charles Sherry, *Wordsworth's Poetry of the Imagination* (Oxford: Clarendon Press, 1980), 97, who suggests something similar.

7. A reader like Geoffrey Durant, nevertheless, would insist on the absence of "'distance' between the valley and Wordsworth's response to it" (*Wordsworth and the Great System: A Study of Wordsworth's Poetic Universe* [Cambridge: Cambridge University Press, 1970], 89).

8. This restoration of the past and of its pleasures, this making the present vanish in the name of regeneration, has a remarkable similarity to Wordsworth's later description of older readers reading bad poetry poorly:

> If it should excite wonder that men of ability, in later life, whose understandings have been rendered acute by practice in affairs, should be so easily and so far imposed upon when they happen to take up a new work in verse, this appears to be the cause; — that, having discontinued their attention to poetry . . . they have not, as to this art, advanced in true discernment beyond the age of youth. If, then, a new poem fall in their way, whose attractions are of that kind which would have enraptured them during the heat of youth, the judgment not being improved to a degree that they shall be disgusted, they are dazzled; and prize and cherish the faults for having had *power to make the present time vanish before them, and to throw the mind back, as by enchantment, into the happiest season of life. As they read, powers seem to be revived, passions are regenerated and pleasures restored. The Book was probably taken up after an escape from the burden of business, and with a wish to forget the world, and all its vexations and anxieties.* ("Essay, Supplementary to the Preface" [1815], in *The Prose Works of William Wordsworth*, ed. W. J. B. Owen and Jane Worthington Smyser, 3 vols. [London: Clarendon, 1974], 3: 63–64; italics mine).

One would also have to rethink the place of the "spots of time" passages in the two-part *Prelude* of 1799, lines 288–96; the 1805 *Prelude*, XII, 257–72; and the 1850 *Prelude*, XII, 208–25.

9. This shift to the unremembered prefigures both the "Nor wilt thou then forget" of the closing lines (which do not precisely indicate simple memory) and also the remarkable way in which "recollection" functions in the Immortality Ode.

10. See Gérard, *English Romantic Poetry*, 104–5.

11. See *William Wordsworth: Selected Poems and Prefaces*, ed. Jack Stillinger (Boston: Houghton Mifflin, 1965), 538.

12. Cleanth Brooks speaks of this as a passage "no longer trying to recapture the childhood joy" "with a hint of amused patronage." Wordsworth, he thinks, might have done well to omit stanza VII altogether. See *The Well-Wrought Urn* (New York: Reynal and Hitchcock, 1947), 128–29.

In any case it is difficult to imagine that this passage could be read as other than an ironic vision of childhood innocence. The distortions of the opening lines of stanza IV as well as the citation of Samuel Daniel's *Musophilus* are the more subtle indications. The dedicatory poem to the latter (from which the "humorous stage" of the Immortality Ode [103] is cited) is an attack on the imitation attributed to the child in "Tintern Abbey."

> I doe not here upon this hum'rous Stage,
> Bring my transformed Verse, apparelled
> With others passions, or with others rage;
> With loues, with wounds, with factions furnished:
> But here present thee, onely modelled
> In this poore frame, the forme of mine owne heart:
> Where, to reuiue my selfe, my Muse is led
> With motions of her owne, t'act her owne part,

Samuel Daniel, *Samuel Daniel's "Musophilus": Containing a General Defense of all Learning*, ed. Raymond Himelick (West Lafayette, Ind.: Purdue University Studies, 1965), 61.

13. Among Wordsworth's readers there is a long history of discomfort with his claims for childhood in light of the details of stanzas VII and VIII, starting as early as Coleridge in chapter 22 of the *Biographia Literaria*. See, for example, Brooks, *The Well-Wrought Urn*, 129–31; David Perkins, *The Quest for Permanence* (Cambridge: Harvard University Press, 1959), 68, 75, 79; also, G. Wilson Knight, *The Starlit Dome* (London: Oxford University Press, 1941), 43–48.

14. See Geoffrey Hartman, *The Unremarkable Wordsworth* (Minneapolis: University of Minnesota Press, 1987), 204.

15. In "Tintern Abbey" that which seems to be the natural in all the specificity of the opening stanza proves to be memory of a previous memory of nature. In the Immortality Ode, too, the way in which nature is said to remember defies any simple link of mind to the external world. Here, after all, that remembering echoes our having become embers in a willed conflagration of the concepts of childhood and human origins so far presented. Much could be said about this in relation to the false nostalgia of the opening four stanzas, where Nature is already human memory, already speaks the language of the poet.

16. See Stillinger, *William Wordsworth: Selected Poems and Prefaces*, 539.

17. Trilling speaks of Wordsworth's using "the word 'realised' in its most literal sense" (Lionel Trilling, *The Liberal Imagination: Essays on Literature and Society* (New York: Viking, 1950), 143.

18. Francis Ferguson, in a highly intelligent reading of the Immortality Ode, emphasizes the appearance of "thought" in the ode's closing stanzas (*Wordsworth: Language as Counter-Spirit* [New Haven: Yale University Press, 1977], 123–25).

19. Reading the stages of life here suggested has been a repeated topos

in the commentary on this poem. For example, Arthur Beatty in *Words-worth: His Doctrine and Art in Their Historical Relations* (Madison: University of Wisconsin Press, 1960), 69–96, reads this as "a scheme of mental development in three stages" which he finds elsewhere in Wordsworth's poetry. See also Rader, *Wordsworth: A Philosophical Approach*, 85ff., and Geoffrey Hartman, *Unmediated Vision* (New York: Harcourt, Brace, and World, 1960), 5.

20. See Paul D. Sheats, *The Making of Wordsworth's Poetry, 1785–1798* (Cambridge: Harvard University Press, 1973), 237.

21. See Sherry, *Wordsworth's Poetry of the Imagination*, 97–98.

22. On "the language of the sense" see William Empson, *The Structure of Complex Words* (London: Chatto and Windus, 1977), 296–97. On the imagination as that which creates see Hartman, *Unmediated Vision*, 21.

23. The figure of the guide is frequently at risk in Wordsworth—for example in "Lucy Gray," in the crossing of the Alps in *The Prelude*, or at the end of book XII of the 1850 *Prelude*, 225–85.

24. Robert Maniquis talks about the use of superlatives at this moment in "Comparison, Intensity, and Time in 'Tintern Abbey,'" *Criticism* 11 (Fall 1969): 373–74. Beyond this particular point of reference, much that Maniquis writes of in this superb essay, despite much disagreement, is relevant here, for Maniquis works out the way in which syntax, structure, and the use of open-ended comparatives contribute to a sense of incremental progression in the poem. This sense of incremental repetition or redundance has been noted frequently. See, for example, Hartman, *Unmediated Vision*, 22; Gérard, *English Romantic Poetry*, 108; and Oscar James Campbell and Paul Mueschke, "Wordsworth's Aesthetic Development, 1795–1802," in *Essays and Studies in English and Comparative Literature* (Ann Arbor: University of Michigan Press, 1933), 32.

25. See Frances Ferguson's shrewd discussion of Jerome McGann's criticism of Wordsworth in McGann's *The Romantic Ideology:* Frances Ferguson, "Historicism, Deconstruction, and Wordsworth," *Diacritics* 17 (Winter 1987): 33–36. Marjorie Levinson's essay on "Tintern Abbey" is of course also of relevance here, in *William Wordsworth's Great Period Poems* (Cambridge: Cambridge University Press, 1986), 14–57.

26. See Gérard, *English Romantic Poetry*, 112.

27. See Harold Bloom, *The Visionary Company: A Reading of English Romantic Poetry* (Ithaca: Cornell University Press, 1971), 140.

28. Harold Bloom, *Poetry and Repression: Revisionism from Blake to Stevens* (New Haven: Yale University Press, 1976), 78. Bloom reads this passage as "a kind of survival through the surrogate of Dorothy" (78) and reads memory as a "trope and/or a defense that overcomes time" (80). Eugene Stelzig sees this gesture as a source of continuity and reassurance (*All Shades of Consciousness* [Paris: Mouton, 1975], 88). Hartman speaks of Wordsworth as a power who "is continually writing his own epitaph" (*Unmediated Vision*, 6), but one need not understand this as a negative judgment. Paul D.

Sheats also relates the end of "Tintern Abbey" to an epitaph but then reads memory as an "agency of redemption" in *The Making of Wordsworth's Poetry, 1785–1798*, 242–45.

29. See Hartman, *Unremarkable Wordsworth*, 42 and elsewhere.

30. John Milton, *"Paradise Lost" and Selected Poetry and Prose*, ed. Northrop Frye (New York: Holt, Rinehart, and Winston, 1961), 391–92.

31. The poem was not precisely written at Tintern but rather begun on leaving it between Tintern and Bristol in the four or five succeeding days. For other slight deviations from the title as well see Mary Moorman, *Wordsworth, A Biography: The Early Years, 1770–1803* (Oxford: Clarendon Press, 1957), 401–2.

In a sense, ironically enough, this and what follows mark an agreement of sorts with Marjorie Levinson's contention that in "Tintern Abbey" one finds "Wordsworth's erasure of the occasional character of [the] poem" where the title would lead us to expect a "loco-descriptive poem" (*Wordsworth's Great Period Poems* [Cambridge: Cambridge University Press, 1986], 15). It is an answer to the question that motivates her essay as to why Wordsworth composed "a title so burdened with topical meanings" (16).

32. The relationship between the boy and the "I" in "The Boy of Winander" as worked through by Paul de Man says much about that between William and Dorothy at the end of "Tintern Abbey." To be sure, the terms of the third person and "I" are reversed, and that has some important repercussions. See especially the footnote that offers an alternate reading: Paul de Man, "Time and History in Wordsworth," *Diacritics* 17 (Winter 1987): 9.

33. See Sherry, *Wordsworth's Poetry of the Imagination*, 102–3, who speaks of making the moment vanish but to conceal "the nature of recollection . . . from itself," "to conceal the present moment as a source of loss." He reads here "a narrative of recompense, where what is lost is more than amply restored." This is the economy of recompense on which Bloom, as well as many other readers insist. Mary Jacobus finds here as in *The Prelude* "an attempt to make permanent the vision that is threatened by the processes of change and growth recorded in the poem" as present is turned into past (*Tradition and Experiment in Wordsworth's Lyrical Ballads [1798]* [London: Oxford University Press, 1976], 130). Yet it is precisely at this moment that other forms of recompense finally give way to a totally different narrative.

34. The question of reading the landscape is soon to be bound to that of Imagination. Frances Ferguson, in reading the Simplon Pass passage that follows these lines, has this to say: "The process of reading in imagination becomes one in which the discontinuity of the act of reading reveals itself— rereading becomes not only a possibility but an inevitability, and betokens the mind's refusal to come to rest" (*Wordsworth: Language as Counter-Spirit*, 82).

35. Paul de Man returned again and again to this passage on the imagination. In "Wordsworth and Hölderlin," for example, he speaks of the re-

lationship between poetry and history and of a projection into a future that is also the remembering of a failure (*The Rhetoric of Romanticism* (New York: Columbia University Press, 1984], 57–59). In "Tintern Abbey" what is remarkable is that the consciousness that remains, the so-called remembering—or, at least, not forgetting—that is to take place, is no longer the "I" of Wordsworth but of Dorothy. In the essay "Time and History in Wordsworth" de Man speaks of the relationship between time and imagination as the key to understanding Wordsworth (16) and sees the contact with nature giving way to the contact with time. This is what also takes place at the close of "Tintern Abbey.": "The imagination engenders hope and future, not in the form of historical progress, nor in the form of an immortal life after death that would make human history unimportant, but as the persistent, future possibility of a retrospective reflection on its own decay" ("Time and History," 14). But in "Tintern Abbey" the reflection on decay seems left behind in the opening of the last stanza and is replaced in the end by the difference that thought—or not forgetting—can make.

36. Moreover, another translation has taken place which one is bound to miss if one looks only to the 1850 edition. The answers of the peasant in the 1805 edition have "sense and substance" (1805 *Prelude*, VI, 522) that appropriately go out in the final version, leaving only words (1850 *Prelude*, V, 589).

37. See Cynthia Chase's superb reading of this blank in *Decomposing Figures* (Baltimore: Johns Hopkins University Press, 1986), 116. Hartman calls this "a disorientation of time added to that of way" (*Wordsworth's Poetry, 1787–1814* [New Haven: Yale University Press, 1964], 46) and relates this to the order in which the three passages of the episode were written (ibid. 62–63).

38. William Wordsworth, *The Fourteen-Book Prelude*, ed. W. J. B. Owen (Ithaca: Cornell University Press, 1985), 129.

39, Robert A. Brinkley, "The Incident in the Simplon Pass: A Note on Wordsworth's Revisions," *The Wordsworth Circle* 12 (Spring 1981): 122–25. This essay is an excellent summary of past readings as well as a careful and subtle consideration of the implications of the several versions. As many readers have noted, it was W. G. Fraser (*Times Literary Supplement*, April 4, 1929) who, already in 1929, spoke of this passage as referring to the 1804 writing rather than the 1790 experience. Although this point has since become a commonplace, there is a vast disparity between readings that locate the rupture simply biographically, say in the 1790 crossing or the 1804 writing, and a reading such as Hartman's in *Wordsworth's Poetry* (46) or Brinkley's, where the relationship among the versions is considerably more complex.

40. Hartman, *Wordsworth's Poetry*, 45.

41. And goes out completely unless one reads here as Empson does in *The Structure of Complex Words*, 294–95, in which case, the "but" of the 1850

Prelude, VI, 601, becomes questionable. See Paul de Man, "Intentional Structure of the Romantic Image," in *Rhetoric of Romanticism,* 15–16.

This is underscored by the passage, another of the gaps left by Wordsworth's rewritings, which in an earlier draft occupied that space following the crossing of the Alps. These lines eventually found their way to the 1805 *Prelude,* VIII, 711–27, and the 1850 *Prelude,* VIII, 560–76.

> As when a traveller hath from open day
> With torches passed into some vault of earth,
> The grotto of Antiparos, or the den
> Of Yordas among Craven's mountain tracts,
> He looks and sees the cavern spread and grow,
> Widening itself on all sides, sees, or thinks
> He sees, erelong, the roof above his head,
> Which instantly unsettles and recedes—
> Substance and shadow, light and darkness, all
> Commingled, making up a canopy
> Of shapes, and forms, and tendencies to shape,
> That shift and vanish, change and interchange
> Like spectres—ferment quiet and sublime,
> Which, after a short space, works less and less
> Till, every effort, every motion gone,
> The scene before him lies in perfect view
> Exposed, and lifeless as a written book.
> (1805 *Prelude,* VIII, 711–27)

The lines above, although altered by what was to follow them in book VIII, are altogether different from the sense-extinguishing Imagination described later. They speak of a shifting, a change, and even a vanishing, a confusion of the senses, but one that, here at least, seems to settle with that which lies in perfect view, and fixed and lifeless as a book.

42. Hartman calls this the independence of imagination from nature (*Wordsworth's Poetry,* 41, 44).

43. See de Man, "Time and History," 14–17.

44. Sherry reads the recollection of the Immortality Ode in relation to imagination in the crossing of the Alps as an "incident in which . . . the poet discovers the natural world to be *other* than it seemed to be" (*Wordsworth's Poetry of the Imagination,* 7). Sherry's interpretation goes on to be very different from this reading, since he stresses conscious significance, a nature heard and read in recollection, and a reading of childhood quite at odds with the one offered here.

45. Only apparently, for the scenes are not identical. See Sherry, 100.

46. On the role of comparatives and intensives in "Tintern Abbey" and their relation to the mind's self-contemplation see Maniquis, "Comparison, Intensity, and Time," esp. 380–81.

47. Wordsworth took with him Gilpin's *Tour of the Wye,* which speaks of charcoal manufactured on the banks of the Wye, presumably by the burning of wood (Moorman, *The Early Years,* 402).

48. See Hartman, *Unmediated Vision,* 9–13.

49. Hartman connects the two passages (*Wordsworth's Poetry,* 167), and the 1797 passage is also cited by Jacobus along with another, similar fragment (*Tradition,* 113–14). Jacobus demonstrates with thoroughness and subtlety the way in which "'Tintern Abbey' is indebted to past poetry—both of others and of Wordsworth himself (104–30).

50. Marjorie Levinson's impressively scholarly chapter on "Tintern Abbey" (in *Wordsworth's Great Period Poems*) openly concentrates its energies on what Wordsworth does *not* say, demonstrating that his "primary poetic act is the suppression of the social" (37) and of the "historical, the ideological" (39). In her reconstruction of an "'extrinsic' referential universe" (1), in her moves to "restore" the "repressed" (11), she artfully reassembles "Lines Composed a Few Miles above Tintern Abbey" by "acts of exclusion," as she might put it (32). While she performs the "critical" act more often as judgment than as commentary—thus the accusatory vocabulary: "disingenuous," "artfully," "morbid," "escape," "blindness," "trick," "perversion"—she shows a far shrewder sense of Wordsworth's enterprise than many others with more direct intent of reading the poetry. Levinson understands, for example, Wordsworth's "determined refusal to let fact supplant fancy"—though "fancy" is not quite the term—his refusal "to let the picture of the place usurp the picture of the mind" (24); she understands the limited nature of the "move toward otherness" (45) in the last stanza of the poem, and that what she calls "the authentic form of the poem" might be a move toward absence.

What she berates Wordsworth for, his "exercise of a selective blindness" (24), is willed by Wordsworth on a far more expansive level than historical context. But in this move neither Nature nor memory is quite as conservative as Levinson maintains: "'Tintern Abbey''s Nature is a guardian of ground hallowed by private commemorative acts—Mnemosyne, a deeply conservative Muse" (23). The concept of guardian and anchor is left behind in the fourth stanza; and the final gesture of something that looks like memory, "Nor wilt thou then forget," has more to do with those comparatives that Levinson finds perverse (41): they challenge a conservative "aura of enclosure" (33) rather than establishing it.

What might seem *Wordsworth's* "reverence for place, for the past" (33) would seem to be affirmed by Levinson's own reading, on a literal level. Might we call this reading 'natural'? Or, reworking Levinson's remarks in another direction, might we call this a "[purging] of conflictual . . . particulars" in the text, leaving a confidence in the "holism of [critical] knowledge" (50)? How else are we to understand the significance of her extensive citations from Gilpin's travel guide and the like, presumably the very models of nonproblematic literal representation of reality, through which Levinson accuses Wordsworth of evading that reality? How are we to understand her use of an admittedly "undistinguished" poem of the period that mirrors the scene, it would seem, with more acceptable accuracy (30)?

Levinson, with great intelligence, closes her essay with a meditation on the impossibility of recreating historical reality as it was. One could ponder how this might apply to the poetical text as well and whether radical political questioning should be bound to a constrictive requirement of mimesis of the factual, too often the oppressive anchor that poses as progress. Wordsworth, like Levinson, was concerned with a crisis of representation, although he seems to regard it with less regret than she does. Levinson's mission is to refuse romantic transcendance (57); my reading of "Tintern Abbey" finds Wordsworth refusing right along with her.

Chapter 8: Time Mirrors

1. German quotations from the *Sonnets to Orpheus* are from Rainer Maria Rilke, *Gesammelte Gedichte* (Frankfurt: Insel, 1962) and are marked by the abbreviation *SO* and the part and sonnet number, where necessary, as well as line numbers. The English translations of the sonnets are my own reworking of the translations from Rainer Maria Rilke, *Sonnets to Orpheus*, trans. M. D. Herter Norton (New York: Norton, 1942).

2. Käte Hamburger, although she does not interpret this poem, provides a learned essay on space and time in Rilke, ". . . und die Zeit ist Raum," in *Zeit der Modernen* (Stuttgart: Alfred Kroner Verlag, 1984), 423–40.

3. One of the most extended readings of this poem is that of Beda Allemann, who nevertheless fails to ponder both the complexities of the opening lines and the radical surprises of the closing lines (Beda Allemann, *Zeit und Figur beim späten Rilke* [Neske: Pfullingen, 1961], 136–57). He reads the "bringing-to-emptiness" as the necessary prelude to a "bringing-to-fullness" (141). Whether what takes place here is fullness is open to question.

4. All German citations of Rilke's literary work (other than the sonnets) are from *Sämtliche Werke* (Frankfurt: Insel, 1965) and are indicated in the text by *SW,* and volume and page number. The English translation of "Turning" is my own with consultations of several translations.

5. We might think back to the lines preceding the Simplon Pass passage of *The Prelude* that openly mock the delusion of poets who function as birds of prey looking for spoils. There are obvious parallels as well between Wordsworth's crossing of the Alps and Rilke's sonnet in terms of temporal structure.

6. All references to letters of Rilke are to Rainer Maria Rilke, *Briefe* (Wiesbaden: Insel, 1950), and are marked *Briefe* followed by letter number.

7. One might think of the figure in Rilke's poetry of the woman who waits at the window. See, for example, *SW,* 2:549.

8. See Paul de Man, "Tropes (Rilke)," in *Allegories of Reading* (New Haven: Yale University Press, 1979), 20–56.

9. "For you / conquered them, but now you do not know them" ("Turning," lines 48–49); "never yet has one knowingly described" (*SO* II-3, line 1).

10. One might also think of the poem that begins "Über die Quelle geneigt, / ach, wie schweigt Narziß" (*SW,* 2:133).

11. Allemann explains this difficulty away by regarding the temporal complexity as a coming to "fullness of time" (Allemann, *Zeit und Figur,* 148).

12. To be sure, it is easier to place "the most beautiful one" *in* the mirror from line 12 on, despite the fact that the poem has all along been written from another perspective. This saves the reader and the narrator and thus is a common narrative ploy for Rilke's critics. See, for example, Marcel Kunz, *Narziss* (Bouvier: Bonn, 1970), 42–43.

13. What this state of initiation meant for Rilke may be seen in a passage from one of his letters written a year after the sonnets:

> Nichts, ich bin sicher, war je der Inhalt der *"Einweihungen"*, als eben die Mitteilung eines "Schlüssels", der erlaubte, das Wort "Tod" *ohne* Negation zu lesen; wie der Mond, so hat gewiß das Leben eine uns dauernd abgewendete Seite, die *nicht* sein Gegenteil ist, sondern seine Ergänzung zur Vollkommenheit, zur Vollzähligkeit, zu der wirklichen heilen und vollen Sphäre und Kugel des *Seins.* (*Briefe,* no. 373; emphasis of "Einweihungen" mine)

> (Nothing, I am certain, was ever the content of the "initiations" but the communication of a "key" which allowed the word "death" to be read *without* negation; like the moon, so life has certainly a side that is always turned away, that is *not* its opposite, but rather its completion to perfection, to completeness, to the really holy and full sphere and globe of *Being.*)

This state of initiation renders the word *death* without a sense of negativity. Another letter of the same period shows a cluster of terms in which such initiation (the term is *wissend,* as in the sonnet) and dying are associated with a "clarifying" "Klärung") of the mind and a release ("Lösung"; compare "klare, *gelöste* Narziß"):

> Seine letzten Jahre müssen voll großartiger Einsichten und Hellheiten gewesen sein—und sein Sterben . . . war eine restlose Lösung des Hiesigen in einer unbeschreiblichen Klärung seines Geistes . . . , er starb *wissend.* (*Briefe,* no. 383, April 11, 1923)

> (His last years must have been full of splendid insights and luminosities—and his death . . . was a restless release of that which is here into an indescribable clarifying of his spirit . . . , he died *initiated.*)

14. Or perhaps "Wesen" ("essence"), along with "wissend" and "beschreiben," is transformed and is to be understood instead as the noun form of the verb *wesen*.

15. Lorna Martens also notes the pun in "Mirrors and Mirroring: 'Fort/da' Devices in Texts by Rilke, Hofmannsthal, and Kafka," *Deutschevierteljahrsschrift für Literaturwissenschaft und Geistesgeschichte* 58 (March 1984): 145.

16. Ovid, *Metamorphoses*, trans. Rolfe Humphries (Bloomington: Indiana University Press, 1955), 72:

> As yellow wax dissolves with warmth around it,
> As the white frost is gone in the morning sunshine,
> Narcissus, in the hidden fire of passion,
> Wanes slowly, with the ruddy color going,
> The strength and hardihood and comeliness,
> Fading away, and even the very body.

See Martens, 145.

17. Mirrors tend to refuse this grasp of self in Rilke. See, for example, the poem "Oft in dem Glasdach . . ." (*SW*, 2:129), which has a similar temporal twist and the first of the three poems entitled "Drei Gedichte aus dem Umkreis: Spiegelungen":

> Wir fallen in der Spiegel Glanz
> wie in geheimen Abfluß unseres Wesens.
> (*SW*, 2:181–82)

> (We fall into the brightness of the mirrors
> as in secret ebb of our being.)

18. See Rodolphe Gasché, *The Tain of the Mirror* (Cambridge: Harvard University Press, 1986), 16–21.

Index

∙ ∙ ∙ ∙ ∙ ∙ ∙ ∙ ∙ ∙ ∙ ∙ ∙ ∙

Designed by Gerard Valerio
Composed by Graphic Composition, Inc.
in Baskerville text and display
Printed by Princeton University Press
on 50-lb. Glatfelter Eggshell Cream, B-16, and
bound in Joanna Arrestox A cloth